Decolonizing Democracy

Global Critical Caribbean Thought

Series Editors: Lewis R. Gordon, Professor of Philosophy,
Temple University, Author of *Existentia Africana: Understanding Africa*;
Nelson Maldonado-Torres, Associate Professor of Latino and
Caribbean Studies and Comparative Literature, Rutgers University;
and Jane Anna Gordon, Associate Professor of Political Science
and Africana Studies, University of Connecticut

This series, published in partnership with the Caribbean Philosophical Association, turns the lens on the unfolding nature and potential future shape of the globe by taking concepts and ideas that while originating out of very specific contexts share features that lend them transnational utility. Works in the series engage with figures including Frantz Fanon, CLR James, Paulo Freire, Aime Cesaire, Edouard Glissant and Walter Rodney, and concepts such as coloniality, creolization, decoloniality, double consciousness and la facultdad.

Titles in the Series

Decolonizing Democracy

Power in a Solid State

Ricardo Sanín-Restrepo

ROWMAN &
LITTLEFIELD
INTERNATIONAL

London • New York

Published by Rowman & Littlefield International, Ltd.
Unit A, Whitacre Mews, 26-34 Stannary Street, London SE11 4AB
www.rowmaninternational.com

Rowman & Littlefield International, Ltd. is an affiliate of Rowman & Littlefield
4501 Forbes Boulevard, Suite 200, Lanham, Maryland 20706, USA
With additional offices in Boulder, New York, Toronto (Canada), and Plymouth (UK)
www.rowman.com

British Library Cataloguing in Publication Data
A catalogue record for this book is available from the British Library

ISBN: HB 978-1-7834-8705-9
       PB 978-1-7834-8706-6

Library of Congress Cataloging-in-Publication Data Available

ISBN: 978-1-78348-705-9 (cloth : alk. paper)
ISBN: 978-1-78348-706-6 (pbk. : alk. paper)
ISBN: 978-1-78348-707-3 (electronic)

∞™ The paper used in this publication meets the minimum requirements of American
National Standard for Information Sciences—Permanence of Paper for Printed Library
Materials, ANSI/NISO Z39.48-1992.

Printed in the United States of America

Contents

Acknowledgements

I have a hope that this book will become a living expression that the *social brain* is alive and kicking.

In the first place I would like to thank Jane Anna Gordon, who opened this door and held it open until I could go through it; Sarah Campbell and Sinéad Murphy, for their patience and always opportune guidance in the editing process of the book; Thomas Meagher, who revised the manuscript methodically and became a wonderful interlocutor who enhanced the power of the book; and Alejandro Morales Henao, who was much more than my research assistant—He was a penetrating and rich intellect who kept my rebel blood young through the creation of this book.

I would also like to thank Costas Douzinas, who drove me to this "point of no return" in critical theory, Oscar Guardiola-Riviera, who helped me to think from the trenches with an open heart, and Lewis Ricardo Gordon, whose intellectual generosity and intensity permanently fuel my work.

A special thank you to Gabriel Méndez Hincapíe and José María Baldoví-Giraldo, exquisite intellects, but above all my fraternal companions through plights and turbulences and always a permanent source of inspiration and beauty in my life. They are the soul-brothers, life gave me the fortune to have.

There are many friends in the academic world that do not inhabit it as a comfort zone of prestige but as an authentic battlefield of imagination and social engagement. They are the ones who somehow are by my side when the barking dogs bite and the fog settles on the soul; it is their presence that keeps me fighting in this world of wonders and tragedies. So always thank you, Maria Aristodemou, José Manuel Barreto, Juan Pablo Barrios, Douglas Barros, Mylai Burgos, Jaime Cárdenas, Drucilla Cornell, Lisandro Duque, Daniel Florez-Muñoz, Juan Felipe García, Eduardo Alberto Gómez, Cristina Gómez-Isaza, Carlos Gómez-Restrepo, Rodrigo Gutíerrez, Paget Henry,

Cristina Hernández, Aleida Hernández-Cervantes, Kojo Koram, Gilbert Leung, Hans Lindahl, Tommy Lott, Vito de Lucia, Emilio Luna, Walter Mignolo, Juan Montaña-Pinto, Juan Felipe Orozco, Simon Ortíz, Alejandro de Oto, Daniel Eduardo Patrón, Jorge Peláez- Padilla, Enrique Prieto-Rios, Willliam Rasch, Marcus Rediker, Felipe Rey, Alejandro Rosillo, Santiago San Miguel, Denise Ferreira da Silva, Ngũgĩ wa Thiong'o, Patricia Tuitt, Camilo Vallejo, Amarela Varela, Roberto Vidal-López, and Illan Wall.

Chapter 1

Coloniality

Decrypting Power in a Solid State

We can only name the world as it is, in all its complexities, pitfalls, and rich details, from coloniality. Nevertheless, and this is the major paradox, coloniality stands as the quintessential organization of power in modernity precisely because it is the prohibition imposed on the many to name the world. The said prohibition is mainly accomplished through the permanent qualification of conditions to access language. However, coloniality is not a fact added to the world, it is the fact of the world. There is no unilaterality, no juxtaposition of planes of the world that fold like symmetrical pieces into each other, or colours that blend in a canvas to create a new texture; it is not, as Hardt and Negri naively call it, an 'encounter'. Coloniality is the brutal understatement of power as domination.

We will prove, then, that power in coloniality depends on the neutralization or utter destruction of politics, the latter understood as the common of language of the being of difference. Nonetheless, the uniqueness of coloniality as *power as domination* is not only the stringent qualification it imposes on access to politics, for this would simply be to give a tautological definition of *potestas*. Potestas as such is the devious art of splitting power apart in order to fix it in a *solid state* from which it conquers the programming codes of language and then surveils all its points of access. Potestas is thus the capture of the power of language and the imposition of qualifications for its use. The element that above all defines potestas is the construction of schemes of unity and identity through the direct cancellation of any being that produces difference.

Nevertheless, our main target is not potestas *per se* but to clamp down the uniqueness of potestas in coloniality. Hence, we will discover that the uniqueness of coloniality is that in order for potestas to act expansively and frictionlessly it must *simulate* democracy and thus necessarily *encrypt* power.

1

Simulation and encryption are the fundamental keys to the enigma of coloniality. Through them, coloniality not only arrogates for itself the transcendent locus of legality, but also bestows upon the world the dreadful fantasy that domination is the only possible measure of power. If encryption and simulacra are the fundamental nuclei of coloniality as domination, they are also our paths to break coloniality from the inside through democracy. Both terms will be deployed throughout the book in order to expound power as domination and open up the conditions for power as liberation. Nevertheless, a third term is necessary to bring out the most acute dimensions of the *power in a solid state*, a new category of politics that necessarily emerges from the fissures of coloniality as its crucial reversal: the hidden people. As we will discover, the negativity inscribed in the heart of coloniality brings to the consideration of power an uncanny novelty: the hidden people are the constitutive exclusion of coloniality and, at the same time, the fundament of its operability. As we will prove, the hidden people are the constitutive substance of politics; they are what define politics as the truth of the *being of difference* in permanent resistance that inhibits the law of identity and unity of coloniality to shutter upon itself. Through the unveiling of the hidden people we will discover that democracy is the only materiality of politics as well as its sole ontological truth.

Democracy, as the only materiality of politics, casts forth the most beautiful paradox of philosophy. Politics is the question of all questions, because it is the question of who can formulate questions. We only have access to the world when we have access to politics. It is impossible to give an answer to politics as long as the possibility of language remains encrypted and its place of enunciation tightly reserved for qualified subjects. Democracy is the only place for politics because it is the non-place where language does not mean anything yet and everything is yet to be decided. Only when every being who makes a difference can communicate her difference through language are we before politics. The ontological condition of politics is that there are absolutely no conditions or qualifications beyond difference to decide what politics means. What questions, then, are hidden when democracy is occluded through coloniality as the production of the hidden people?

COLONIALITY AND COLONIALISM

Coloniality is both the foundation and the pyramidal construction of modernity; modernity can only be understood as an expression of coloniality. The *West*, as the self-imagined axis of power, thinks itself on its own solitude, on its own epic quest to conquer the limits of nature and the human spirit. Its historical *magnum opus* is modernity. Nevertheless, modernity exudes a centripetal history that absorbs every molecule of what it considers foreign and flushes it back as culture, development, and civilization (meaning, in reality, war, domination, and the suppression of everything that would stand in its way). Not only capitalism but all elements of the package that go along with it—the law, the modern state, constitutional law, etc.—would hold no ground without the dyad of coloniality and modernity. The aforementioned are neither the inventions of a pure spirit in seclusion nor a production in the midst of a battle to conquer the *good*; rather, they are the structures that have made possible that queer and unbalanced unit of modernity/coloniality. All the institutions that come in the package of coloniality are the expressions of *power in a solid state*: they are, above all, institutions that mutate back and forth from liberation to domination. All of these products of modernity are thus not the products of a higher cultural praxis but a praxis that builds itself on the need for domination. It is not the gift of a demiurge but the choking point of difference. In short, they are a force-feeding (a *gavage*) of civilization, culture, and history. Modernity and all the light that it expels is but a poison injected into the stream of our fragile planet. It is the tropic where episteme, metaphysics, politics, and aesthetics come to a boiling point and galvanize in a portentous structure of domination that leaves no stone unturned and no corner unscathed by its might.

One of the backbone theses of this book is that coloniality is the *hegemonic* form of the organization of power in modernity which trickles down and *overdetermines* every form of politics, knowledge, epistemology, and being. Hence, any work attempting to create a politics of liberation that forsakes the central formational role of coloniality turns out to powerfully reinforce it. At the end of the day, we are left to tragically regard the sad spectacle of all the ingenuity of those works that, no matter how earnestly concerned with liberation, nonetheless carry coloniality on their obedient and docile backs. We then begin to develop a premise: It is not only full-size institutions like capitalism, international law, the nation state, citizenship, and constitutions that become unthinkable outside the symbiosis of modernity and colonialism; but the fundamental dimensions of ontology, ethics, politics, become unnamable outside of the symbiosis. In other words, doing constitutional or political theory outside this symbiosis is not only to perform theory in a vacuum of darkness, but also to reinforce the relations of coloniality. Forsaking the constitutive force of coloniality sends every project of liberation and transformation astray, not only eroding their own potential but turning them, functionally, into instruments of coloniality.

The dyad of modernity and coloniality has shaped the world in a bizarre dynamic of imposition, resistance, experimentation, transplant, and syncretism. This dynamic locates its protagonist in the euphoria of law, the fanaticism of science, the barbarism of development; it is to persist in a continuum of motion and rest, of acceleration and precipices, of fascination towards the body and its dismemberment. The greatest ploy of coloniality is its capacity to retrieve itself, to hide in plain sight while it reproduces itself exponentially. In coloniality, the problematic other—the black, the poor, the women—are put in the ghastly parenthesis of a state of exception, and are turned into the excrement of a 'universal history'.

Coloniality, as Nelson Maldonado-Torres explains, is different from colonialism:

> Colonialism denotes a political and economic relation in which the sovereignty of a nation or a people rests on the power of another nation, which makes the latter an empire. Coloniality, instead, refers to long-standing patterns of power that emerged as a result of colonialism, but that define culture, labor, intersubjective relations, and the production of knowledge well beyond the strict limits of colonial administrations. Thus, coloniality survives colonialism. It is maintained alive in books, in the criteria for academic performance, in cultural patterns, in common sense, in the self-image of peoples, in aspirations of self, and so many other aspects of our modern experience. In a way, as modern subjects we breath [*sic*] coloniality all the time and every day. (Maldonado-Torres 2007, 243)

Coloniality does not simply denote a chronological succession, or the overcoming of colonialism, but something more encompassing and total (Dussel 1995). As claimed by Argentine semiotician Walter Mignolo (2001), conceptually, coloniality is the hidden face of modernity. The dyad of modernity and coloniality means that coloniality is constitutive of modernity, and therefore there is no modernity without coloniality. For example, the Americas were not incorporated into a pre-existing capitalist system; rather, capitalism simply would not have existed without the Americas (Tlostanova and Mignolo 2009). As Gabriel Méndez-Hincapíe has stated, the first global monetary system was not bred at the port of Antwerp or at the stock exchange in England but in the Spanish mines of Potosí in today's Bolivia. This strange but coordinated duality allows modernity to have two confluent faces. Inside the West, modernity spreads the biopolitical fantasy of evolution, what Boaventura de Santos Souza calls the logic of regulation/emancipation. Modernity hides under the guise of an arrow of history that demolishes superstition in the name of the light of reason while accomplishing freedom and prosperity for all through technologies of power and an emancipated will whose best representation today is the idea of the 'free' market. However, its necessary converse, in the colonial world, is extraction and racism, domination and exclusion (Santos 2010). The colonial subject becomes what must be civilized, the superstition that must be superseded in the name of the freedom of reason.

The colonial subject stands as the perverted and barbaric underside of the fantasy of reason. A hideous paradox is thus created in the bosom of coloniality. Modernity's dream of emancipation and reason can only be fully accomplished when it rests on a kind of internal destiny to convert the impious to reason and to civilize the barbarian. Nevertheless, the dream may only bare all the thickness of life under the condition that it never materializes. In other words, it functions as long as the subject of coloniality is never actually converted but kept in a sempiternal state of submission, as the utter negativity of reason and emancipation. Maybe the best image to describe this logic can be found in the new version of the film *Mad Max*. Max is captured and, when recognized as a universal blood donor, he is hung head down in the back of a truck as a blood bag for a decrepitating War Boy. The boy can go on and perpetuate carnage as long as he has an immobile living blood bag feeding him life. In the case of the emblem of the *War Boy* of coloniality, the fate of modern man is to liberate mankind, a destiny that can only be fulfilled when the world is liberated from archaism (through law, science, economy). Nevertheless, the completion of this logic of liberation is impossible, for if the aim is to free the *blood bag* that keeps him alive, with the fulfilment of this aim a catastrophic systemic failure would befall the liberator.

We are thus faced with a fact that is much more powerful than a mere coincidence of strategies of domination or a succession in some particular history. Following Peruvian sociologist Aníbal Quijano (2001), we can only conceptualize the present world-system when we understand that coloniality is basically the very *matrix of power*. Coloniality is a matrix in the most rigorous sense; it is the *hegemonic* strata of meaning that *overdetermines* every other meaning. There is no pristine meaning of anything in modernity unless any meaning is contrasted first with the colonial matrix of power. As Maldonado Torres explains, 'Modernity as a discourse and as a practice would not be possible without coloniality, and coloniality continues to be an inevitable outcome of modern discourses' (Maldonado-Torres 2007, 244).

Another fascinating fact about coloniality is that it is very hard to capture, to bring to its own terms; we cannot grasp it entirely at one given moment, for it always eludes us as it shapes every corner of our reality. Coloniality is so powerfully subtle that it would not even do to consider it as the screen through which we see reality, a kind of machine installed in the environment which distorts and translates a different reality; for coloniality is something more physical, organically creased to the body, closer to a membrane in the eye which sees reality, not *'instead of me'* but *'as me'*.

As Anibal Quijano (2001) explains, the West as the carrier of coloniality stands on two founding myths. The first is the idea that the history of human civilization is a linear and necessary trajectory that springs out of a fuzzy state of nature and culminates in Europe as its unique model, as the chosen place of fate. This model is then fraught with all the brutality of physical and symbolic violence over non-European worlds, which are therefore considered non-worlds, that is, the utter negation of the world. The second is that the differences between European and non-European are natural-racial and not the consequence of history and power.

When in Europe science awakens from religion, this will mean the imposition of an even harsher leash on the colonized world. As science is believed to be the product of an autonomous language that does not depend on hierarchies or opinions, on particular wills or hidden principles, but on a fully objective method, domination will be exercised under the pretence of absolute and universal truth. This is what Santiago Castro-Gómez dubs the constitution of a zero point of coloniality (Castro-Gómez 2005). Through science, domination will reach its climax as a pure '*idea Mathematica*'.

When the absolute other is created through the coloniality of being and the coloniality of knowledge, what is extended as facticity is thus a negative fantasy: the fantasy of pureness in race, of straightness in reason, of wholeness of law. Coloniality holds itself as a dominant power through the need to create an *absolute other* that defines defectiveness, the one to be ordered and straightened. What is projected onto the model is nothing less than the fetishization (and, by perverse extension, facticity) of such a fantasy. And, as in Marx, the producer of the fantasy as a commodity must remain invisible, trapped in the sheaths of the fantasy. What is naturalized in this process of becoming facticity is the order of hierarchies, of masculine/feminine, white/non-white, and proprietor/non-proprietor. Nevertheless, when this order of hierarchies is dissolved in the point of its creation, the dissolution reveals its nature as but a decision of exclusion, a decision harnessed in power. The primordial hunger of power in coloniality can thus be reduced to the need of *constituting the other* permanently through exclusion so that the fantasy/fetish may stand as the only possibility of truth. As Ramon Grosfoguel teaches us:

> This epistemic strategy has been crucial for Western global designs. By hiding the location of the subject of enunciation, European/Euro-American colonial expansion and domination was able to construct a hierarchy of superior and inferior knowledge and, thus, of superior and inferior people around the world. We went from the sixteenth-century characterization of 'people without writing' to the eighteenth and nineteenth-century characterization of 'people without history', to the twentieth-century characterization of 'people without development' and more recently, to the early twenty-first-century of 'people without democracy'. (Grosfoguel, 2011)

Race becomes the abstract universal equivalent of right and might; it defines access to the world (Balibar and Wallerstein 1991). Facticity becomes the image that represents all images, a unifying mechanism that condenses and dilutes difference. Such a facticity is a construction whose origin, stages, and deployment in time can be traced and identified. The key point is to know that such a constitutive aperture is not the coy mistress that reflects a blast of illuminating forms of being, but a dark whirlpool intended to alienate them. What is fetishized through facticity is not only labour as actuality, but labour as being. As affirmed by Lewis Gordon (2005), the shift of political conflict into the severe codifications of the law creates vast populations that are in strict submission to the orders of the law. This is the world of coloniality, where conflict is shuttered in magical formulas defined by an elite, leaving the rest of the people in a syntactic form of existence dependent upon the protocols designed in the words of the law. The validity of this game of differences between inside and outside is protected by a theodicy (Gordon 2005) that proves the kindness of god (now displaced onto modern, supposedly secular institutions) despite the perversity of the world, where evil is external and foreign to god. Each and every modern rational mythology starts with this theodicean division: Nazism outside the liberal project, *ethnic cleansing* outside any Western construction of race, the slaughter of the indigenous as a simple sacrifice on the road to evolution and progress. It is precisely the belief in the completeness of the system that allows its members to deny the horrors that inhabit and are produced by that system (Gordon 2005).

THE DECRYPTION OF POWER

In an article that I have co-authored with Colombian philosopher Gabriel Méndez-Hincapíe, we proposed the concept of the 'Encrypted Constitution' as a novel and incisive interpretation of the complexities of the relations of power, coloniality, capital, law, and democracy (Mendez-Hincapie and Sanín-Restrepo 2012). The main claim of the article is that modern constitutions are highly sophisticated power structures designed to tame and wilt (true) democracy. *Encryption* supposes a progressive entanglement of the language of interpretation, not only of the constitution and the law, but also of all sorts of images and of every information chain that constitute reality. Such a feat is commanded by an elite of experts dealing in esoteric and unintelligible languages who claim to hold the sole truth of the world. Hence, when we confront reality and its excruciating magnitudes, all we receive is an encrypted echo of life that can only be solved by the minute fraction that encrypted reality in the first place. Consequently, this elite of experts have hijacked politics as the order of common conflict and creativity.

Encryption snatches reality from common knowledge to make it an exclusive capital of experts. Encryption involves a shift in decision lines where decisions happen each time less and less inside politically open forums and increasingly more in expert forums divorced from the most basic rules of accountability for public discussions, where acts of power are visible but unintelligible. Encryption glues together power and knowledge, state and capital, and politics and economy as impenetrable spawns, where the key to all rests in the simple fact that democracy must not be. It is at this point that we find that modern constitutions are the utter negation of true democracy, built as the stringent structure that holds the liege of capital and state as an indestructible and necessary order of all things deemed possible.

The encryption of power goes far beyond the simple entanglement or deliberate concealment of language, which could be solved by simply applying methods of interpretation that would clarify the obscure or unify the polysemic. The problem is deeper, for the conundrum is political. Encryption does not signal an atrophy or obscenity in the system that could just be attuned by better methods and straightened by stronger programmes or wills. On the contrary, encryption secures the smooth functioning of the system and guarantees the destruction of democracy in its name, hastening the process of colonization, famine, wars, racism, legal expropriation, and the empire of capital. Let me be clear: capitalism and its horrors depend on the encryption of power; it depends on the neutralization of true democracy as its sole condition of existence.

Therefore, what we are pointing at is something completely different from a mere hermeneutics or method of interpretation. *Decryption* is the lens that produces the aberration in the system and through it creates the possibility and the *potency* of the new. Thus to decrypt the constitution (or any form of power in a solid state) is to revert exclusion as the primordial form of domination and to rehabilitate democracy as the only conceivable space of politics and the only order of truth. In this sense, we cannot understand decryption as a simple form or variable of *deconstruction*, for although there is some methodological proximity to it, the former is far beyond the aims and methods of the latter. We can also think of decryption as dealing with the concept of *ideology*, which it does, but decryption takes ideology to new and unsuspected reaches and significations. Decryption, far from being a 'new method' or another analytical theory of language, is substantially the theory of justice immanent to radical democracy.

Through decryption we do not only perforate the thick constellations of the state-capital liege in order to find the 'hidden treasure' of reality, or to unearth what has been mysteriously buried. Rather, the act of decrypting is the original act of liberation, the putting forth and becoming of a true democracy. In short, decryption is to democracy what air is to sound.

Let us remember here a punctual description made by Michel Foucault: '(Modern) power is tolerable only on condition that it masks a substantial part of itself. Its success is proportional to its ability to hide its own mechanisms' (Foucault 1978, 86). As will become clear, the key feature of law as domination in our globalized pseudo-democratic world is its encryption, specifically through contemporary liberal constitutions, whose main function is the direct frustration of democracy through its simulation, and the preservation of oppression as an exclusive manifestation of power. To decrypt power is to reverse the liberal agenda and its monumental machine of privatization of the commons that carries the depoliticization of conflict as its main characteristic. This is why decryption means not only a critical or semiotic tool, but fundamentally the primordial act of liberation and the first exercise of politics.

It is essential to differentiate decryption from Derrida's deconstruction. Deconstruction is a semiotic analysis of the text intended to upset the binary definition of Western metaphysics (Derrida 2004, preface). Its internal technique does not hold any kind of necessary association with an ethics or politics, which means that it would have to presuppose a transcendent idea of justice to link its deployment with politics. For encryption, politics and the idea of justice are immanent; they are its essence, because decryption is ultimately about the reversal of exclusion as the primordial form of power. To decrypt is to render language possible. It is to recognize that power as domination depends solely in the blockage of the access to politics.

In the sense that coloniality stands for the denial of language as the first common of politics, *encryption* is a scheme not merely for hiding language but for occluding politics. The problem of language that decryption targets and which fashions its capacity and reach is, first and foremost, a political problem entrenched in language. The problem, simply stated, is that in coloniality there is a primordial prohibition (political, juridical, racial) to the access and use of language. Encryption is not a simple problem of one type of struggle among others, but is instead the core problem of politics. Another way to say this is that coloniality depends absolutely on its power to deny language as the first common of politics. Therefore, coloniality exists because it encrypts.

The archetypical manoeuvre of power as domination is to turn law into an enigmatic event, to make the experience of the encounter with law not only traumatic but mediated by the impossibility of understanding it, for its language is always uncanny, hidden or, in a word, *encrypted*. From this it follows that law must always embody an esoteric meaning, a very precise knowledge that only an elite can master. The judge, the initiate, the expert, holds the key to the meaning of the law and therefore of reality itself. The problem becomes more acute with the emergence of liberalism, as a condition of democratic politics the law is supposed to be *democratic* and thus completely open to the people, to the common person (the illiterate even). Law, being supposedly democratic transfers a deep sense of frustration to individuals as they are the authors of something that is beyond their means of comprehension. It is here where we begin to understand that the *encryption of law* in the modern sense carries an even deeper and more intricate feature:

that of impeding the realization of true democracy through the entanglement of the meaning of the law. Encryption, then, not only serves the purpose of upending democracy, but also severs politics, as it privatizes it to the sole dominium of experts. What is encrypted is not only the formal sense of the words and constructions of the law, but every chain of communication, every code and point of access to interpretation, through which we identify reality. It is here where we finally recognize that encryption is at the basis of the separation between politics and economy. Encryption is thus the main circuit by which power as domination operates under the code names of 'democracy', 'rule of law', and the 'open market'.

Law in modernity absorbs all the electric charge of political conflict and achieves a major shift in the transformation of the meaning of politics. Politics understood as conflict is overcome and eliminated by a law that codifies conflict, thereby suppressing it fully. From there on out, entrance to law as the only measure of reality is dependent on the capacity of conflict to be included under the precise meaning of the law. Conflict comes to be defined as that which can be codified. The remaining forms of conflict that express exclusion, racism, sexism, etc., are dumped in the margins of culture—and, of course, will return in the form of pure violence. Conflict disappears (or so it seems) into a thicket of liturgies, regulated in the bowels of the dogmatic institutions of the law as difference is expelled from language by language.

The illusion that there is no other truth than that uttered in the name of the legal text by a qualified interpreter marks the beginning of the institutional game. There can be disagreements on the meaning of the aspects of the law, but there can never be disagreements regarding the process through which such a meaning is attained. Legitimacy is converted into a procedural law and a mechanics of power, while interpretation is severed from its political intensity and openness and converted into a gatekeeper of processes.

Encryption is language as state of exception, where the law means nothing but its non-meaning, the fact that it means nothing but blind obedience. The law outside the law is the structure of capitalism. To transmit language is to obey it; to translate it is to pacify it. What is at stake is the continuity of a historical process called oppression. In encryption, to speak out is in reference not to an exteriority but to the exteriorization of the law, that is, to the expansion of its due obedience.

The encrypted text becomes one clear moral command: *obey*. But the text is a blurred and impossible completeness; each of its layers is cast in speech, so the legal hermeneutics of the Western text fold in upon the text itself. The optimization of its function is to subtract its meaning in the sacred lamina, in the *protocol* (Protokollon, the Greek name for the glue that pasted the envelope containing an order), and so protocol becomes a ritual, a saying of speech in certain and defined combination, with the narrow capacity of opening the crypt of the law to decipher the lamina flooded by a blinding light. The text of the law, the book, remains always afar from the body of the law. This vacuum, its impossible completion, is deferred to the obedient subject. The natural habitat of the subject is the void where the command of the law is fired at her like cannons at close range. Law becomes a metaphysical essence embodied in an embroiled speech that demands the obedience of the body to the ritual, while asserting itself as the first pedagogue of reality.

As Deleuze brilliantly puts it, 'There is a confusion that compromises the whole of ontology; the history of a *long error* whereby the command is mistaken for something to be understood, obedience for knowledge itself, and Being for a *Fiat*. Law is always the transcendent instance that determines the opposition of values (Good-Evil)' (Deleuze 1988a, 24). Knowledge is enmeshed in the command, so in obeying we supposedly gain knowledge, when truly what we are obtaining is the habit of obedience that simulates our knowledge of the law. Ultimately, the ritual of obedience becomes knowledge.

This kind of tradition begins by verifying that before transmitting anything, the first transmission is language. Encryption must be transmitted—as myth, as culture, as scientific truth, but specifically as the law that binds all the subspecies together. What is occluded by encryption is not language itself, but the process of its transmission, the norms by which it operates, and the means by which it is distributed and through which it may change. Time, through the tradition of history, is kept in a crypt, reconciled with language as the form of truth. The first transmission of encryption in coloniality is the hierarchy of knowledge.

Encryption does not consist solely in hiding the true meaning of things, but hiding them in a way in which the meaning becomes a non-meaning or absolute meaninglessness. What encryption inhibits is the bare possibility of communication of meanings that are not programmed from a model where the political lexicon is fully hierarchized.

In coloniality, there is no origin beyond the repetition of the formula 'there is no origin'—which becomes the origin in itself. Language is but a translucent receptacle and a vehicle of the truth of *others*, to the extent that communicability as a condition of language depends on the capacity of a particular language to express fidelity to the master's message. Discourse can speak of everything, but under the condition that it speaks first of the fact that it speaks about itself. The original sin is not disobedience, nor the poisoning of the body, (Deleuze) but interpreting the command and thus projecting language beyond the command. In this simple action rest the possibilities for language to supersede the name in the command.

The constitution as the climax of the law becomes the archetype of encryption. The constitution may only be operated by the slickest elite dealing in hyper-sophisticated languages, and thus it becomes a sort of oracle that is entrenched in total exteriority. When the order of the law descends on us mortals, it does so in the form of religious ecstasy, as an epiphany of language. As Angus McDonald sees it, 'A constitution is an architecture, a temple' (McDonald 2104, 84). It is a temple that houses the complexity of the law in an even more complex structure, a visible definition of the inside and outside which is the main feature of the law, the abandonment, where law begets law in an erotic arch of origins. The law is the shrine of idolatry, where sovereignty is unleashed from the labyrinth making the world its own. Most will be crushed in the passage, but some of us gain our place under the sun in the 'law' of the free market of the free state, where we can indulge in the debauchery of the other and of all. Language as command becomes the carnival without Lent, a speed without motion, the vertigo of the fall without space, the smell of the kill, the final leap of lust.

What is encrypted, in addition to the languages of law, symbols, and images, is nothing less than the origin of being. What is denied by encryption is the possibility of difference as the regulatory idea of the world. Encryption defines the impossibility of even naming injustice and envisioning change; it defaces the mere possibility of saying 'Here I am, this is me'. What liberalism has broken, as a precondition of its existence, is the possibility of a community, and the being-in-common that supposes it. It is impossible to give an answer to politics as long as the possibility of language remains encrypted and its place of enunciation is tightly reserved for qualified subjects. Philosophy and politics would merely hear their own echo, bouncing off like sound waves from the wall of encryption.

The specificity of the decryption is to perforate into the conditions in which the origin of being is simulated. Its primary mission is to transform disobedience into resistance and to lead it as the method that destroys the place of the false origins of the community. Decryption only succeeds when it unearths the codifying apparatus, when it penetrates the nest of vipers where the demiurge that produced the simulacrum dwells. As we will clarify, it is crucial to understand that the *simulacrum* is not the image produced, but the very mechanics of the production of that image; it is *the machine*. The simulacrum is the encoding of 'being with' of the *being in common*. Decryption cannot rest, pause, or be satisfied with the decryption of multiple layers of simulacra. The central objective of decryption is to decrypt the very source of production of modern biopolitics of *being* where politics as the precondition of language is severed and reserved for a few that will command obedience.

As we perfectly know, language can neither be surprised nor surpassed. When searching for the principle of language, we find it bent upon itself, collapsed upon its own possibilities; hence, to try to extract it is to use it and therefore to acknowledge that it anticipates us in its use and possibilities.

There is no doubt that where there is language there is encryption. Nevertheless, as we will discover progressively, within the liege of coloniality and capitalism, encryption holds the fundamental concatenation of power and liberation.

The purpose and main target of decryption is not to subvert meaning *as if* there were a primordial and pure meaning at the base of language that is merely encrypted and must be recuperated at all costs. There is no *Alpha* meaning that has been smothered by encryption and that we must unveil as if something primordial had been taken and re-signified, and thus overturning the construction would reveal not only the caveat but the inert truth. If the latter were the case, then decryption would fall back as the obedient servant of a mystical metaphysics of power. Decryption is aimed solely at unclogging the production of language. What decryption acknowledges is that language, as the means of politics, is created based on a fundamental exclusion, and hence the target is to revert the exclusion that makes domination possible. Decryption would fail miserably if it were only seeking desperately to restore the correct meaning; it would be just another molecule of thin air, trying to find its meaning within the closure of meanings. The sole purpose of decryption is to open politics as the place where meaning is yet to be decided.

DECRYPTING POWER IN A SOLID STATE

Nevertheless, the big game in the hunt of the encryption of power is what we define from now on as *power in a solid state*. Power in a solid state is all about the inhibition of power through its concentration in artificial structures, and its aim is the utter destruction of difference. Domination is as much about discipline (Foucault) and fear and exception (Agamben) as it is about libidinal bonds (Lacan) and imitation and love (Legendre). In any denomination, shape, or form, we will show that domination is crystalized when power is transformed from the *un-stratified labour of producing affections through difference* into a solid state. Power becomes domination when it is solidified in a structure whose pretension is to concentrate power—and, through it, to garner absolute control of bodies and minds.

There are people you control by simply sitting them in front of a TV set or a constitution, a shopping window or a smart screen; others require cages and bombs to be controlled—though cages and bombs are also plugged as a spectacle into the TV set, the constitution, the shopping window, and the screen. All of these expressions are simply forms of domination through the solidification of power.

One of the chief conclusions of Michel Foucault's massive and profound investigation regarding power is that if we focus our efforts on big institutions, in *molar* apparatuses of power such as the *law* and the *state*, we miss the specificity of power and we become vicars of power as domination. What is the specificity of power for Foucault? In his own words:

> The exercise of power is not simply a relationship between partners, individual or collective; it is a way in which certain actions modify others. Which is to say, of course, that something called Power, with or without a capital letter, which is assumed to exist universally in a concentrated or diffused form, does not exist. Power exists only when it is put into action, even if, of course, it is integrated into a disparate field of possibilities brought to bear upon permanent structures. (Foucault in Dreyfus and Rabinow 1983, 219)

Power is created in its exercise. Foucault´s almost obsessive dedication to a microphysics of power is fundamental to understanding power. According to his work, if we are ever to theorize power we must descend to its microphysical layer where power is pure strategy, movement, a series of innumerable points of confrontation, of nodules of instability, and innumerable intersections of forces. The great apparatuses of power (state, law, the market) may never be known in their final state; they can never be described as a concrete figure or described in their total interactions. When we attempt such a feat, we end up describing a hollow body or the edges of a silhouette, but never power on its own order of being. Hence, as Foucault shows us, what must be extracted from these molecular structures is how they actually perform and create concrete forms of reality, how they organize statements and discourses and how they exercise violence and punishment. In other words, what is important when engaging structures of power is not their corporality but their expressions. The description of their structures will always be superficial compared to the fields of reality that they create and the cartographies they design (Foucault 1977, 1978, 1980, 1995). One fundamental finding in the work of Foucault is that power cannot be localized in an apparatus; it is not the tendency of power to localize itself in an apparatus but, on the contrary, it is the tendency of apparatuses to concentrate power and make it pass as their own attribute (Deleuze 2014, 114).

Power, then, is diffuse and incalculable; it circulates through the whole of the social body, it is exercised without being possessed, and it produces linkages that are dependent only on receptiveness. In that same sense, we can establish without a doubt that power is not a *form* that can be structuralized or measured but the permanent production of *affections*. Power is not a form but rather what produces forms, and so power is intentional, dispositional, modal, mobile, heterogeneous, opaque, and strategic. Hence, power is communication, and, as we will discover gradually, communication depends solely on the production of difference as the axiom of politics. Nevertheless, power is turned into potestas when all of these characteristics are centralized and objectified in solid structures of power such as the state or the law.

We may distinguish between power and the structures that build themselves through the solidification of power. The greatest trick of domination is to confuse one thing with another and to show itself as the only constitution and generator of power. Foucault captures perfectly what we are expressing in the following formula: 'This relationship of domination is no more a "relationship" than the place where it occurs is a place; and, precisely for this reason, it is fixed, throughout its history, in rituals, in meticulous procedures that impose rights and obligations' (Foucault 1977, 150). Power in a solid state consists in how to discipline the masses, how to impede the collective through the creation of the individual and to impede the individual through the image of the law as the threshold and limit of beingness.

All the aforementioned explains why encryption is ever more evident in the processes of solidification of power in the hands of potestas, and, moreover, why it is increasingly evident in the latter's capacity to exhibit power as if it were a concrete form, a measurable thing that organizes and orders every combination of power. Why does domination have to solidify power? Because in doing so it absorbs all the energy that is proper to singularities expressing difference. Hence, domination begins to regularize the access to language and to define qualifications for the encounters of singularities—that is, it begins to qualify politics. When the encounter of singularities is *mediated* by an external form of power that proclaims to hold the norms that decide the outcome of the encounter, we are before domination. The principle of power in a solid state is to frustrate difference, to organize encounters and hierarchize singularities. That is why the problem of power in a solid state is how to regularize the access to language and, from it, how to establish a system of counting and of distributing subjects and their voices. As maintained by Foucault, domination 'operates according to the simple and endlessly reproduced mechanisms of law, taboo and censorship' (Foucault 1978, 84).

In conclusion, power cannot be a matter of immense and finalized structures of power, because they are precisely constructed to consume power and to generate obedience, to devour difference and regurgitate identity. Hence, as Deleuze concludes: 'The theory of power must be local and not global, molecular and not statistical. Power is molecular agitation and not statistical organization' (Deleuze 2014, 92).

The state incarnates the perfect symbol of power in Foucault's diagram of power; it becomes the Vortex of power as it takes its place as the sole propagator of language. The finality of the concentration of power is to distribute meanings and to determine who can use language as power and for what purpose (Foucault 1995, 27–28). The state and the law are 'molar' powers; they are designed to absorb the fluidity of the practices of power and to turn them into a pre-programmed process within very rigid codes of language. The existence of these molar structures signals a very definite movement to concentrate power in an act that is tantamount to a need to frustrate the mobility of power within singularities. Power is diffuse: it disperses through the whole of the social field, and it circulates intensely between all forces, the dominant as well as the dominated. The idea in the concentration of power is to take power out of its free circulation in order to organize the encounter of every singularity from prefixed and pre-codified matrices of communication.

Law as a prototypical form of solidity of power does not limit power—this is a physical impossibility. What law does is to distribute and institutionalize its own force as the only available power. It defines what power is legitimate, and thus determines who possesses the power to exercise power. This is the deepest and most definitive split in the heart of modern politics. As Foucault elucidates, 'The crowd, a compact mass, a locus of multiple exchanges, individualities merging together, a collective effect, is abolished and replaced by a collection of separated individualities' (Foucault 1995, 201). Power in a solid state is the technology that absorbs energy from the exterior and transforms it to an ordered stratification of subjectivities; it is the contracture of all circulation where every relation becomes prefixed, and language becomes the constitution of politics. Power in a solid state distributes the circulation of power in the factory, the gymnasium, the screen, the street, the battlefront, and even in our gaze. The purpose of domination is to immobilize energies and bodies and to separate individuals, qualifying their strength. Thus Foucault declares that 'in a sense, only a single drama is ever staged in this nonplace, the endlessly repeated play of dominations' (Foucault 1977, 150). Hegemonic power—whether it is solidified in the state or the market or is distributed among an invisible set of powers—has the primordial purpose of accounting for difference. It is, above all, a mechanism of census; it is the counting of the heads of singularities.

Nonetheless, there is another dimension that is crucial to the solidification of power. When power is fixed in a particular institution, necessity, as a trademark of power, is built retrospectively from an origin that hides its exterior validation. As Foucault proves, the theory of state is a metaphysics of power that intends to infuse the state with the utter necessity of monopolizing power and thus sets power as an autonomous entity in itself, clothed with divine qualities that must be adored by its sufferers. When power is solidified it becomes a fetish. Power is posed as a self-originated power, as an ever-actualizing actuality, and then becomes its own cause and effect. Power as domination becomes *causa sui*, the metaphysical being of beings, the godlike figure in the organization of the world.

Accordingly, power in a solid state is the nullification of singularities in a universality that stratifies power. We have before us one defining characteristic of potestas: potestas is the negation of power through the stratification of the conditions of power. This is the reason why decryption always begins to confront supposedly coherent and meaningful signs, because the intention is to unearth all the relations whose signs are prohibiting. It is in this sense that encryption is very close to a *hermeneutics of suspicion* (Ricoeur 1981).

Power presupposes multiplicity. Its constitutive form is the permanent communication of difference. It is amorphous, not a form but a relation of forms. Power in a solid state is built to control the interaction of the forms and to produce a final form of communications, a matrix that controls all communications. Power in a solid state therefore transforms living labour into dead labour and *Energeia* as the unqualified power to participate in politics into *Entelecheia* as the fundamental split of ethics and politics through the qualification of the conditions to use language. Again, we will discover that decryption is not about descending in search of an interiority of meaning that is pure; it is rather an endeavour to allow the non-stratified generation of meaning to burst through the seams of politics.

Chapter 2

First Definition of Democracy

The Hidden People as the Dark Energy of Power

By renouncing God, transcendence, and veiling its own principles, modernity has set forth a paradoxically divine force: its own nihilism. From within the carcass of divinity, a flood of power-thirsty deities struggles to subdue the production of time and space and to harness every kind of creation of life as its own creation. The dogmatic slumber becomes the linguistic (nihilist) psychotic awakening. Their enemy: any living form that produces difference as the trait of its own existence, because such a thing defies both the deities' control of the creation of life and their claim to dominate space and time through transcendence. The antidote to difference: to solidify power in ever greater and more sophisticated machines that simulate politics in law and culture and trace origins to aberrant communities. The finality of this machine: to grind bodies into automated units and to scorch the earth clean of difference. Its psychedelic architectural model: to create a centre of light as positivity and then ignite the centrifugal fuse at its core, creating peripheries of negativity where the perverted infra-human must dwell under the cloud of error while transfusing every ounce of energy to replenish the centre. Coloniality is the name of the form of power we are describing.

THE ENCOUNTER AND THE SINGULAR PLURAL

Jean-Luc Nancy establishes the dimensions of the problem when he affirms that the community as the foundation of being (and the city as origin) has always been tainted by transcendence; this is why philosophy is the problem of the city, and the city is the aporia of philosophy (Nancy 2000, 23). Logos, God, social contract, state, market, always refer to a community in the void, without origin, as the encryption of all origins; all of these are then condensed into a metaphysics of hegemonic and exceptional sources, founded on exclusion and shuddered in self-referentiality. By now it is obvious that liberal democracy imposes a *simulacrum* of community, one whose origins are clogged by the purported transcendence of false universals.

The great feat of modernity is to disassemble subjectivity within language. The final goal is straightforward: to deny access to the creation and transit of multiple existences within politics. In modernity, language is deprived of communication through the gentrification of its points of enunciation and codes of programming. The prevailing move in law and politics is to attach the meaning of subjectivities to hidden meanings, to afford language a status that places it above perceptibility and to reduce the relation between subjectivity and knowledge to an impersonation, an adaptation of conducts and personality to the occult forms of the law. Law emerges as *the* form of subjectivity. This is first elaborated as a sub-species of language, but eventually comes to oversee the norms of the entirety of language. These norms are in turn furnished in grand structures of power that disseminate subjectivity in murky statues, as inanimate lumps of flesh and blood that must try to mimic an inscrutable language. To learn the language of being is to gargle the acid spirits of being's own destruction.

Nevertheless, there is something even more insidious and powerful in the coming of age of modernity as coloniality: the negation of *being*. This is the blood that runs through the veins of every modern enterprise. The constitutive simulacrum, the act of primal violence of modernity occurs in the destruction of being. The disintegration of being is the centrepiece of modernity. Its primary purpose is to separate, to maul the singular, and to disseminate its pieces in the extreme edges of the *state* and *society* as transcendent and ineffable models. The modus operandi of modernity is to agglomerate individuals in atomized entities, to turn us into isolated creatures, terrified with the absence of being, totally dependent on a *Big Other* that commands us with the encrypted law of unity and identity. However, the problem is not the impossibility of a plural being, a *people* or *a multitude*: what modernity prohibits from its base is the constitution of the singular. The 'I think therefore I am' truly hides an 'I think what the other orders me to think in order to survive in his swarmed Law of Desire'. As announced by Žižek, the constitution of modern being is the utter absence of being (Žižek 2001, 46). This is the fundamental seismic fault that structures reality. The artifice of capitalism, as the form of modernity, is to trace the very origins of *being* to the hollow transcendental schemes such as state, market, or constitutions. The being of modernity is the non-being of politics. The quintessential feature of modernity is the encryption of being and its destitution within the structures of power in a solid state.

Our task is thus to decipher the network of relations in tension, to find the breaking points of that tension, and to determine how compound practices of the destitution of being become sedimented and operate as the vectors of all other practices of social engineering. Our task, in short, is to smoke potestas out of its burrow. Our aim is to prove that democracy as difference is the absolute opposition to capitalism, in democracy being produces herself from radical difference, without the destructive need to recognize her being as a mere caricature of a transcendent model that commands that being to remain outside herself in a perpetual logic of oscillating dependence.

FROM LEVINAS, THE FACE-TO-FACE
TO THE COMMON OF BEING

For Levinas, the face-to-face is the original opening into the world. In the face-to-face, the individual does not yet exist fully, and language is but a remote zone of non-configuration. In the face-to-face, being arises out of the vapours of time, where it is spatialized; thus the meaning of *coming together* arises in this point of original encounter. In the encounter, the intermediary cannot be measured in time and space for it is the coming into being of time and space. The encounter is not mediated by lack of difference, where a structure would come in to assign a point in the map with intersections and properties, with divisions drawn by the meticulous scalpel of analogy. Rather, the encounter is the creation of a light that becomes difference, a tearing of the ancestral tissue of the structure of knowledge in favour of language that rises as the bridging of distance. As Derrida articulates it 'Beneath solidarity, beneath companionship, before *Mitsein*, which would be only a derivative and modified form of the originary relation with the other, Levinas already aims for the face-to-face, the encounter with the face' (Derrida 2001, 112).

For Levinas, the corruption of ontology is that being is a category of knowledge (Derrida 1968, 116). To be is to know otherness which is to trap otherness within the compounds of a knowledge that ordains, a knowledge that is maintained external to the relation. In this precise sense, knowledge is nothing but power in a solid state. The other for Western knowledge is like the freak of Victorian medicine, the uncanny *thing* put in the centre of an amphitheatre which has to be stripped down to the bone, described, and lightened from above with a prefixed knowledge. An anomaly, a puzzle of defective organs, which must be cramped in the catalogue of knowledge that speaks for subjectivity, that casts its sombre shadow of recreation of itself.

For Levinas, an encounter mediated by a previous knowledge not only brings out the fangs of power in knowledge but also forces the encounter to descend into the waters of identification to receive a baptism of self-consciousness, which turns out to be yet another name for consciousness of knowledge. It is here where Derrida asserts that the only way to overthrow history as the Hegelian centre of reason is to reconsider historicity with this light of otherness. History as knowledge deprives one of the possibility of going beyond oneself; as such, *beyond* would be condemned by history as a prefixed knowledge that must turn the other into its object. As Levinas raises the stakes, 'The knower neither participates in nor unites with the known being' (Levinas 1979, 64). History as a privileged point of enunciation, as the moment of sameness and continuity, is not only suspended but also dissolved in its capacity to account for a spacing of time as knowledge, where nothing is put in its place but the mere possibility of time within the facticity of the encounter, of difference as the *being* of self. If history is to become something different than a tautology of the order of language in its accounting of itself, it must be retold as '*once upon a now*', once upon the encounter of differences. History as the impassive retelling of the norm of the same and identity is just a representation of time in a normative stratum, what a clock's movement is to time.

Totality always involves a project capsized in itself. Its finality is that the other-object cannot step out of herself as subject, as a predefinition of the body of knowledge. Relations are thus marked by their own intimate negation, where the finality is to convey the other as object of knowledge. To know within the totality is not to know about oneself but to know the functions that objects play within a destination that remains occluded in the totality (Derrida 1973). Hence, to know is to know that the object is a representation of my own place of dependence within a power system of knowledge; it is to mystify signification as the true economy of power.

The encounter does not neglect that power is a *ready-made* of language, but nevertheless it traverses language with the virtuality of the new. The precise role of the encounter is to render knowledge impotent as the force that orders bodies and things in language. 'We name this calling into question of my spontaneity by the presence of Other ethics' (Levinas 1979, 43). Knowledge thus comes after ethics; it is surpassed by ethics in the encounter. Language becomes infinite with the other, the other always throws language off track, over itself; it exceeds language, turning it to a codifying machine that never reaches its limits: a machine that can only interpret what it has to say about the interpretation, *on its own grounds*. It is always a step too far back, so language must literally jump out of itself into a space that it cannot designate. Language must wait for the time infused in the other, so it may become a tool of its own imagination. The encounter produces the failed projection of its capacity to reinstate order and meaning within *sameness*. Language can only become so, a starting point, a fusion of its possibilities in the recognition of its failure to anticipate the other. Thus decryption as the common of language becomes visible; it becomes a possibility, not of difference, but through the operation of difference. Thus every encounter with the other becomes a separation of language from itself, and thus language is not a fishing rod set out into the obscure waters of knowledge, but the openness of time submerged in the present of otherness. It is not that history is autistic, but time in itself is made deaf and mute as a product of knowledge.

There is no way to conceptualize the encounter, as the encounter is the only possible outlet of the work of conceptualizing—work in its deepest meaning as potency. It is not a retrospective naming of the event as truth, as Badiou would have it, but the leaning over the future in the uncertainty of knowledge and the certainty of being other than language. In Derrida's language, it is the presence of the *trace*, which is to say the question of the validity of language as becoming time; the question of history as an account and a meta-narrative of subjectivity and knowledge; and, in the bottom of it all, the quintessential question of being as self-other-than-self. Time and space not as the total possibility of a universal intuition, or the marking of borders of an autonomous being, but time and space as the becoming whose tremulous and viscous melting pot is the *I* in the other. It is by this juncture that immanence achieves its plane.

Ontology in neglect of the other becomes a philosophy of power (Derrida 2001, 119). Thus resistance, the resistance of the other to be packed into the shallow compounds of a pre-given knowledge, is what makes possible the joining of ontology as ethics, that is, politics. Ontology abandons the obsession with the *one* and the *absolute* only when it searches for its fundament in the relations of multiplicities as its sole possibility of expression. Ontology may only communicate meaning when it springs out of the entanglement of potentials in an encounter. Without this primordial kind of resistance of the other that cannot be conceptualized or driven to the safe haven of knowledge, ontology remains the name of solitude battling death. Ontology can lead us to politics only when it is infused with ethics, which is to say when it confronts otherness as the basis of becoming. Otherwise, ontology is left to take the pulse of stones and isotopes. But also, facticity would remain the cold brute fact that there is a knowledge, any knowledge. Knowledge seen in this fundamental light becomes the encryption of every and any possibility of the common, and of the latter to create anything which has not already been created in the corruption of *things as they are*.

It is not that the encounter is neutral, emptied from any givenness, standing in a point of indeterminacy. Rather, the very option of neutrality, givenness, and indeterminacy becomes an object and therefore a possibility in the encounter. Thus, only in this precise site can we speak of an encounter of potentialities *qua* potentialities, where power is power in itself and not the power to indulge in the self qua other. Only here may we recognize the speaking subject. The encounter is not language impeding the totality of the other, but the other as the impossibility of the totality of language.

Derrida describes the face as infinity: 'The face is not only a visage which may be the surface of things or animal facies, aspect, or species. It is not only, following the origin of the word, what is *seen*, seen because it is naked. It is also that which sees. Not so much that which sees things—a theoretical relation—but that which exchanges its glance' (Derrida 2001, 122). Very close to Derrida, one of his more learned pupils, Costas Douzinas states 'In modernity, to comprehend is to make something my own, my property, but the face of the other resists this form of apprehension, it cannot be domesticated or consumed' (Douzinas 2008, 423). The face is the imperative, the only possible breakthrough of language. There is no possible synthesis; to be is to be dislocated in the future, since the future is open to the stakes of the encounter. It is the looking glass which Alice must traverse, since staying on one side would render reality as just a representation of sameness. The piercing through the looking glass is the understanding of our otherness in the other; the bizarre becomes our side of the mirror, where we departed as something other than ourselves.

Think of the immigrant, the refugee, as an absolute other—in the reason of punishment of law; the other must be branded and packaged as nationless, poverty must be criminalized, race must be qualified, before the other may enter society through the garb of law.

The face-to-face is not sight as light but as an oscillation of sound, an all-encompassing tract that fetches the inner region of lack and despair. In the words of Derrida, it is a moment of intensity of senses and language that produces an ethical fusion of difference that constructs a common space, (Derrida 2001, 125). Ontology creates being at the expense of the other, that is, it creates being on the condition that it betrays itself.

What comes before the encounter? The faces that meet are already loaded guns, smoking of language, but language and knowledge (and history, and art, and passion) can become accessible only as the friction of the encounter takes place. The faces are but a preterit urgency, a dim surface where actuality is inscribed as a contingency. Nonetheless, when the encounter presupposes a split between object and subject, a split between one who already knows and will test the viability of the object to be inscribed within the frame, the encounter is dominated by the time of potestas, a time where epistemology is the blind screen that determines ontology by putting it under its wing. Derrida rounds out the idea perfectly: 'I could not possibly speak of the Other, make of the Other a theme, pronounce the Other as object, in the accusative. I can only, I must only speak to the other; that is, I must call him in the vocative, which is not a category, a case of speech, but, rather the bursting forth, the very raising up of speech' (Derrida 2001, 128). Hence, the only case of speech is where difference is a norm—a highly paradoxical norm, for it informs the encounter only as long as difference is its product. Letting go of the self, Kierkegaard's leap *to* faith is not diving into an unknown: losing footing of one's self is diving into the other as far as the relation bears the possibility of infinity.

Capitalist coercion of value is precisely designed to limit the other, not only to brand it and commercialize it as an objective commodity but to negate its capacity to touch upon another. It is the isolation of the being that must communicate only through exchange value, a residue of otherness, and so the other is only allowed an existence, a phantasmagoric texture of its own, through the property of others. Being becomes trapped in the swamp of indifference or the metal jacket of domination, as an extension of the self or an object that must be shaped as commodity. The hydra of capitalism and ego-philosophy as the measure of reality makes me feel the other as something predetermined; it makes me see the other as something to be possessed and exploited. This is why Albert Camus in *L'Étranger* expresses in dismay 'I Opened myself to the gentle indifference of the world'.

History enforcing the past and therefore the determinism of language and reason is what Derrida calls the 'transcendental archi-factuality as violence' (Derrida 2001, 165). It obeys the necessity that the other does not appear, that the other be subjected to a prefigured time. Time is turned to violence, and the spacing of time becomes a property of power as potestas and thus the limits become insurmountable walls within which a specific model of man dictates the rest.

Where language or any pre-existing model commands the encounter, we are inevitably faced with a void. It is the angst of nothingness that pervades a norm that seizes what cannot be fully accounted for. In this sense, such an impossibility is followed in the act by the encryption of being. Here we come to understand perfectly the dimensions of *the crypt*. 'No crypt presents itself. The grounds [lieux] are so disposed as to disguise and to hide: something, always a body in some way. But also to disguise the act of hiding and to hide the disguise: the crypt hides as it holds' (Derrida 1986).

Isn't the law precisely the way to precast communication, to limit the ways in which things are said, so discourse does not occur between otherness but within the interior of a discourse that is already established as the end of discourse, as the mathematical prediction of formulas and their content?

It is in the opening, in the welcoming of the stranger, that language is redone from its foundations, that it loses any predictability and with it the predominance of science and law. The sight becomes language when it abandons its panoramic futility, when the gaze forces the self to come to the other in a streamed reciprocity of creation of language, not finding the language that is common but involving the common as the first language, thus finding that language, in itself, is and has always been another form of otherness.

Desire for the absolute other is a hunger; it means not to walk known paths of anaesthetic security of the totality. The encounter is not a predisposition (as the regime of action or as the Aristotelean *thaten*) but an inevitability, an incommensurability lacking any measuring rod, any possibility to enact a composition of quantity or quality.

Žižek's critique of the face-to-face runs in the following lines (Gousis 2011). The face-to-face is never truly a face-to-face but always mediated by the symbolic, thus it is not authentic and the subject is always the lack, the crack, in the order of being. 'What happens when the face of the other is the "Judeo-Freudian" monstrous other, the "inhumanity"' (Žižek 2011, 167). The figure of the Muselmann, a starving body, a rotting living flesh was the name given to people in the concentration camps who achieved a threshold of death. The Muselmann for Agamben is an impossible other, whose humanity is degraded by horror to a point where it cannot give testimony of the horror or of itself inside any symbolic order.

Yes, the symbolic order is definitely at the base of the face-to-face. The face-to-face is nevertheless a relation of struggle, of permanent redefinitions. As we will uncover, power as domination (potestas) is the facticity of subjectivity in our times of coloniality. The face-to-face reproduces a vicious cycle of inscribing the symbolic order over and over, and over and over to make it mean something different than the first time. Hence, the condition of the approximation of the faces turns out to be a relation of utter indifference that cannot be detached from the symbolic order. The symbolic is the facticity of the relation, a pre-supposition, but never the legal order that commands it; if it were, the very meaning of *encounter* would be irrelevant. What Žižek fails to see in his *Parallax view* (Žižek 2011) is that the symbolic other is already vibrating as an implicit limit with my relation to the other, and thus a third other is irreducible to the encounter but stands on her own two feet as its precondition.

The face is not made up to stand as the ontological fact for Levinas, but the fact that opens up the possibility of ontology. In the face, the ontological pretension of the symbolic is suspended in favour of the infinity of modes that the encounter is capable of producing. The lack of the subject as a fissure or a crack in the order of being is precisely the ignition of the encounter, what allows the Muselmann to step out of her condition of a mute and impossible witness and to become the incarnation of horror as a speaking other. It is not that the symbolic order abjures its possibilities, but rather its possibilities as an *impossible totality* are unveiled, and with it, its impossible duality of inside / outside is thwarted. In other words, the crack in the order of being that is fundamental for Žižek's philosophy can only be detected as constituent *within* the encounter. The other, contrary to what Žižek holds, is neither the place of authenticity for Levinas, nor the only receptacle liable to authenticate my truth. This latter idea presupposes that there is a truth beyond the other which must be ceased by the relation that must be objectified as if the relation was a mathematical formula destined to bring light to an enigmatic figure. Levinas does not propose an encounter between two translucent and symmetric faces that would create the ecstasy of recognition. Far from that, a traumatic encounter is always mediated by the symbolic which establishes the point of friction and the obstacle to be overcome. The face-to-face is always a suspension of the symbolic order; it is always the judgement that runs at its core. We cannot immerse ourselves in the encounter without the symbolic order of totality, but the immersion is the unsettling of the order, it is the proof of its impossibility to account for every encounter, it is the sign of its own incompletion. The face always stands to the symbolic as the *totality minus the singular*, which, as we will prove, is the definition of the totality and thus of potestas. The relation of the encounter is always an encounter of the minus of the totality where the faces facing each other are in truth the confrontation of the truth economy of the totality. The face-to-face suspends the possibility of the totality; it marks the possibility of politics but only after reckoning with the fact that there is power as domination inscribed as the sign of the totality.

As will become evident in the following chapters, the totality must repeat itself in the monstrosity of the face that it expels as it keeps it paradoxically inside (this is the sign of sovereignty). *The other* is what distorts the symbolic dimension, it is the spike in the wheel of its motion, not as a complete form that stands next to it but as a supplement that cannot be interiorized, a presence of an expression that divides the ontic edifice of totality. This is why Levinas describes metaphysics as 'to die for the invisible' (Levinas 1979, 35). In the encounter and its relation to totality, we do not find correspondence of the same but reciprocity of difference; we see identity not as a system of references and equivalence but as the possibility of creation of the basic particle of the proposition, *to be is to be different.*

The other, not as a relative, a familiar other but as the absolute other is what guarantees meaning. For Martin Buber, and his philosophy of dialogue, reciprocity is only an exposition of the asymmetry. The *I and the Thou* (friend, partner) are not involved in a veil of ignorance (as in Rawls), they do not communicate through a language that is defined by the need of consensus, they are not in psychotic mission of reconstructing the ideal forms of dialogue which are enclosed in a universal need of achieving a pre-performed reason (as in Habermas). Rather well, the condition of the encounter is the asymmetry itself; the encounter can only happen when the asymmetry is the conflation of meaning. Asymmetry is the transition of potentia to politics. The pretence symmetry of the other is the result of an interpellation through power as potestas, as domination. The formal structure of the interpellation is suspended in the encounter. The voice that calls out to the other is an affection, a curvature in the straight line of the structure that bends it to achieve the space with no name. It is the coming into presence of the negative other—the other that is excluded from the systems of accounting rather than the objectified other that can only be in knowledge.

The face-to-face is the place of both facticity and actuality, the merging of potentiality into act, of stillness into the movement of becoming. The impossibility of fulfilling with singular acts the enigma of the totality is what turns desire to guilt, freedom into obedience to knowledge, and its neglect into failure. It is what transforms ethics to a metaphysics devoid of another principle than its name; this is the basis of any economy of power as potestas. Mediation of the encounter, be it through a meta-language, a structure, or a model, is always the mediation of totality and thus we are before the intervention of power as potestas. Seeing without being seen is the nature of knowledge in modernity, the fate of Gyges (Derrida 1997).

The Muselmann cannot come to me in her nakedness, in her expressive silence, precisely because she has been distorted by a foreign language, a mediator that has designed her as such. That silence, those pustules of the body make silence extensive to her soul as an utterance of being. Encryption begins when the mediator is imposed as the measure of the encounter. What is encrypted is the encounter taken out of its own space of infinity and driven back to totality. Nevertheless, we will discover that without such a mediator, the work of a politics of liberation becomes impossible. As Buber states 'When one says You, the I of the pair I-You is said as well . . . "you" has no borders. Whoever says You does not have something; he has nothing. But he stands in relation' (Buber 1996, 54).

As indicated beautifully by Buber, 'All actual life is encounter' (Buber, 1996, 62). The relation created in the encounter is the actualization of the *between*. A between that does not occur between knowledge and experience, or totality and structure, but only in the *in-between* of the encounter. Not the gap, but the bridge made out of the breath, of the calling of the other. It is the clinamen of potentiality, it is the fluid limpet teeth of the political. It designates a brand new consideration of time, time as presence, and presence not as a measure of use or productivity of materials, but presence as the self-actualization of potentia. Melancholy, for Buber, pervades when the other is treated as an *it*. Some *others* become noble objects, treated as prized wines, gleaming jewels with the colours of the rivers of the world, but objects no less, with a price tag always attached around the neck as noose.

In Jean-Luc Nancy, we find the essential architecture of ontology as first philosophy, according to which the nature of every being, of any being, is being in common (singular plural). Where being can only be called as such when it is in common. We are not before a whim or a particular political teleology; we are before the essence of the world. Being is only being in common; in other words, being is always *singular plural*. It is no wonder that Heidegger writes, if 'Dasein is at all, it has Being-with-one-another as its kind of Being' (Heidegger 1996, 163).

Being in common is the order of being. Consider that there is no meaning that is not shared and communicated, and not because there is a supreme or first meaning that all beings have in common, an eternal meaning that produces truth and trickles down the walls of souls anointing them, but because meaning is, in itself, the very form of being in common. It is being in common where all meaning appears (Nancy 2000, 2). In this becoming of meaning, which is the becoming of being, language cannot be anything other than the physical exposure of being to the world, this is to say, actuality. The relationship among the multiple singularities builds every relation of meaning (Nancy 2000, 84). Therefore, and this is the crux of the matter, if meaning is created symbiotically in the encounter of singularities in a *common*, then there is no final or original language that organizes, from its universality, all the relationships. On the contrary, *being in common* is the origin of all meaning. Thus, language is not the limit of the world, but *being in common* is the boundary of language and therefore the boundary and consistency of the world. Insofar as this is the case, language is not simply an instrument of communication, and communication is not an instrument of being, but rather 'communication is being' (Nancy 2000, 93).

The failure of language, of communication itself, is at the same time the only opening to resist the totality of image, the oppression of actuality as the silent form of finality. Language is communicable and thus common where there is no language that claims to ordain all languages, an alpha (Aleph) language. Language as a constitution, as a structure that organizes the movement of all language in a definite and precise direction, is the sign of potestas. Hence, the failure of language is its own potentiality: language becomes communicable when it ceases to obey. Every space reconstitutes itself in time. Seeing without being seen is the impossibility of being: it marks distance as a graveyard. As Levinas puts it, the knowing subject in his isolation is the 'limitrophe of nothing' (Levinas 1979, 61).

Why are the face and the being in common always discourse? Because they are a living presence, they are expression. As Levinas holds, 'the life of expression consists in undoing the form in which the existent, exposed as a theme, is thereby dissimulated' (1979, 66): discourse not as an object that has already been thematized and that enters reality in order to give it order, but discourse as simultaneity of the origin of meaning. Discourse as present in the presence of the face of the other which immediately snatches the function of meaning away from any mediator that would claim such function in the name of the encounter. Discourse is always in a problematic relation to exteriority and therefore with difference; if discourse were to remain interior to thought or intuition it could simply be traced back to *the same*. Therefore, it could not share any meaning as it is expressionless. What is to be known about the same is equal to the totality, as a part of a machine can be retrieved, disarmed bit by bit like Theseus' ship, and then put back into normal function. Meaning always supposes a relation with an exteriority: for something to obtain meaning it must be said twice in the same order. Meaning only exists multilaterally, and interpretation thus enters as a separation of the statute, as what the statute cannot foresee. This is the reason why science will always remain obscure and in frank opposition to politics: science can only refer meaning back to an inert statute in a repetitive production of cases by the number, redirecting the strange to the uniformity of the law of its mould.

Accordingly, it is not that being possesses certain attributes, among which one of them is being singular plural; on the contrary, singular plural is the essence of being (Nancy 2000, 8). This is exactly what Lewis Gordon is referring to when he states that 'For communities to exist, membership must be possible; but for membership to be possible, there must be something already available for admission or something constituted as available for future admission' (Gordon 2006, 51). Being singular plural means that the continuous essence of things is always a coexistence. Being consists in nothing else than the continual existence of all existences, being in common is then the general situation of the world. Nothing pre-exists the meaning given by being in common. A world is not external to existence, but it isn't an extrinsic addition to other existences either: the world is coexistence. Coexistence joins existences, not to cancel them as singularities, but to potentiate difference *in and for itself*.

Consequently, the difference between two persons is the difference between things in general, and difference is the source of being. Being singular plural means that the essence of things is always coexistence; being does not consist in anything other than the existence of all existences. It is then within co-originality as the structure of any consistency that being in common defines the general situation of the world. According to the law of difference, not only are people and things different, but they are different from each other and not in a contrast of dependencies before an archetype or a generality that concentrates all meaning of unity and identity, but within their own co-originality, which is the originality of the world. Thus, Nancy affirms, we do not have access to things or to a particular state, but only to a becoming: we have access to the access itself, where each singularity is the 'access to the world'. This is why the world always consists in as many worlds as are required to be the world (Nancy 2000, 15).

To the extent that the primordial ontology of *being* is a being-singular-plural, the encounter between beings is always the encounter between different origins of the world, and the world is the multiplicity of origins. If the above is true, then the creation and origin of being takes place always and everywhere (Nancy 2000, 17). Following the logical thread of the construction of the originality of being, we will find in co-originality, in the multiple and infinite encounter of diverse and unique origins, the general structure of consistency of the world and the establishment of all consciousness (Nancy 2000, 41). This is the stuff of the world; this is the specific matter of being, of all beings. Co-originality as the aperture of the world and the possibility of meaning therefore depends on one single feature, difference. The encounter of singularities can only be deemed as such as long as what is brought to bear meaning is the expression of difference. Difference is the essential condition of communication: to communicate is to communicate difference. Levi Bryant emphatically puts it as the axis of his object-oriented philosophy: 'The claim that there is no difference that does not make a difference is an *onto-logical* claim. The claim is that "to be" is to make or produce a difference' (Bryant 2011a, 263).

Nancy defines the prefix '*co*' of coexistence as the unrepresentable, not because it occupies the most remote and mysterious region of being, the region of nothingness, but simply because it is not subject to the law of representation. The 'co' is the origin without previous origin; it is therefore the singular plural condition of *presence* generally understood as co-presence. So the *I* or the *other* or any other mode of presence cannot take place; it would be a factual impossibility if the co-presence does not come first, as the origin of all presence (Nancy 2000, 40). If being is being only coexisting, then the 'co' is not a simple prefix or connection between an existing relationship, but rather what constitutes being—the being of Being. In other words, being *with* or coexisting is the condition of the aperture of the world (Nancy 2000, 83).

Therefore, the problem of the place of enunciation, the possibility that we say *We* is not a problem of enunciation in itself, trapped in a temporal-spatial logic, but an ontological problem that presupposes the very possibility of enunciation! Insofar as any utterance, any action, presupposes a singular plural, the singular plural supposes the communication of differences. The coexistence of the origins is the essence of being, where the world is born out of the womb of difference. However, for there to be *identity* it is obvious that difference must come first, as the principle that defines originality.

Being-singular-plural is not an abstraction displaced from reality, but is the very order of being which contains within itself the reconsideration of the meaning of *politics* which is nothing more than the need of ontology as a first philosophy. Again, Bryant helps us clarify the stern ontological scope we are pursuing: 'We affirm the thesis that being is composed of nothing but singular individuals, existing at different levels of scale but nonetheless *equally* having the status of being real' (Bryant 2011a, 270). The fundamental grid

of beings as singularities is that difference is always in a relation of productivity of meaning; thus, the status of things that express difference is always
in a relation of power. As Deleuze expresses sharply, 'An individual is first
of all a singular essence, which is to say, a degree of power. A characteristic
relation corresponds to this essence, and a certain capacity for being affected
corresponds to this degree of power' (Deleuze 1988a, 27). Thus, power as an
affection and determination of beingness must meet two entwined commit-
ments: (1) not to destroy alternative differences (for it would be destroying
any possibility of communication); (2) not to count the singular within the
plural as a simple species or genera, or to include the singular in the plural as
a flat composite part. Nations, the laws of coloniality, and corporations are
beings that make a difference (as affections of power) but are not themselves
beings of difference. On the contrary, their existence—as we are demonstrating—depends on overshadowing difference, in absorbing it in order to
survive as units of sameness and captors of identity. They create meaning—
and spaces of meaning—but they do so in order to bottle up difference as a
precondition of their own existence. They are the parasites of difference, and
this is the definition of power in a solid state. Hence, the litmus test of a being
of difference is that whatever makes a difference cannot deny an alternative
difference and compose it as its own functional part. This is what Levi Bryant
calls the principle of translation:

> If we accept the hypothesis that there is no difference that does not make a dif-
> ference, then it follows that there can be no object that is a mere *vehicle* for the
> acting differences of another object (...) The concept of a 'vehicle' denotes the
> concept of one object being *reduced to* the carrier of the difference of another
> object without contributing any difference of its own. (Bryant 2011a, 275)

The true fabric of the things in modernity is that the *apparent* dissociation
between *us* and *I* that defines the ontology of modernity is really anchored
in the impossibility of saying *I* in the midst of the desert of being where the
self is a socket of reality, a maimed subject, a being in permanent exile from
herself. Here we find two measures of the incommensurable. A first measure
is defined by unity and identity, in which to say *I* is already calibrated by an
ascription of being the *Other*, the other of society, the other to the law, the
other as model; this is the schizophrenia and void of being. According to
the second measure, the I can only belong to an us when the *us* is a deeply
delimited, divided, and qualified *us*. It is then 'us the consumers', 'us men',
'us Europeans', 'us as a unit of production'. The other extreme of commonality through the communication of difference is regulated according to the
'co' where each singularity becomes from itself and communicates only as a
'Being in common'.

Thus, Nancy holds that capitalism is the alienation of the plural singular. In capitalism, every demand for equality necessarily has to refer to a generic identity (Nancy 2000, 24). Thus, the presence of the singular is split and distributed in immense representational circuits that cancel the mere possibility of saying 'I', for 'I' is condemned to the gloom of her own emptiness, of her own nothingness. According to the simulacrum of capitalism and its liberal law, we can only exist in disintegrated spaces of imagined communities, where existence is marked by loneliness and panic caused by the presence of other singularities, where we are refugees of being living in frozen temples of fear.

In the singular plural, in the being in common of radical democracy, the task is not, as in liberalism, to stack anonymous and weightless singularities under an order of arithmetic integrity. What is important to understand here is that the simultaneity of singular plural origins is the source that cannot be registered within an order that simulates the origin. This is the reason why the *people* become the excess, the surplus of modern legal systems, the deranged mass that simply does not fit in the immaculate accounting systems of subjectivities. Following Lewis Gordon's concept of 'problem people', these are 'people who disrupt the system. Under this view the system ultimately works, which means that the people who suffer within it ultimately don't' (Gordon 2006, 40). To the extent that liberal legal systems are indeed systems of accounting and constraining of the democratic excess, radical democracy is always the excess overflowing the system of accounting. It is at this point where we will find the ontological foundation of politics, in the void that runs as an incurable wound splitting the centre of systems of accounting and regularization. Therefore, we will discover, the being in common is the law of the destruction of the law of the simulacrum.

DEFINITION OF THE PEOPLE AS THE
EXCREMENT OF DEMOCRACY

Let us anticipate the first definition of '*the people*' and unfold it gradually. The people incarnate the struggle for the right to become a commonality. The common is an inexhaustible source of innovation and creativity of social production, or as Lewis Gordon would have it 'Part of politics is the facilitation of spaces through which the unpredictable can leap forth and the creative can shine' (Gordon 2006, 27).

So let's put before us the fundamental question that will be settled from here on: What is the specificity of democracy? Let us advance our results as follows: Democracy (radical, not liberal) is the power (potentia) of the people (the people as difference, the excluded, people as multiplicity) to define within our own becoming what is absent in democracy as actuality (simulacrum) and therefore the power to actualize ourselves as a new form of legality.

Until now we have shown that every system can only declare itself complete in a voracious act of exclusion. The question that remains unanswered is whether, in ontological terms, a system can constitute itself avoiding that such constitution supposes a constitutive exclusion. Or in terms of the political, we intend to answer the crucial question: Can the *potentia* of the constituent power actualize itself without falling into the performative contradiction of becoming power (potestas) as a synonym of domination? This is the kernel of the political question; the monumental barrier that has always arisen before the power of the people; the contradiction that has been wedged in the core of philosophy since Plato; the terror of democracy as an incarnate of an insoluble logical contradiction.

In modernity, but specifically with the advent of liberal constitutions, the concept of the people is not simply another category adjoined into a uniform structure that shares its attributes with another series of elements within a homogeneous group with which it forms a unit of meaning. Since Hobbes, but especially with the inauguration of liberal constitutionalism, when we invoke the people we call forth the materialization of nothing less than the origin and irreplaceable source of legitimacy of liberal modernity. The concept of the people in modernity is not just a part of a whole, but its binding element, the element that brings meaning and texture to the rest of the elements that are thus in a state of subordination to it. However, and this is the great simulacrum of democracy, modernity as an idea, as an economic, historical, cultural, and political organization can only function as it does under one inexorable condition: the annihilation of the people.

Moreover, the very condition of existence of the state and modern law is precisely that the people be left out of its constructions, so that everything is done in the name of the people without the people ever being present. The climax of the contraption is that the validity of modern law depends entirely on the most severe encryption of its popular legitimacy. How is this paradox even possible? How can something be the legitimacy of a structure, when the structure can only function provided the cancellation of its own legitimacy? We are treading into the threshold of the simulacrum and encryption of democracy.

Following Giorgio Agamben (1998, 221), the concept 'people' in Western modernity can mean one of two things. On the one hand, it means people as a totality, the entire body politic, that is, the constitutive political subject, the absolute integration of free and sovereign citizens, the *all* on whose name law, human rights, and the state operate. On the other hand, it means the marginalized and condemned, the *bare life*, the *homo sacer*, those who are *de facto* and *de iure* barred from politics and law[1] (whom I will hereinafter identify only as the *hidden people*). That in its first meaning we are before an impossible totality is proved by the mere existence of the second meaning and its paradoxical coexistence.

However, this is not a minor and surmountable logical contradiction installed on the fringes of democracy; it is the vital anatomy of modern politics. This is the milieu that fashions the symbiosis of modernity and coloniality as we know it. This is why these two definitions are implications and mutual dependencies. Hence, the *totality* of the first meaning requires maintaining itself as a failed entirety, as an unfinished shape that never reaches its final form and that affirms its identity only through the recognition that there is an outer zone to it, which defines it. In layman's terms, the totality of the people of the first meaning depends on an excess that is outside of it, an excrement that is not included in the totality. The paradox is that the said excrement makes the totality, both impossible as an entirety, but operational as the criterion of separation between the two meanings of the people. Without that missing piece, that excrescence, the people as the *totality of the body politic* could not be called as such. Without that *abandoned* outside that is required to affirm an inside which is thick and self-sufficient, the state and the law, and all its manifestations—but basically the violence that preserves the law (Benjamin, 2010)—would be meaningless. They would wither away in their own vacuous ooze, but, more importantly, they would lie bare in its naked monstrosity.

We stand before the constitutive paradox of the legitimacy of liberal constitutionalism. On the one hand, we discover the rigid zone of codified law, of codified reality, that manifests itself in archetypal concepts such as the *totality* of the people as constituent power ("We the People"), or the *totality* of the human rights model (everyone) that announces an abrasive universality that holds together the fruit of reality. On the other hand, we have the excess that is compulsory in order to make such totality work as such, the *all but one*, the *all minus one*, as the exact mathematical formula of liberalism, the totality minus what it needs to exclude to keep itself immaculate.

The operation is simple and we will describe its logic in the following chapter. Just as the model who is called forth to faithfully embody the totality is a fallacy, to the extent that the universality of the model is nothing but its substitution by an *iconic* copy, a surplus is needed to fully structure the model. As we have demonstrated, in the origin of modernity and coloniality, there was no abstract and pure model of the civilized white man, so it could only be invented by placing the constitutive absence outside the model. The black and the indigenous serve to mark the absolute and contradictory difference that would justify the model. Henceforth, the absolute difference is then expelled from the model in order to construct and affirm the model. This, as we already know, is a sheer act of violence justified retroactively only from the invented and distorted model of the white civilized man.

Sovereignty is fundamental to understand the split of the people at the heart of power in modernity, and we will fully develop this concept in chapter 5. Nevertheless, let us begin to shape its contours right away and transpire what is fundamental for the present theme. The sovereign is he who declares the norm, and its outside, and thus possesses the power to suspend their relation at any given time. Whatever constitutes the exception of the norm must be both outside the norm and included as its negativity as the catalogue of what the norm must never be. In liberalism, the totality of the people is the norm and the hidden people are the exception where law is suspended, and therefore absolutely anything can be brought upon it. A new legal structure arises from the shadows of the formal constitutions and legal practices where the aim is to maintain the hidden people in a legal vegetative state. In the analytic of power of modernity, the hidden people inhabit the paradox of sovereignty. The hidden people are at the same time the regime of the possibility of sovereignty and what must remain paradoxically outside of what the sovereign declares as normality. The decision of the sovereign regarding the norm and its outside—normality and abnormality, order and chaos—is made possible only when the sovereign is outside the norm and declares the exception that constitutes the norm. Hence, the hidden people are constructed in a constituent act of exclusion from normality and inclusion as the reverse of the law. The vital point is that the sovereign, in order to declare the taxonomy of inside/outside, cannot be inside or outside the norm, but only in the state of exception may he declare the norm and its suspension. William Rasch explains the taxonomy of the sovereign decision: 'A decision about a distinction, therefore, cannot reside wholly inside or wholly outside the space of that distinction, it must be *of* it and somehow also act as if it were outside of it at the same time, as if it could truly 'see' the unity of the difference that it creates, though the only name it can give that imagined unity is sovereignty' (Rasch 2008a, 2).

Sovereignty as the primordial expression of domination is mechanized through an exception that is neither inside the norm nor totally outside of it. The hidden people are the exception to the rule of the sovereign. Hence, the state of exception that separates the inside and outside of the law is the niche of the hidden people as that element that makes impossible that the totality shutters upon itself, but at the same time makes the totality operational within the norm. As Agamben explains 'The exception is a kind of exclusion. . . . But the most proper characteristic of the exception is that what is excluded in it is not, on account of being excluded, absolutely without relation to the rule. On the contrary, what is excluded in the exception maintains itself in relation to the rule in the form of the rule's suspension' (Agamben 1998, 18).[2] Henceforth, the hidden people, as the part of no part (Ranciere 2006), as the compound of exclusion that is impossible to fit within the totality, become the problem of democracy. The odd one out, the aberration to the system must be kept under a permanent disposition towards death. Every extension and production of the hidden people is a direct threat to the uniformity of the system; every expression is a denial to its order and every gesture a deformity of the model. The problem faced by problematic people is thus how to be actional within a dynamic that denies their own existence—better yet, a dynamic of law and suspension that is structured *from* such denial. As Lewis Gordon clarifies, 'The problem faced by problem people is how to be actional. Such people live in a world in which the assertion of their humanity is structured as a contradiction of the system. To assert their humanity, then, is already structurally "violent", "unjust", "wrong", "ill-deserved" and "ill-liberal"' (Gordon 2006, 92). As we will clarify in due time, sovereignty is the central paradox of power in modernity, and the state of exception is the bizarre place where the dominator, its law, and the hidden people meet, granting us a uniquely transparent view of power and ontology. Hence, even though all the radical manuals of democracy will summon us to avoid sovereignty, to leap over it, we will discover that the only possibility of democracy is to lock horns with this ineffable beast.

The Dual Logic of Modern Democracy, the Dissociation of Law, and Market

While capitalism has refined its methods of expansion and control, and liberalism is a persuasive and almost hermetic ideology, the simulacrum of totality continues to operate under the same method but with evermore subtlety in the details to which it conforms. The universal totality of the people of liberalism fully depends on a constitutive exclusion, that is, it requires a nameless excrement. Nonetheless, the perverse logic of the people as a totality and the people as exclusion (hidden people) operates in two diverse but proportional senses, in an input/output logic, that are the hard components of the simulacrum of coloniality. Let us analyse this dual logic of the democratic simulacrum in turns.

First. The people as a totality is the promised land of freedom and equality and therefore it is the law of desire which throbs at the heart of ideology. Capitalism, as the force of unity and identity, requires a permanent construction of an ideological supplement of difference; it requires the construction and maintenance of a legal framework that serves almost literally as the theatrical stage of difference. Jouissance and the Shock Doctrine blend to create the self-fulfilling fantasy that every act of terror perpetrated for the sake of capitalism is founded on the principles of democracy. The atrocities of capital (and those of the state and the law as its mercenaries) would be an unpalatable reality if not for a simulacrum that appeases its horrors while internalizing them. In other words, capitalism needs to simulate democracy to legitimize itself. The horror of global warming and the 'humanitarian' wars are digestible only when they pass through the bowels of the greater good of freedom and legalized ways of life, and when the violence is filtered through the spectacle of the screen as erotic gore. Capitalism is the most deceptive and sophisticated of the machines of encryption. It allows us to stomach as natural the fact that the only country that has used weapons of Armageddon would be the police of the world under the canopy of civilization. It allows us a new arithmetic: that the death of Palestinians or Somalis can be counted as an infinite zero, while the death of a civilized person is worth the wrath of revenge under the flag of liberty and fraternity. The simulacrum of democracy is what inhibits the intrusion of the Real within a controlled symbolic space; it is the ideological mediator that legalizes its brutality while at the same time transferring to the ambit of democratic legitimacy its true destructive power. Without the simulacrum of consensus, of participation, without a democratic society of the spectacle (Debord 1977), capitalism would present itself in its entire monstrosity and would be outright unbearable. The simulacrum of democracy is then the interface between capitalism and its horrors, that which legitimizes its actions in the totality of the We of the totality of the body politic. This is the systemic function of capitalism. We are thus before ideology in the precise terms defined by Costas Douzinas: 'Ideology is not false consciousness. . . . It is the imaginary way through which we experience our real conditions of existence, a set of fictions that create our reality' (Douzinas 2013, 93). Through the court and the opinion poll, the suffrage and the interactive screen, capitalism reproduces the spectacle of consent and participation in order to internalize its social production of dispossession and violence.

Second. Beyond the aforementioned, the failed totality of the people in liberal democracies functions in a more consistent and appalling reality. Capitalism uses the law to permanently expel beings, commons and territories, towards the *no man's land* of the laws of the market so that capital, without any obstacle whatsoever, may dispossess them freely. Thus, the hidden people become the rule of what David Harvey calls accumulation by dispossession (Harvey 2011, 48–49). However, this does not refer merely to economic expropriation, but the expropriation of knowledge, culture, politics, race, and gender as the basis for the creation of the simulacrum of legality.

Liberalism is anchored in a very specific and bizarre combination. On the one hand, it connects political economy and law to ensure the utter separation of economic and extra economic powers; on the other hand, it allows them to act in completely separated spheres with a single point of connection, expropriation. Liberalism divides social life into two domains. The first one is the domain of law, encumbered not only with the capacity to mirror society, but also with the infinite power of creating it. Law lures in the social through coercion and guarantees; fabricating subjectivity through personality, and aberrant communities through fictions, establishing harsh limits on freedom in the form of legal prophylaxis and cultural multiplicity. Nevertheless, the safeguards of legal institutions, and any hint of their capacity to protect its subjects, gradually vanish when we enter the domain of the economical. Here, the subjects are expelled from the statute and the courts to the mayhem of the *laws* of the market so that it may act as truly *free*: free to dispossess, free to crush subjectivities. When this latter step is accomplished, all that remains of the law are its symbols of violence and coercion: the national border, the prison, the police, the negation of subjectivity—in a word, sovereignty.[3]

In the bizarre passage from law to the market, a further consequence can be drawn: the subject must be transformed into what Michel Foucault called a *docile body*. What we may term as the *dissociation* of law and economy serves to underline multifaceted modes of domination—that is, power as domination in modernity depends, in all its variants, on this dissociation. Classic sovereignty and its transformation into bio-power and *panopticism* and its further conversion into the most acute features of immaterial labour in post-Fordism all share a common feature: their point of departure and vessel of dominance is the dissociation. All the forms of power just mentioned are fundamentally forms to organize the body that correspond to diverse historical compositions. Nonetheless, their base is a common goal of domination through the prohibition of being. Every relation of power creates a proper form of knowledge; the theatre of knowledge is then to diffuse, dissect, categorize, divide, and inhibit the movement of bodies. The consequence of this operation is the transforming of subjectivity into docile bodies, but this is only possible after the circuits of subjectivity are severed from language, and labour is detached from creativity and transformed into surplus. This is why, as Foucault explains, the body and 'its constitution as labour power is possible only if it is caught up in a system of subjection (in which need is also a political instrument meticulously prepared, calculated and used); the body becomes a useful force only if it is both a productive body and a subjected body' (Foucault 1995, 26).

Law and its chameleonic essence deploy multipurpose forms (as cluster bombs) of intense regulation or intense deregulation according to the dictates of the market. It is a revolving door that distributes the prey of capitalism to meet its hunger. Henceforth, as we stated elsewhere, 'It is not simply that capital controls the workplace under its own standards and regulatory regimes. The truly shocking feature of this dissociation between 'law' and 'economy' is that the exercise of biopolitics is increasingly the case in a de-regularized market, it is where dispossession and the degradation of nature, of man and his rights occurs' (Mendez-Hincapie and Sanin-Restrepo 2012). In capitalism, the subordinated subject can enjoy freedom and legal equality without depriving capital of its vast power of expropriation (Meiksins-Wood 2002). Formal democracy, with the display of all its institutions of freedom and rights, leaves class exploitation intact (Meiksins-Wood 2004, 224). Politics—as action and as the basic question of who can speak and think—is neutralized, first in economy as an autonomous realm that produces reality under the iron umbrella of supposedly scientific and rational decisions, and then in a legal structure that regularizes every relation of meaning.

As Hardt and Negri put it: 'Capital too functions as an impersonal form of domination that imposes laws of its own, economic laws that structure social life and make hierarchies and subordinations seem natural and necessary' (Hardt and Negri 2009, 7). On the side of the law, the reduction of the people is even worse. The people stand as the fundamental subject of modern constitutions, the living energy that instantiates all forms of normative life, the elemental particle that produces every stretch of possibilities within the normative design. Nevertheless, once the blood has been washed from the walls and the constitution is established as a mere norm, the people are disintegrated and attached to formal institutions until they become zombie life forms, the subservient organization of the *norm of norms*. Through judicial review, representation, rights, and all the cornucopia of the networks of law, the people are bled out of their life and converted into normative automatons. For example, regarding representation and in the words of Etienne Balibar, 'Parliamentary representation was presented by liberal political science as the touchstone of democracy in the name of the organic unity of the people' (Balibar 2014, 28). The people become trapped within a crushing tautology, and defending oneself against the government can only be accomplished by the same will that ordered the government in the first place: law becomes a knife that cuts both ways. As Illan Wall reminds us, in order for the people to speak, they must be first organized legally as a people, a pure and exact extension of law (Wall 2012, 102). In the eyes of Antonio Negri 'Constitutionalism poses itself as the theory and practice of limited government: limited by the jurisdictional control of administrative acts and, above all, limited through the organization of constituent power by the law' (Negri 1999, 38).

The ambush of the people that renders them 'constituent power' follows a simple logic: make the people the sovereign, devolve sovereignty to a norm, deactivate the people within the norm, capture its energy in legality, deny their access to language, and expel their bodies to the triturating machine of the market.

Perhaps the best illustration of what we are trying to bring across was given more than 150 years ago by P.-J. Proudhon in 'The Philosophy of Misery':

It is said that the people, naming its legislators and through them making its will known to power, will always be in a position to arrest its invasions; that thus the people will fill at once the role of prince and that of sovereign. Such, in a word, is the *utopia* of democrats, the eternal mystification with which they *abuse* the proletariat.

But will the people make laws against power; against the principle of authority and hierarchy, which is the principle upon which society is based; against liberty and property? According to our hypothesis, this is more than impossible, it is *contradictory*. (Proudhon 1846)

Capitalism is a creature that can only bear life and mechanize its full extension within the piston of law and economy. But the crucial point is that the symbiosis of economy and law serve the greater purpose of capitalism, to keep the people—the antithesis of capitalism—in a permanent state of despair. The bond law-economy, as the ambush of democracy, creates constitutions as the celebration of the status quo: they incorporate an encrypted totality and make it pass as a truth of the world that does not disturb in the slightest the basic reality of property, social hierarchies, or labour as production of zones of non-being. Again Negri hits the mark: 'Constitutionalism is transcendence, but above all constitutionalism is the police that transcendence establishes over the wholeness of bodies in order to impose on them order and hierarchy' (Negri 1999, 322). Conflict is condensed and deactivated in law through the state as the filter and the site of power. On the other hand, coercion is defined by capitalism through an autonomous set of logics abstracted by the law and resolved in the sanctuary of economic laws. As Gilles Deleuze thoroughly explains 'In capitalism only one thing is universal, the market. There's no universal state, precisely because there's a universal market of which states are the centers, the trading floors' (Deleuze 1990). This is a phenomenon ever more intense in neo-liberalism and accomplished through more sophisticated methods of bio-power, disciplinarity, social control, and governmentality. Explaining Wendy Brown's theory of democracy in neo-liberalism, Balibar says, 'As a result, it becomes possible to combine market deregulation with constant interventions by the state and other agencies into the field of civil society and even to the intimate sphere of subjects, which tends to create out of nothing a new citizen, exclusively governed by the logic of economic calculation' (Balibar 2014, 21). Take equality, for example: when constitutions do not establish hierarchies, equality is perversely called upon to keep historical social hierarchies intact, such that equality becomes the weapon of the powerful.

In conclusion, capitalism as an insatiable machine of accumulation depends on vast geographies of legal deregulation, as a permanent exercise of sovereignty, where it can expropriate freely, where it may appropriate labour and turn it directly to profit. If this is the case, the direct victims of such dispossession cannot belong to the *totality* of the people of rights and constitutions but must remain in a permanent *state of exception*, in a grim threshold outside the protection of law and subjected to a direct connection with death. This is the hidden people, the excrement of liberal democracies.

We have thus described the dual logic of the simulacrum of the people within liberalism. First is a logic where liberalism, through a colossal deployment of institutions, simulates conflict and difference to naturalize and legitimize the horrors of capital. The court, the screen of a smart phone, the law, the false sense of expression and the fantasy of dissent create a monumental stage for the spectacle of difference that enervates the capacity of power as domination to thrive on its own. Second is a logic where the uncanny symbiosis of law and market creates the ideal conditions of expropriation of commons, peoples, territories, and every kind of subjectivity. This second logic operates at different speeds and intensities but remains the vital metamorphosis of power that explain diverse concatenations such as bio-power, disciplinary control, immaterial labour, and geo-politics of power. In other words, the symbiosis is at the root, of all possible combinations of power as domination. In consequence, the concept of the people is trapped between the walls of the spectacle and expropriation which neutralize the people while making it irrelevant for politics. Nevertheless, the vital feature that we must grasp is that this split within the anatomy of the people acts simultaneously as the core of the negation of democracy and the lifeline of capitalism. Yet again, the main feature of liberalism is that in the utter frustration of democracy—through the occultation of the people-lies the truth and stamina of capitalism.

Deleuze is very close to the hidden people when explaining the difference between minorities and majorities:

> The difference between minorities and majorities isn't their size. A minority may be bigger than a majority. What defines the majority is a model you have to conform to: the average European adult male city-dweller, for example. . . . A minority, on the other hand, has no model, it's a becoming, a process. One might say the majority is nobody. Everybody's caught, one way or another in a minority becoming that would lead them into unknown paths if they opted to follow it through. When a 'minority creates models for itself, it's because it wants to become a majority, and probably has to, to survive or prosper (to have a state, be recognized, establish its rights, for example). But its power comes from what it's managed to create, which to some extent goes into the model, but doesn't depend on it. A people is always a creative minority, and remains one even when it acquires a majority. (Deleuze 1990, 3)

Rule of law, validity, market, human rights, economic development, humanitarian missions, preemptive wars, interventions in the public space and the nation state exist not as abstractions but as real presences in the modern world, all anchored to an origin and a particular teleology: democracy. Without it, they would be in permanent lack of political and normative value. But when we retract the links of the chain of this particular history we begin to understand that the democracy to which they refer is a hollow democracy: it either refers to an impossible totality or what's missing from it, the parts that in fact and in law, are outside the norm. So the axiomatic subject of democracy has been obliterated and what remains is but a nominal entity under whose name that particular *universe* was built and continues to strive. The sovereign people, the people as the constituent power, is the fallacious origin of Western modernity.

However, the people as a totality and the hidden people are not static and fixed normative sets. It is not about a permanent division of us and them. The *Global South* is everywhere; the division is then malleable and unstable and depends on the intimate dynamics of capitalism. The people as a totality is a mere hypothesis, a floodgate that opens and closes at the ratio of capital needs. As the peoples of the South of Europe are learning through fire and sword, the floodgates can expel even the most entrenched person in the 'Welfare state' when she becomes irrelevant to the market or her very existence becomes problematic for the system. There is no guarantee of permanence in the system of the people as a totality, at best, when we clinch onto the totality is to understand oneself as a domesticated ideological and economic creature feeding blood to the unity and identity of capitalism, that is, to reproduce the simulacrum as an entrenched habit.[4]

The hidden people are precisely the unrepresentable excess of liberal democracies, both what escape its accounting and symbolize what has to be beyond the representable, and yet—and this is the sorcery of modernity—it has to be falsely included in order to grant consistency to the fantasy of totality. The hidden people are the scum, the intimate enemy, which by definition is abandoned by any system of representation. But precisely because of this abandonment, in its necessary but paradoxical exclusion, it becomes the *means of universal representation*. As explained with great precision by Žižek (2012, 23), whether we speak of the state, of international law or human rights as agents of capitalism, they all require the same, to elevate themselves above classes, so that they do not seem to act in the name, and for the sake, of one in particular. In this eerie twist of politics, they turn out representing, symbolically, precisely the class that is not constituted, which cannot be represented—that is, they symbolically act on behalf of the hidden people, because only in the hidden people lies the common denominator of classes, and to the extent that the totality is a false totality it is unrepresentable.

We stand in the centre of the labyrinth of modern politics. The hidden people are both the exclusion of the system and its symbolization. The element that symbolizes and gives sense to the wholeness and integrity of the system is also the one that has to forcibly stay on its hinges, in a permanent state of exception. The hidden people are then the vital absence of democracy, they are then its concrete universal, where incompleteness becomes the intimate order of the order itself. This order can only be complete under the sole condition of excluding from its inside what would truly make it a complete order, its false totality depends in its fundamental absence. In short, the hidden people are the radical absence of democracy. This is why Ranciere understands that politics is not an everyday event: 'It occurs rarely when "the part of no part" ruptures the everyday sense of the political and demands equality in a radical sense' (Ranciere 2001, 93).

Thus far, we have discovered the composition of the people in coloniality and the emergence of a hidden people as its necessary negativity, that which is absent but constitutes the very possibility of the totality. Politics is then made impossible by this double conjuncture: the concept of totality of the people is the key element that encrypts politics and disables any possibility of communication; the hidden people are the element that keeps the logic together in its ontological seams by being outside its composition. Politics becomes impossible precisely because a false subject incarnates it as the very means to deny it. The people, as a process of legal organization and of subservient subjectivity, hide the true being of politics (the hidden people): the one that would render politics *universal*, as the absolute communication and becoming of all subjectivities of difference. We have then a first and decisive composition of politics, the hidden people form the *basement (crypt)*, the libidinal architecture of liberalism, locked up in a dungeon that is itself the foundation of the building.

The work that awaits us is to determine the precise ontological contours by which we may transpose the missing space of democracy, to alienate the gap that separates the hidden people from the people as a false totality. As we will prove, we need to universalize negativity (or the missing space of nothingness). In other words, democracy can only produce itself through a dialectical approach that recognizes the *constitutive* contradiction between the totality and its hidden counterpart. As we will ascertain, the democratic synthesis does not involve the reconciliation of opposites, but first the total alienation of the false opposition (Adorno 2004, 18) and second the structuring of a true ontology of difference. What follows in this book is to build a path to show that the hidden people are both the means of alienating what stands as the simulacrum of politics (totality) and the means of actualizing difference as the primary order of the being of politics. When the constitutive absence of democracy (the hidden people) is universalized, this is coextensive to the universalization of difference as immanence in such a way that the exercise of difference always constitutes the actualization of power. With the actualization of difference, we will produce radical democracy; in radical democracy everything that produces difference without eclipsing it counts as being. If identity is derived from unity, we are before the ontic as the closure of the opening where there is no difference that produces difference.

Difference as the ground of ontology transforms objectivity radically since difference is not an exclusive trait of subjectivity. We are not before the pre-eminence of a co-relation (Meillassoux 2008), where objects are just utensils of the sovereign subject, but before a horizontal line of difference where objects and subjects communicate solely by difference. Hence, difference radically transforms the links between subjects and objects, where there is no preference among them that does not pertain to difference. The conventional legal standard of qualifications and hierarchies of forms of human life and its interaction with objects is utterly subverted, where difference becomes the only measure of the relation. Henceforth, difference and simulacrum replace identity and unity as the columns of reality. And this is so, not because we do not know difference beyond objectivity or cannot know it (Kant) but because difference is the formal condition of existence. Hence, we do not choose one thing over another because one being of existence is primary and the other secondary (Heidegger), but because one is difference and the other simulacrum, in the sense that one is being (singular plural) and the other is unity as the barring of being.

Encryption happens on two complementary moments. First, it is the ideological support that holds the entire legal apparatus, which at its turn separates the people as a totality and the hidden people. Second, the liberal simulation of democracy encrypts power so that each act of violence exercised by capitalism can be drawn back to the place of democratic legitimacy. In this state of things, reality seems foreign, traumatic, because we are already part machine, part of the dream of another; we are created in a production line where reality is the state, the society of the spectacle, virtuality in the sense of unreality, where everything, even the eyes of the beholder are encrypted.

We find ourselves before a preliminary division of the people which we will take to its most extreme consequences in the following chapters.

DIVISION 1 The division that is the fault-line of modernity between people as totality and the hidden people. This is the anatomy of power in a solid state.

DIVISION 2 The totality of the people are in turn divided into different forms of legal categorizations and the concept itself serves as the floodgate that opens and closes according to the hunger of the market. The people slide in and out of the spectacle and expropriation, in and out of legality and communication, in and out of living and dead labour. At any expense, the concept of the people stands for institutionalization, legal subservience, and processes of accounting and organization of bodies as the key to deactivate political power. The technology of power is in essence a technology of how to organize the people, to diffuse its problematic flow and coagulate it in structures of power.

DIVISION 3 The hidden people as the absolute excrement, the dividing threshold of the line of inclusion/exclusion, the grand paradox of power and sovereignty. The hidden people are what the *totality* lacks to become a true totality, what impedes it and makes it operational and at the same time, what is constitutively absent in the definition of politics and democracy. On the one side of the line, a perverted inside, the prison, the neo-colony, the informal worker, the migrant; on the other, the negative symbolization of the false totality. Only when the hidden people become the universal may we speak of politics as the creation of democracy. Paradoxically, the hidden people are the zero where the totality fits in.

NOTES

1. 'One term thus names both the constitutive political subject and the class that is, de facto if not de jure, excluded from politics' (Agamben 1998, 100).

2. We will not pursue this issue further here as it will be fully developed in chapter 5 when considering the problem of the state of exception and sovereignty.

3. A very good example of the disassociation in which human rights are adapted according to the necessity of exploitation of capital is in a recent case in Brazil. The Awá, a tribe of just 355 people in Brazil, has been assassinated by *pistoleros* (hired gunman) who follow instructions of land-grabbers, who, in turn, follow instructions from logging companies interested in exploiting the rain forest in this country. This is an outcome of the logic of capital imposed on the hidden people, as asserted in a research article:

> Their troubles began in earnest in 1982 with the inauguration of a European Economic Community (EEC) and World Bank-funded programme to extract massive iron ore deposits found in the Carajás mountains. The EEC gave Brazil $600m to build a railway from the mines to the coast, on the condition that Europe received a third of the output, a minimum of 13.6m tons a year for 15 years. The railway cut directly through the Awá's land and with the railway came settlers. A road-building programme quickly followed, opening up the Awá's jungle home to loggers, who moved in from the east. (http://www.theguardian.com/world/2012/apr/22/brazil-rainforest-awa-endangered-tribe)

4. In the words of Jacques Ranciere,

> Democracy indeed signifies, in this sense, the impurity of politics, the challenge to governments' claims to embody the sole principle of public life and thereby to circumscribe the understanding and extension of this public life. If there is an 'illimitation' proper to democracy, this is where it resides: not in the exponential multiplication of the needs or desires emanating from individuals, but in the movement that unceasingly displaces the limits of public and private, of the political and the social. (Ranciere 2001, 61)

Chapter 3

Difference and Simulacra

The Poisoned Gift of Platonism

We are chasing the possibilities of an ontology of democracy not as technology of the isolated subject but as the possibility of the truth of being in common. We are pursuing the possibility of meaning within an infinity of difference. In order to pave the road that may lead us to an ontology of democracy I will execute a *turn of the screw* on one of the most revolutionary intellectual projects of our day, Gilles Deleuze's *Difference and Repetition*. Deleuze's project of unleashing difference in a world obfuscated by unity and identity is beautifully crafted and sturdily grounded. Nevertheless, I believe it is incomplete and meets an intrinsic limit when the project is examined in the light of power. It is crucial to clarify that my project is not *Deleuzian*. Rather, I will use Deleuze as a kind of Archimedean lever to move difference from potentiality to actuality, and thus pulverize the thick cluster of identity and unity that blocks the gate of ontology. Hence, the *turn* is the bore that punctures power as domination and lets us gain entrance into a fresh and entirely new consideration of being through difference. What is a turn of a screw? It is above all an optic device that causes an aberration in the regime of truth, distorting the solidity of images that have settled themselves before our eyes by the ferocity implicit to the passage of time; or, better yet, it shatters the illusion that such images compose the fullness of reality. A turn of the screw melts colours and forms, dimensions and textures in a whirlpool of time and space, and yet we can only capture the vertigo of the lack of words that is immersed in its process of becoming nothingness. Hence, a turn of the screw is a violent change of perspective that expels us from language, giving us the obligation to name everything anew. It is both a trauma and a primal opening, where the common becomes unnerving and the uncanny becomes our home. In the turn of the screw, there is no omniscient first-person narrator who could be able to move the building blocks of reality and to accommodate them at whim granting us the comfort of familiarity. On the contrary, to peek inside through the *turn* is to acknowledge that anamorphosis and parallax belong to the things of the world and are not properties of our position towards them. In conclusion, in the turn of the screw, things talk to us through the crystalline membrane of their ghostly appearance, things talk to us through their immemorial silence, and just before we are out of breath and lucidity, we realize that this is all that there is; we realize that the fracture of reality was always before our eyes.

The main purpose of Deleuze's ontology is to subvert Platonism and hence to destroy the Western tradition in the production of truth which is built upon rigid models of identity, resemblance, analogy, and opposition. Plato's work divides the world between *ideas* that govern every regime of truth and *simulacrums* which distort the unifying order of ideas and therefore are doomed to disappear from the world. Deleuze denounces such models, which can be traced back to the *'Parmenides'* of the Dialogues, on the grounds that they lead to a severe division of the world between *unity* and *difference*, where unity, *The one* of the 'Theory of forms', governs every possible worldly relation from an impenetrable nucleus, which itself supposes the annihilation of difference. This is where Deleuze identifies the collapse of all ontology. To achieve the objective of debunking Platonism as the hegemonic method of the formation of truth, Deleuze emancipates the power of the simulacrum as the internal function of difference against the unifying force and unalterable power of the *idea*.

Nevertheless, my project of executing a turn of the screw on the work of Deleuze does not mean a return to the Platonic idea; it is not a Copernican turn if you will, but rather, I intend to radicalize it in a direction that would be forbidden by Plato and even by Deleuze himself. Hence, my *Einsteinian turn* does not consist in merely inverting the composition between the orders of the *idea* and the *simulacra*, which would suppose a total overturn of the Deleuzian project. Deleuze liberates the power of the simulacra against the unity of the Platonic model, but this is done within parallel planes of reality that are incommensurable to each other; hence, they rotate in individual fields without a proper system of affection that would produce a mutual interaction such that communication becomes impossible. Instead, my turn consists in a profound rearrangement in the composition of power and ontology. My destination, then, is to arrive at the heresy of fixing difference as the privileged place of the *absolute* and revealing the simulacrum as the usurper. Hence, the simulacrum is any *power as domination* that possesses, as its central function, the closure of difference and the violent imposition of identity. We will thus understand simulacrum as any form that denies the absolute of difference. Let me be clear on this: after the turn of the screw, we will come to understand difference not simply as a *universalizable* component of reality, but as its absolute and undisputable truth. The aforementioned is not a strategic sleight of hand on my behalf; the task is simply to illuminate the history of difference and identity with a new ontological light, which in turn produces a paramount historical proof: democracy is the immanent order of difference.

The crux of the matter is this: there is a perpetual tension between power as domination and power as *resistance* whose modern representation is the struggle between capitalism—embodied in liberal democracy—and radical democracy or, in other words, between capitalism and its liberal simulacrum of democracy and radical democracy as the immanent order of difference.

The turn of the screw allows me to demonstrate that democracy is the absolute of being that resists a history built upon hierarchies and, therefore, to show that democracy is the same as the permanent and irrevocable exercise of difference. Democracy as a *place of absolute differentiation* means that the constituent power possesses difference as its essence, the constituent freedom of the people as its most radical presence, as its ontological trait. With the radicalization of the Deleuzian investment, we overcome the hideous, absolutist dichotomy between transcendence and immanence, which is at the base of the edifice of being in metaphysics and ontology. To install democracy as the single order of difference has immense implications, but the one that inclines the balance of ontology is to recognize that the power of the constituent power is immanent to itself and hence does not require any *a priori* universal foundation. Transcendence has always been the hex utilized by power to dissolve difference. We will thus prove that the only absolute power resides in democracy, for democracy is the only viability of politics, inasmuch as being, as singular plural, communicates only through differences. As stated by Antonio Negri, 'Constituent power is tied to the notion of democracy as absolute power. Thus, as a violent and expansive force, constituent power is a concept connected to the social pre-constitution of the democratic totality' (Negri 1999, 10). With the actual and necessary fusion between difference and immanence, transcendence as a divine and occult origin is terminated in its own conditions of existence, and the presupposition of validity of liberal democracies and modern constitutions is demolished along with it.

The turn of the screw will also allow us to counter a dominant postmodern strand that produces a kind of messianic gridlock, according to which democracy is merely a truth to be realized, suspended in a remote and uncertain future. I will demonstrate that democracy, as a unit, consists of a continuity of its becoming in its own time, and to that extent, it possesses a triply integrated nature. Democracy is first difference as the origin of the world, but simultaneously it is also resistance as a result of the exercise of its potentia, and finally it is a permanent vocation of actualization (actuality) of a new legality that distributes difference in the world as an absolute law of the production of truth. The aforementioned integration of the triple nature of democracy will allow us to dispel yet another postmodern ghost, according to which any updating of the power of the constituent leads inevitably to power as domination (Negri 1999). What will become evident is the opposite: that the actualization of potentia as the distributor (*'the piston of reason'*) of difference synthetizes power as the immanent exercise of difference. In other words, the actualization of potentia is not only urgent, but a necessary consequence of democracy as well.

Here we are taking to heart the value of what I call *Agamben's challenge* and turning it into the scope of our enterprise. The challenge is both our barrier and our platform, but, above all, I believe that in it lie the scattered pieces of any thought that seeks to overcome our complacent times in which power is at once both loved and feared. *The challenge* is formulated by Agamben in the following terms:

> Only an entirely new conjunction of possibility and reality, contingency and necessity, and the other *pathē tou ontos,* will make it possible to cut the knot that binds sovereignty to constituting power. And only if it is possible to think the relation between potentiality and actuality differently—and even to think beyond this relation—will it be possible to think a constituting power wholly released from the sovereign ban. Until a new and coherent ontology of potentiality (beyond the steps that have been made in this direction by Spinoza, Schelling, Nietzsche, and Heidegger) has replaced the ontology founded on the primacy of actuality and its relation to potentiality, a political theory freed from the aporias of sovereignty remains unthinkable. (Agamben 1998, 31)

Certainly it is an enticing challenge, one to which I can only hope to offer some articulating elements, to draw some routes of possible access in order to achieve at least a sharper view of its contours. A massive amount of work awaits us and it is all uphill from here on. In order to begin to outline our direction, it is necessary to sketch the roads we must travel.

As we revealed in chapter 2, the construction of the normative truth of liberalism is structured upon a sharp division between people as a false totality and people as an *excrement* (hidden people) of the said totality. The fundamental fact to grasp at this point is that the excrement functions as the index of validity of the totality, so the totality could not be counted as such if it were not for the excrement that *totalizes* it. In this sense, on the one hand we encounter a false totality, the central hypothesis of liberalism and its rules, and on the other hand we encounter a people who are neither inside nor outside legality but instead suspended in a paradoxical state of exception. This division, which is not accidental but rather defines the legal anatomy of modernity, forms the tandem of the *simulacra* of liberal democracy (simulation of conflict, simulation of the *universality* of human rights, etc.) while it expels from law the majority of peoples, of territories and of commons so they can be expropriated by the brute force of capital.

It is here that we find ourselves at the centre of the labyrinth of modern law and politics, a *Gordian knot* that must be undone. It is therefore essential to find the conditions of possibility of a qualitative leap that alienates the gap that separates the people as a (simulated) totality from the hidden people (in a permanent state of exception) as the condition for the *actuality* of democracy. We will see how the universalization of the hidden people not only alienates the gap, but also, in the same act, defines democracy as the authentic universality, that is, as the absolute of being. What will become evident with the turn of the screw is that when the constitutive absence of democracy (hidden people) is universalized, what becomes universal in equal extent is the power of difference and immanence, so that the exercise of the difference constitutes the actualization of power.

The final step is then to establish that only through the Einsteinian turn that I have executed on the ideas of difference and simulacrum may we obtain a genuine dialectics of democracy as the exclusive method of achieving the ontological order of the political, where the *hidden people* is both the antithesis and the mediation of the universalization of democracy. At this stage, we will come before a highly complex and problematic compound: the need to universalize difference supposes the ontological need to actualize power. This affirmation is nothing short of the subversion of every tradition of radical political thinking from Machiavelli and Spinoza to Negri and Deleuze. Nonetheless, we will not only insist on its importance but also set out to prove that such an ontological operation is the fundament of a new consideration of power. This will be the matter expounded rigorously in chapters 4 and 5, which in itself is the fulcrum of the theses of the book.

In short, the turn of the screw I propose will allow us to traverse the nuclear dimensions of democracy, generating a chain reaction of its dynamic elements, which eventually will reveal the authentic *ontology* of the political and hence the emergence of a brand new legal model that contains it.

THE ONTOLOGY OF DIFFERENCE

For Plato, truth corresponds only to the supreme idea of the *Model*. Therefore, all things can copy integrally the model, and hence deserve to live, or they can betray the model and constitute mere *simulacra* that must perish. An intense selective process establishes the truth of things and determines the validity of their development in the world. Thus, the very substance of the world is rendered through an intense selective process consisting first of the division between models and copies, and then of the division between faithful or *iconic* copies and simulacra. What this selection process aims to recognize, beyond any questionability, is who or what is the true claimant to the truth (Deleuze 2004, 75; 1992, 47). The selection seeks to establish a legitimate *lineage* that things have before a pre-established model of truth. Therefore, within an infinite ocean of things and facts, the selection method filters out those things and facts that conform, in their configuration, to the *form* of the supreme model. The task of the selection, as the construction of the truth of the world, seeks to ascertain who is courageous according to a superior and static model of courage; who is virtuous according to the transcendent Idea of virtue; and who deserves to be the true shepherd of men within a plethora of candidates. The selection is defined stringently according to a direct and gapless correspondence between the fact and the superior Idea of the model.

The Idea, the pure origin, the universal—in other words, *the model*—denotes the supreme *will to select* and to retain the thing in its pure and absolute state, as the only beckoning of the true existence of things. Hence, the normative content of this will to select is translated into the immutable fact that from the model or the universal idea follows the incorruptible duty imposed on the world to produce iconic copies, copies that are mimesis of the original model. It is the *line of production* elevated to moral reason, or, if you prefer, moral reason degraded to the line of production. The relationship between model and copy simultaneously generates an inexorable boundary line which serves to expel copies that deny or adulterate the model from the world. The model is then the absolute demarcation of the world and of all knowledge that it produces, where the allocation of the truth is ultimately a matter of *lines* and *hierarchies* of how things relate to transcendent models which enclose truth in themselves.

The kernel of truth then rests at the source, on the Idea that controls the lineages and the creation of iconic copies. It is an endless production line that controls all possible cases of creation of reality and its membership (validity) to the original idea. Consequently, according to Plato, no-thing, outside of the very idea of the model, can be immanent to itself and must follow a precise transcendent model of production. A severe canon of qualification separates the pure from the impure, the original from the copy (Deleuze 2004, 72). The demarcation line is defined by the stretching of the line towards a nuclear focus of membership, where to speak of contraries within a genus is forbidden, and what is left is a petrified distinction between the pure and impure, the good and the bad, the authentic and inauthentic.

Here we come across the four figures of dialectics in Plato: the selection of the difference, the installation of a mythic circle, the establishment of a foundation, and a complex relation between the question and the problem of identity (Deleuze 2004, 79).

For Deleuze, the poisoned gift of Platonism is the introduction of transcendence to philosophy (Morris 2004, 128). Plato inaugurates what Deleuze called the *long history of the error of representation*: a massive machine in the production and qualification of truth that expands the vast territories of the West, forming the mythical and incontrovertible tribunal that divides the world between the authentic and the fake as the only way of being *in* and *with* the world. Transcendence, as the zone of absolute demarcation, will not be confined to philosophical speculations, but rather, like every hegemonic philosophy, it will serve as the basis and method for fixing the truth in every sphere where *being* is to be conditioned and assembled, expanding its formidable pincers until it engulfs politics, law, and all strata of subjectivity. Coloniality and its shrill divisions of race are all referred back to a model that determines lineages and hierarchies, and, when infused with modern science, difference becomes a matter of sin and error. As Aimé Césaire beautifully proves, when Cortés conquers Mexico and Pizarro el Cuzco they do not claim themselves as the bearers of a superior order; they bring spears and death, extraction and greed. It is only when the *science jurists* of Christianity arrive that the blueprints of brutality are laid down as a paramount legal model, where Christianity is equated with civilization and paganism with savagery (Césaire 2000, 33).

Let us think of dramatic examples that are very close to one of the identity crisis in modernity. According to what we have described, what does sexuality (or gender identity) mean? What is *ethnicity*? In Platonic terms, and hence historical and current terms, it means that there are two manifestations in an open and irresolvable contradiction. On the one hand, we have a transcendent model that is external to each experience but defines said experience from its externality—and without any margin of error. Hence, the transcendent model defines every infinite case in which a particular manifestation fits the model (lineage) as its iconic copy, and henceforth acts as the sole regime that establishes what is authentic. On the other hand, things are produced as copies and hence are aberrations because they do not copy the model in a faithful manner—that is, they are not iconic, and therefore are not eligible for any kind of identity, which makes them illegitimate forms of the world.

Therefore, we have the model and its iconic copies, a transcendent model where the resemblance is given not from one thing to another, but from the thing to the corresponding model. So you and I are alike or different only when the point of differentiation is the model, only when difference or similarity is awarded by the model. Thus, the difference is cancelled at the origin, in the model of identity that ensures infinite reproduction and dependence of things to the order of truth. The central problem is that Platonism only allows *difference* when it is knotted first and exclusively to the principle of the identical. Accordingly, any difference is external to the thing in itself and can exist only under a direct relationship that defines its authentic lineage in absolute dependence to the original.

For Deleuze, the primary distinction made by Plato is between the model and the copy. Nevertheless, the copy is far from being a mere *appearance,* a degraded image of the original, and, moreover, the copy belongs to the internal and ontological structure of the model. Furthermore, the second and more profound distinction really occurs between the *iconic* copy and the *phantom copy* (the copy that does not copy the model)—that is, the *simulacrum.* Therefore, what is truly significant for Deleuze is that the model-copy relationship is aimed principally at obtaining a unique criterion of selection that allows the separation between *iconic* copies and the simulacrum.

The simulacrum then fails on two interconnected levels. It first fails as a fake copy of the model, but more importantly, it also fails because it possesses no identity or resemblance with the iconic copy (Deleuze 2004, 333). From this point on, it is obvious that the place of the model really begins to be occupied by the iconic copy. Thus, given the void and impossible place of the model, the copy erects itself as the model. In the absence of a true model of *courage of man,* etc., what follows is that a particular and finite version begins to fill the void place of the model. Henceforth, the *white* man occupies the model of the *human* of human rights, and *virility* the place of the model of sexuality.

For example, think of the role that the model of human rights plays in the *humanitarian wars* of the century and in the battle against *terrorism* and its racist correlate, Islamic extremism. Human rights are essential to defining who shall be considered human and according to which model of humanity. If, on one side of fanaticism, the ascription of humanity is defined by the capacity to recite the Quran, on the other side it is decided instead by subscription to the democratic values that keep the horrors of capital intact. Obviously, as in colonialism, the meaning of human is retracted to a very particular strand of a set of beliefs and practices that define the modern western man, which can be reduced to the *consumer of democracy*, and whatever does not meet the standard is put in a state of vulnerability, in a state of suspension of humanity. One can only think of humanitarian interventions around the world (Iraq, Afghanistan, Syria, and so on) in which the world is an open field where the Western powers can arrogate the position of the defence of a model of humanity.

This is where we can understand fully the true meaning of the controversial *great Other.* The psychotic requirement imposed upon us to copy impossible models engenders the collective psychosis of the severed *desire* of the Other as inability and failure of *being.* Desire manifests as the punishment of incompleteness, which always involves an unreachable beyond, an unattainable belonging and matching with another that remains silent and hidden behind the walls of the model. The model is always in an elusive beyond, in a kind of Augustine of Hippo's *City of God*, from which it looks down and mocks our failure. It is the constitutive absence in the centre of being which can only be counterpoised when we depose our language and direct the enigma to the oracle, the judge, the expert, who holds the key (encryption) to appease (in war, in the orgy of consumption, in the spectacle of the Courts) the fury of the archetype of the Big Other.

In Plato, the model has no further justification other than *myth*, and its historical extension has no other means of dispersion and affirmation than violence, especially the blind violence of law. Deleuze tells us that finally the copy must be constructed by a selective method in which, between two opposite predicates, full correspondence with the model is attributed only to one of them. In such a proceeding, copies are distinguished from simulacrums only when every difference is first subordinated to the principles of the *Same*, of *Resemblance*, the *Analogous*, and the *Opposite* that the model dictates (Deleuze 2004, 334). In other words, the existence of things in the world depends on a full submission of difference to the unity of the model. Things can only be different between themselves when they are first identical to the model. Difference is thus a consequence of identity, rather than identity being a consequence of difference.

It is at this time that the ontology of *Difference and Repetition* really begins to gash the underbelly of Platonism and to structure the true shape of an ontology of difference, whose emancipatory capacity will be in the imperative idea that we can only think when thought is forced to think difference. We can then define a simulacrum as the *phantom* copy of an *iconic* copy whose relation to the model 'has become so attenuated that it can no longer properly be said to be a copy' (Massumi 1987, 91). A simulacrum is then a copy without a model, where any *lineage* or line of demarcation between the copy and the model completely disappear. The central feature of the shuttered relationship between model and copy involves primarily the need to subjugate difference—every difference—to the impenetrable unity of the model. Nevertheless, as we are now becoming fully aware, the model can only be defined when identity is assigned to a copy as the essence of the model, and the representation of resemblance is marked within its body as the only way to attain *sensitive presentation* in the world. What is attributed to the iconic copies are the qualities that would really be internal to the configuration of the model, and thus the iconic copy becomes the model of the definition of truth in a bizarre leap of reason.

We have the definition of our first problem: the Platonic idea of copy and simulacrum is aimed at removing all differences that are not submitted first and foremost to the identity of a thing with the iconic copy. In the absence of a material transcendent model, the iconic copy takes the place of the model.

There is no possibility that difference exists *in itself* or *for itself*: this is the petrifying curse of identity. What is the concept of difference within the relation of a model and a simulacrum? To ask for a concept of difference is to impose the same as the binding concept of difference, that is, to know what the same means in order to expand it to difference. Difference as a fundamental principle debunks the very idea of principle as something holding together at the base, retrieved from thingness but giving identity to the thing from beyond the thing.

Consider two statements and let's focus our attention on their subtle differences. The first states, 'only what is alike is different' and the other states 'only what differs is alike'. The first sentence reveals the subjection of every difference to a unitary model. Hence, things, in order to be considered as different, first, as a *sine qua non* condition, must refer to a model of identity and likeness. That is, to be different, they first have to be identical to the model. The second statement is the elementary particle of difference that Deleuze potentiates in the diluting power of the simulacra, where things are different *in themselves*, and for them to be deemed as similar it is necessary to first recognize their difference, where difference relates to difference through difference itself. Henceforth, when confronting Agamben and Negri in chapters 4 and 5, our wager is that being is univocal (univocal not in the sense that we can recall all beings to a primordial being that gives each particular an identity, but univocal in the sense that it has the power of difference). A being of difference is thus where difference is not said as a category but as a foundation, where difference is not a property of diversity among other properties, but difference as the *being at work* in its own expression of sustainability—a sustainability that does not refer to the common traits of a kind or a species, but of itself *qua* itself. In conclusion, the power to affect and to be affected is not determined beforehand by a substantiality of being which must be held in a model, but by the work that stems from difference and difference alone.

The concept of the model forces us to live in the world of *representation*. Representation means that things are not in themselves and that, amusingly enough, all existence must be validated by a transcendent model, where the identity of the thing must be granted by a pre-existing model and any likeness established by the iconic copy. Precisely to the extent that things cannot have an existence for themselves, they lack *presence* in the sensible world: they are disjointed from time and thus require a device that brings them to the world—in other words, they require a device of *representation*.

Deleuze denounces the four *shackles* of representation in Western philosophy: identity in the concept, opposition in the predicate, analogy in the judgement, and resemblance in perception (Deleuze 2004, 330). For Deleuze, the will to eliminate simulacra follows a moral motivation: to condemn freedom and to subject the authenticity of difference to the strict obedience of deafly replicating the model. A perverse cliché of 'I am the measure of all things, to the extent that I am identical to the measure of things, which has no other measure than the measure of things themselves' is the circle that draws a shadow over the vicious cycle, the infinite zero of being.

The selection between lineages, pertaining to the Platonic model, lacks an essential element: mediation. Between the model of the *beautiful* and the beautiful copy (and in order for the simulacrum of beauty not to belong to the relationship), we lack the catalyst that would allow the operation of unification of their contents and the affiliation of characteristics from the species to the genus. Thus, we lack an objective criteria of selection. How do I know what to do with what falls on my lap or with what I create, and how do I know if I must compare it with the model of beauty and not to the model of virtue? How and where does the rule that relates the copy to the model operate? How am I to establish, as non-contradictory, that copy X belongs in model Y and not Z? Given the objective lack of a mediator, only myth can fulfil the role of mediation. This is to say, only a model hidden behind the model may authorize the connection between the model and the copy, a *Deus absconditus*—but the model, as we saw, is the same iconic copy that by this gesture becomes the mythical transcendent foundation of itself.

Plato joined myth and dialectics and melted both in representation, granting the fundament of dialectics to the mythical division (where there is no possible mediation). While in Plato's world the transcendence of the model could only be anchored in myth, as a model hidden behind the model, in the modern world transcendence is rooted irremediably in theology. Modernity, unable to overcome its divine origins, intensifies them, enthroning divine models such as state, law, market, sovereignty, or liberal democracy, in the place of the divine Model of God.

That is why for Deleuze, the most striking effort of philosophy has been directed towards making an infinite enterprise out of representation, where all that there is must be redirected to the original place of representation. Representation thus becomes an immense and thick web that captures both the largest and the most infinitesimal difference (Deleuze 2004, 331). The aim of it all is to conquer and tame difference in itself. According to Deleuze, this monumental effort found its climax in Leibniz and Hegel. The work of the first representation conquers the infinite because it captures the infinitely small (monadism), banishing any residue of difference from the sacred pyramid of the *best of all possible worlds*. The work of the second representation conquers infinity, capturing the gigantic differences that are incorporated into a rational history, where difference is transformed into both contradiction and the place of dialectical negativity. Finally, difference is dismantled in the unity of a monumental narration of truth that is impenetrable to any contradiction.

This is also a good place to formulate our own dialectical enterprise and once and for all sever it from the Hegel's construction. Hegel's conception of freedom as self-determination produces difference only when it is knotted to the unity of the universal and subjective will. The subjective will is but a faithful reflection of the universal will. There is no greater apparatus to pacify difference than Hegel's absolute spirit, a herculean movement of reason in history to unify the individual to the totality. For Hegel, to think of being in itself is finally to think nothing, because it presupposes that what is valuable is in the relation between positivity and negativity, a tug of forces that must be decided in favour of a rational spirit that embodies the positivity of being (Hegel 1991, 56). Philosophy thinks of negativity only when it asserts that the failure of the formula to think the other (because the other is not the same as the model) demands an effort instead to think of the other only in terms of the same and the identical, with the result that difference is blacked out beyond any reference to sameness. The result is that we can only deem the unbridgeable gap between sameness and otherness as the vacuum of being. The other, being a non-being, is reducible to the same and thus becomes negativity in itself. From this point on, the impossible is demanded from otherness: to be thought only in relation to a pre-existing measurement of sameness, to be thought only as a relation to the subject that sees it, that measures it, and qualifies it, which transforms the positivity of subjectivity into the omnipotent legislator of things. Hegel's dialectics is the embodiment of a demiurge that chooses from an objective set of conditions marauding the negative as an apparition of the demonic in history. The negative is a beast that must be hunted and expelled from the inner circle of history. This is what Negri calls 'an unbearable absence of being' (Negri 1999, 23). This is the operation of philosophy as a legal statute that produces the malevolent and salacious desire to impose the negativity of being upon the colonized.

Here, we must ask ourselves, what purpose is served by representation remaining infinite (Deleuze 2004, 331)? The answer is quite simple: that representation is infinite means that all creations, all discoveries, all alternative forms of being, all manifestation of the surplus of difference can be accounted for and redirected to the place of the identical, of the similar, of the analogue, and the opposite. In other words, the place of unity and of closure of the model. In the words of Levinas, 'For the philosophical tradition the conflicts between the same and the other are resolved by theory whereby the other is reduced to the same' (Levinas 1979, 47).

Representation operates the miracle of the self, the possibility of determining the other by the *same* without the same ever being determined by the other. Representation is the sanitary wall of the same, serving as intentionality that which keeps intentionality within the frames of thought. The self is determined by representation without being touched by otherness; it is the void of time. On the other hand, the encounter with the other denudes the fact that the subjects involved are also a representation, and that, as such, the encounter is never neutral but rather is contaminated with otherness from the outset, which implies the impossibility of representation as a pure act of apperception of what is held to be in an external relation to self. The constitution of the representation as an act of intentionality dissolves into the relation which not only absorbs it fully but dents its centre with the excess of presence. In other words, it expels representation as the only communicable form of the *I* and turns it into a reciprocity which is up for grabs, that cannot remain safeguarded in individuality if real communication is ever to take place. The *I* that says 'I' is making a stake in and through the world, representing an image of thought that is launched to the relation to be reckoned, not as a representation of a full being that enters intact and pure but shaken and shaped by representations he cannot command. The 'I', and not the relation, is by its very definition contradiction and not reconciliation, a layered mechanism of traces but not spontaneity. The 'I' is always eccentric in its pure mathematical form; the 'I' is what lacks the quality of being a centre. The 'I' looked at from the other of intentionality can only become an object of representation (Levinas 1979, 127), that is, it is reduced to the same as other, indifference in its purest strain.

As a first conclusion, we can affirm that difference cannot be thought within itself as long as it is subjected to the requirements of representation. Deleuze's wager is that if we release the formidable differentiating power of the simulacrum, the empire of identity and resemblance will collapse at its feet. The subversion of Plato is thus on the table. Its guiding light is to collapse every foundation, and claim the world where the being of difference is the simulacrum, and where every simulacrum is its own model. The simulacrum is not simply a copy, but that which subverts all copies as it subverts all models (Deleuze 2004, xix). But before executing the subversion of Platonism, one of the boldest and most penetrating acts of thinking of contemporary philosophy, and in order to move from there to estimate the turn of the screw I intend to give on the Platonic subversion of Deleuze, it is essential to understand with more detail the scope and depth of the Deleuzian project.

Let us remember the four *shackles* of representation announced by Deleuze: (1) identity in the concept, (2) opposition in the predicate, (3) analogy in judgement, and (4) resemblance in perception. What does it all mean? That when the subordination of difference to the model operates, it does so through the four categories of representation that supplant the substance of thought. Hence, thought itself becomes a subordinate to representation, and the very possibility of immanence and difference disintegrates. Following this train of thought: (1) Identity is tied to the conceptual force of the model, which means the primacy of pre-established concepts over the originality of any idea stemming from any manifestation of difference. (2) Difference is taken to its extremes: it is either compressed to infinitesimal proportions (Leibniz) or stretched to enormous dimensions (Hegel) with the sole purpose of transmuting difference *in itself* into absolute oppositions between identities derived from iconic copies. This is where the strength of the negative in dialectics runs unconstrained. (3) To the extent that the iconic copy occupies the place of the model, all that remains for judgement is to rebuild the puzzle of the world from analogies drawn out from iconic copies, where to think is forbidden as an original act and suspended in the necessity of judgement to assign identities to the model. This is nothing less than judgement reduced to an industrial tool of distribution of the truth. (4) In the field of perception, we can only grasp things (ideas, facts) from the similarity that things have with the iconic copy and never the thing itself, in its *selfhood*.

These shackles, which form the crux of representation, will be an umbilical cord of this part of the argumentation: some will be treated in greater depth, and the second one will be especially vital to address the problem of dialectics and therefore the ontological foundation of democracy. However, each one develops a specific problem of ontology that we will not touch directly. Let us then face the first shackle, identity in the concept, because here lies the joint of problematic thinking as the basis of difference.

Perhaps the error of the philosophy of difference, Deleuze tells us, from Aristotle to Hegel, lies in confusing the *concept* of difference, with a mere *conceptual* difference (Deleuze 2004, 30). He concludes that when philosophy is content to inscribe difference within a general concept we cannot access the singular idea of difference and thus we remain snarled to a difference that is mediated by representation. Which is to say that we remain subdued to the identity of a model that obstructs any possibility of true difference (Derrida 1993, 119). In this same line of thinking, a concept can only become a universal in a relation of concepts. It thus needs a background, a context, a constitutive web, a language game, a determination from outside of the concept. A concept is thus always in a relation of power determined from the externality of the concept.

There is an abyss between defining difference with reference to a general concept and *creating* the concept of difference carved out from difference itself. The former means that the concept is in a position of primacy to difference, it is previous in time and logos, and as such it is a model under which difference must be modelled. Hence, the concept works as a framework that defines a specific identity prior to difference. In the latter case, the *concept of difference* emerges from difference itself: difference creates the very conditions of evaluating the concepts that it creates and the conceptual consistency of external concepts. In the first case, to be similar or equal is always to be equal or similar to something that is supposed to be identical with itself, something uncanny that enjoys the privilege of the original identity (Deleuze 2004, 368) without the original sin. Thus, the action of assimilating or equalling something means *identifying* it with a general concept that pre-exists both the *Idea* of difference and the possibility of a being that stems out from its own immanence.

Consequently, for example, my identity has to refer first and utmost to the concept that defines any and all identities (sexual, ethnic, etc.). The conceptual identity has already been fixed and standardized from a model and concentrated in the form of a general concept. Only then can I descend to the uniqueness of my difference, so that what constitutes me as a singularity is the concept, and not the difference.

It is crucial to understand that when the difference—of human acts per example—is referred to a conceptual difference, it cannot be difference for itself, because it does not proceed from an immanent decision, from the freedom or autonomy to claim the difference by difference. Precisely because the rule of conceptual identity is imposed upon it, it has to fit within the margins of a concept prefabricated in the law of identity. Therefore, difference may only be difference within the concept that forces it to be *part* of the concept as the element of integration of differences. Difference as an integral part of the concept loses all possibility of difference *in itself* because its fate is locked up in the sole possibility that the concept assigns the thing the difference that corresponds to it according to the law of identity. Here, as we will discuss below, the encryption of power can be seen in its fullest dimension.

The conceptual obstacle imposed on difference is that the conceptual order precedes any idea and thus the possibility of thinking. Consequently, the concept is something given, fixed as a rock-solid reference to reality which inhibits the mere possibility of *being thought as something* before it appears to schematize thought. As Lewis Gordon positions it, 'Where there is no thinking there is no distinction, and where there is no distinction, we collapse under the force of sameness or mandatory sameness (where thinking is indecent)' (Gordon 2006, 26–27). Deleuze's aim, in releasing the power of the simulacra, is that immanence in difference itself becomes the engine that generates the concept and any conceptual frame thereof. This means breaking with the Western philosophical and political tradition according to which difference always comes after the concept as something given and defined in advance.

Any agenda of the destitution of the model begins with the demolition of the privileged shrine of concepts and the liberation of our power to think about the dimensions of the problems that fashion life. Any agenda of liberation begins with the liberation of language—language understood not as an analytical composite of pre-given rules, but language as the primal opening that is yet to be decided. Hence, ideas (as a product of difference) oppose concepts as the locus of definition of language. Ideas are not concepts; they are a form of eternally positive differential multiplicity, distinguished from the identity of concepts, and thereby from the resemblance of perception. Ideas create divergence, disparity, and decentring; they create objects of affirmation which rupture the framework of conceptual representation. As Deleuze beautifully puts it, 'Ideas imply the always excessive Idea of poetry' (Deleuze 2004, 363).

Representation is the place of the illusion of transcendence, where identity happens in the form of concepts that overlap the idea. The problem that needs to be removed is not then the *concept of concept* but the action by which any reference to difference must be inscribed within a concept that explains it.

DELEUZE'S COPERNICAN REVOLUTION OF DIFFERENCE

Deleuze's Copernican revolution is nothing less than a total overturn of hegemonic Western thought. The heart of his ontology is deputized to establish the immanence of difference as the only viability of *being* and thus to depose unity and identity as the rigid models of the world. His strategy is to raise the simulacrum to the space of its own truth, so that the formation of reality does not obey the pairings' essence/appearance or model/copy but only the coupling of difference/immanence. We begin to inhabit another universe of being, the universe of extreme and ontological freedom—and here we are already scratching the edges of democracy.

To the extent that the simulacrum is the distortion of simultaneity, the word *modern* from its etymology means a petrified infinite instant. That is why we argue that the law of the simulacrum perverts the origin of reality—the simulacrum is the fundamental adulteration of the *being in common of difference*. The simulacrum as the order of unity and identity, imposes an interface, a simulated state of existence structured in law as its ideological image, as its symbolic duplicity. This is why the law of capitalism, which is essentially the law of the simulacrum, is not the law of existence, but the law of *subsistence*. And the loss of self in the simulacrum is the place where you live inside the Other (state), for the other (market), and because of the other (law).

In difference as the order of being, and repetition of difference as the immanent order of time, we find dialectics as the only theory of ideas that inaugurates being in its autonomy emerging from a genetic and problematic basis of difference. Such a dialectics is worlds apart from a theory of ideas based on Plato's identity, and the regulatory model of the Kantian unity, as well as the Hegelian model of contradiction (Smith 2012, 19). For Plato, difference exists as long as it has a direct representation, a hierarchical claim in the model. For Kant, difference exists as the product of the structuring of our understanding which itself can only warrant the correlation between subject and object as the condition of the coherence of the objective world. For Husserl, difference must be made relevant through the governing principle of consciousness, a correlate of concatenations of conscience. In short, Deleuze's project is the most promising theory to overcome the prison of identity in Western thinking; nevertheless, as we will see, it falls short for its lack of a mediating agent, leaving power as domination unfettered.

The traditional Platonic model, which has, beyond its creation, taken on immensely protracted dimensions and physical limits—including its manifestation in the more capillary structures of the Western world and its colonial extensions—is based on the transcendence of absolute models imposed on beings. The essence of Plato's transcendence lies in the submission of difference to the unity and identity of the model, where each manifestation of the world that does not correspond to the copy of the model must perish or be redirected to the riverbed of the prevailing model. This is a model that, as we have shown, is fallacious and is actually occupied by a particular that subdues the space of the absolute. So we discover that behind transcendence, an unfounded act of pure violence is concealed, forcing the world, in its richness and difference, to be reduced to a grey copy of an iconic copy.

For Deleuze, only simulacrum may be the sounding board of difference and only within it may difference be immanent to being. Deleuze concludes that the simulacrum affirms divergence and decentralization, where the only unity and convergence of the differential series is an informal chaos in which every difference is included (Deleuze 2004, 348). When the simulacrum overthrows the model as the origin of truth, it destroys the very idea of model in the same act (Deleuze 2004, 348). There is no series that enjoys a privilege or hegemony over the others: none possesses the identity of the model, or similarity of the copy, and everything is constructed by difference and communicates with others only through the difference of the differences (Deleuze 2004, 348).

To destitute the model and in the same act to consecrate the systems of simulacra as the source of truth annihilates the model/copy dichotomy and means a definitive break with any hierarchical equation. Difference as immanence does not build a new and solid foundation, it is rather the event that demolishes all foundations, as it means the universal collapse of the exercise of grounding. Difference in itself is difference liberated from all metaphysical identities. The overturn between difference and unity obstructs the model of unity and identity. In the latter, difference would be but the result of a simple empirical relationship between two terms that already have a previous identity ingrained in the model. So if it is true that representation is the element of identity, and similarity its unit of measurement, in the simulacrum only difference is its own measure, and presence is the only seal of difference (Deleuze 2004, 83). As stated by Bryant, 'A difference is *inter*-ontic when it consists in making a difference with respect to another object. A difference is *intra*-ontic, by contrast, when it pertains to the processes belonging to the *internal* constitution or essence of the object as a system of ongoing differences. The key point here is that if a difference is made, then the being *is*' (Bryant 2011a, 269).

In this order of things, difference is not what a being is—that is, it is not the recognizable stamp or emblem that being exhibits to the light in order to be commensurable, but rather, difference is what being produces through its difference. Levi Bryant makes a strong point here, that whenever knowledge fails in attaining the necessary information of a thing, when it cannot be squeezed far enough as to fill the relation with the subject, the thing in its undistinguishable difficulty is discarded as being beyond our knowledge so it becomes indifferent to knowledge (Bryant 2011a, 277).

Deleuze's genetic model of difference means the emancipation of difference as the true order of the world. It means the destruction of transcendence as the ground of truth. Therefore, we can say that Deleuze executes a substantive transformation of ontology as first philosophy. So if the question of the Idea for Plato is *What is it?*, and if the question for Wittgenstein is *What is it? In which cases?*, then for Deleuze the question is *Who this is? In which cases? Within which process of difference?*

AGAINST THE GRAIN OF RADICAL THINKING: THE NECESSARY HERESY OF ACTUALIZING DIFFERENCE

Deleuze (along with Foucault, Althusser, Derrida, Lyotard, and Blanchot) belongs to that tragic European generation that, while standing on the ashes of Auschwitz and Hiroshima, is hit by a lethal lightning of conscience that not only war, but even coloniality and racial and gender submission—that is to say, the structure of the world—follow the miserable failure of *instrumental reason*. A will to dominate that lurks behind the absolutes, the models, the universals on which the West was built. This revelation is followed by a primordial nausea towards major linear projects of liberation and perpetual peace, and an instinctive revulsion to the concept of power as the form and vehicle of domination. Central Western concepts such as progress, evolution, civilization, enlightenment, humanism, are its monstrous fingers smothering the world to the edge of apocalypse. This generation, in its anti-foundational turn, falls in a sort of intoxication of the world that pushes it towards the need to find in fruition, in the removal of foundations and in contingency the antidote to anthropocentric, androcentric, and Eurocentric totalitarianism.

The Einsteinian turn I intend to give to the ontology of difference in Deleuze occurs in this symptomatic turmoil of his time. The operation is simple, but its complex deployment and its consequences are profound. The primary destitution executed by Deleuze means the end of transcendence and the recuperation of immanence as the order of being, with the result that the only basis of things in the world is their total difference. However, an absolute process can also be the process of absolute nothingness. Without any criteria of specificity, the absolute difference can enclose the horrors of political hegemony. Without an articulation point, absolute difference may fade into an ethical and ontological fuzz of white noise. But especially without an element of contrast, without a matrix from which to evaluate infinite differences, difference itself can constitute its own negation. But most relevant is the recognition that when difference gravitates in its own orbit, it lacks the aptitude (potentia, strength) to produce an interference that disrupts the dense orbit of identity and unity. Therefore, without a foundation that actualizes and distributes in the world the physical mass of difference, it would remain a weightless indifference, which would then fail to modify the world of unity and identity. The task is not only to discover how the world of difference can operate within its own logic, but much more importantly, how this logic may indeed transfigure a world eclipsed by the logic of unity and identity. What is required is simply to discover the historical-political conditions of praxis under which difference is already a dense reality whose primary function is that of stubbornly opposing the force of unity and identity. From there on, the aim is to find the conditions under which difference may finally constitute a legality based on itself, that is to say, in its immanence.

But the limitation runs deeper, since the idea of an infinite number of singularities communicating through difference forsakes the fundamental building block of reality: power as domination. Precisely the first gesture of power as domination is to condition differences in language, to qualify them and thus to render them dependent upon valid forms of allocating meaning. In other words, there is no language game of difference that occurs outside the limitations of power as a legal standard of communication. How can we reside in a world of differences? We cannot ignore that what happens inside any game of language is determined by power. If and only if we assume as true the conditions of the production of rules that define the field of truth and falsity may we participate in the game. The intersection of sets in the production of language is determined by power, but if the only field of production of language is *difference in itself* then we are confronted with an extremely open—indeed, infinitely open—field. Consequently, what happens if and when these fields collide? Where may we find a rule, if any, of the measurement of the confrontation of differences? Where is the element of mediation that transforms unity into difference?

Here again philosophy forsakes the most pressing element in the conditions of difference, power as domination. Deleuze imagines a smooth surface of immanence where difference sprouts out of a virginal cocoon already encumbered with the conditions to create the world. Nevertheless, as we will keep insisting, in a plane of facticity, difference is already corrupted by potestas. To potentialize difference as the true category of transformation of politics, a further step must be taken: we must figure out the conditions under which difference becomes actual and may challenge the world of domination on its own turf. This point will become ever more clear in the following chapters, when we open a discussion of the impossibility of immanence within a world fractured by power as domination. Nonetheless, our point is that constructing difference as the order of the world requires an immersion in the dimensions of power as an already existing construction of the world.

What happens when we assume, as does Deleuze, that difference may only be the simulacrum of a concept of unity and identity? Exactly what we have just described, the inability of difference in itself to alter and hence be the source of reality. Hereinafter, what becomes urgent and primordial, the first degree of the turn of the screw, is to actualize difference as the sole source of difference.

Difference as actuality means that difference is the order of the world and the source of truth. Subsequently, if identity and unity remain dependent upon the idea of a model they become orders of simulacrum whose genetic code is programmed to abolish difference while arrogating for themselves the place of origin of the world. We have then the first degree of displacement of the Deleuzian project: the need to actualize difference. With the turn, potentia actualizes itself, inhibiting the possibility of a self-referential power. What we need henceforth, as a first requirement, is a qualitative leap: to recognize that what is truly universal is on the side of difference and not on the side of unity and identity. This conclusion is obvious because what we are coming to terms with is that if we keep evading universalist projects, we are withdrawing our power to face them in different terms than their own closed presuppositions. Such evasion thus also forfeits the possibility of establishing true universal projects that deny and suppress the farce of any project of domination. We have encountered, head on, the sham of the supremacy of universal models, based on unity and identity, for we can clearly acknowledge that their universalism fails ontologically—not because of universalism itself, but because of its preposterous abduction of the universal idea. They fail because they are the negation of the universal. That is, the failure occurs in a purely ideological dimension; it occurs at the level of the simulacrum. Where they promise difference we find homogenization, where they promise inclusion it is instead exclusion that functions as an essential condition for its operation. But specifically, where they mark the force field of the universal, we discover a vicious particular fraudulently filling the space of the model. There is no evidence that universal normative ideas are impossible or inconceivable. What bears unquestionable evidence is that the West erects itself as an apparatus of domination by fraudulently raising particulars to the place of universality, where universality is an inaccessible place of divinity and where the place of the origin is forbidden as an essential condition of the operation of the model. This is why, with piercing lucidity, Gordon states that 'The fact of the matter is that different communities of people do manage to communicate with each other, and since they are able to do so, there must be cultural universals' (Gordon 2006, 82). It is evident that the primacy of the world of unity and identity over difference is purely a phenomenon of violence, of un-reason—that is, an act of imposition that works at the level of ideology, duplicated in massive production scales of reality such as law, image, spectacle, and science. The world of unity and identity is the factory of the subject in modernity (biopower) with the pervasive mission of skimming difference, in order to include it falsely, until it disappears completely.

If we already acknowledged the need to actualize difference, what follows, necessarily, is to find the subject and method of such actualization, which is to say how, and under what conditions, can we make a qualitative leap from an order of things overshadowed by unity to one founded on difference. This quantum leap begins with the awareness that it is in a political plane where *power as domination* is the wall that maintains the worlds of difference and identity in isolation. The question of the quantum leap is the question of the subject of the leap, in other words the subject of the revolution and of a new law that is built based on difference and from difference itself. Thus, what we need is the *agent* of difference, not the agent where difference occurs, but the agent that produces difference as immanence.

Our twist on matters will be a radical one, as it will suppose a new foundation of politics and a new constitution of the agent of change. Thus agency and structure will be reconstructed from its foundations. The core of a metaphysics of power from Aristotle to our days has been drawn out from the tight interaction between the concepts of potentia and actuality, and ever since Spinoza from the relation between potentia and potestas. These are the deep-clustered dimensions of power that must be brought to a new light and examination. Constituent power vibrates within this alignment of power, finding the meaning and the limits of its own possibilities. But it is not only power that is ingrained profoundly in these compositions, but every order of objectivity and subjectivity, every determination of the possible and the virtual, and every definition of the necessary and the contingent. Within the walls of potentia/actuality and potentia/potestas, the fate of the world and the things in it is decided. *What can we do? How far we can go? How thick is the sheath of reality that prevents us from breaking through to the other side?* These are all questions whose answers lie in the composition between potentia, potestas, and actuality. Thus far, in the history of philosophy, the composition has been kept in a tight balance, as a precious chemical compound that can be upset by the slightest tremor. Its volatility is extreme, but precisely because of this, the answer to power as transformation, power as fluctuation, power as the access to a new set of possibilities to the world lies within in its chemical reactions. We have already accomplished a great bounty in our quest through Deleuze's destitution of the iconic copy, but we have only travelled half of the way towards discovering radical democracy.

Our thesis is that difference within its own becoming is a weightless difference that forsakes the monumental symbiosis of power as domination of coloniality/modernity/capitalism. Henceforth, the only possibility of uniting difference and democracy and thus opening up politics as the order of the world passes through the necessity of locking horns with sovereignty and all its productions of power, in short, with power as domination.

Fathoming Aristotle's metaphysics we will find that the true order of politics lies in the construction of politics as a non-qualified actuality. Energeia, as work, is the sign of the people; this will prove that Agamben's dominant interpretation of actuality as synonym with qualification of life is wrong. From there on, we move to challenge Negri's interpretation of Spinoza's ethics where we will discover that the evasion of a point of friction in power relations destroys the political in its own terms.

The fundamental order of constituent power is its potentia, while actuality is its contingent, secondary, and possible concretion (constituted power). Potentia is the primary order, whereas actuality is its probable consequence. Thus, the relationship between potentia and actuality is not antithetical but complementary. Actuality is the consequence of potentia, of the way potentia realizes itself, and therefore actuality is subjected to, dependent upon, potentia as its condition of validity and legitimacy. What happens when potentia actualizes itself? According to the capitalist historical and political narrative, its political philosophy and constitutional law, *potestas* deposes potentia and all that remains; as a compact reference of reality is actuality, and therefore we can only understand power with reference to domination for it is the illegitimate substitution of the origin. I believe that a strong variant of postmodern thinking falls into the macabre hustle of capitalism when it assumes the loss of potentia as something natural and allows actuality (constituted power as the antithesis of potentia) to be the resilient and undisputed locus of power. My point is that power as domination, in other words, as potestas, does not emerge from actuality, but rather from the fact that actuality affirms itself as the origin when it arrogates itself the place of potentia. Hence, the true postmodern terror of power does not come about because power is *actual*, but on the contrary, precisely because power does not become from an authentic exercise of potentia as its original creative force.

Thus, in terms of reality, a mere potentiality that does not result in the creation of concrete spaces is a potentia that revolves in an ultra-mundane orbit, distant from reality and unable to produce itself in the world (Alice has to transpose the looking glass). I am not saying by this that the potentia belongs to the world of the unreal and actuality to the world of reality. What I am saying is that in our state of affairs, actuality appears as the only dimension of reality, as a *causa sui* of reality, the only transcendent cause of the world, precisely because it is severed from the potentia of constituent power. However, the fact that potentia is realized in actuality does not imply its loss—as has been the instrumental and false assumption of liberalism—but on the contrary, the realization ratifies the original power in potentia, its place as the first *Idea*, as a matrix of truth whose actualization is the necessary result of its power to compose reality. Therefore, we must emphasize that the postmodern terror regarding power is really towards power as domination, towards power as the order of unity and identity that is only actuality in itself. This manifestation of power is not only a particular version, but also the particular and isolate feature produced by unity and identity, which, when it operates, occludes the original potentia of the constituent power.

What the postmodern terror and evasion of power achieve is to disconnect two planes that are intimately connected, potentia as origin and actuality as its result. Said disconnection would mean that potentia is a mere epiphenomenon incapable of affecting reality, and we are then left in a state of utter prostration to transform actuality. When this fundamental relationship is severed, as Negri does when he establishes that the denial of potentia is actuality (Negri 1999, 21), a vaporous parallelism is imposed where the two lines do not touch each other's reality. Therefore, actuality is presented as the only viable concrete reality. In other words, the only possibility of producing an actuality that denies power as domination is when we refuse to burn the causal bridges between potentia and actuality and we let the latter be the immediate consequence of the former.

Under the conditions raised by Deleuze, precisely to the extent that an intrinsic ontological unity in difference does not, and cannot exist, everything that exists exists in a constant becoming, a pure potentiality that makes the planet of actuality uninhabitable. Becoming as a condition of being, when transposed to the political terrain, means the constitutive lack of a measure of an element of distinction, which allows us, in actuality, to distinguish the just from the unjust. This *Chaosmos* (Deleuze and Guattari 1987) avoids the moral order, for each simulacrum would be tied to its own game as its own exclusive truth, each molecule sustaining an isolated life form, locked up in an inferno of plasmatic solitude. Becoming, as simply becoming, not only skips over conflict as the order of politics (which is precisely what we seek to recuperate) but also precludes the realization of power as an instance of political praxis.

However, with the turn of the screw, when difference is actualized as the source of politics, actuality will be deprived of its character of domination, because that character is not specific to actuality, but to the absence of difference as the source of power. The turn of the screw that we will execute by investing the place of difference and of the simulacrum, allows us to prove, without a doubt, that such system is democracy as origin and deployment of difference. Not only will our *turn* prove that the democratic impossibility is a false conundrum but that democracy is the only possible foundation of politics. Let us observe the problem closely. This will be the task of the fourth and fifth chapters.

Chapter 4

The Plastic Soul of Democracy

Power Between Potentia, Potestas, and Actuality

Thus far we have established the urgency for a problematic proposition: the need to actualize difference, which is immediately transformed in an even more taxing statement, the need to actualize power. The latter, on its own, instantly flashes an intuitive proximity with potestas—that is, power as domination—and so the alarms of radical democracy turn to burning red. Until now, we have walked on a slippery slope, dangling between manifold manifestations of power that seem to cancel each other out. Accordingly, on the one side power, typically denoted as potestas, means domination, an impossibility of being and becoming beyond subjugation, as well as harsh lines that delimit or utterly negate conflict. On the other side, potentia stands as the generic right of all unto the world of the being in common of the democracy. We have encountered a monumental blockage for difference as the order of the world, its incapacity to move beyond its own constitution and affect the world. That is, to transverse the world constituted through domination and the denial of difference, a world we have proved is constructed under the single premise of the cancellation of difference. The vicious cycle must be broken from inside. Therefore, we are seeking a way to establish the *necessity* of difference to become actual, that is, to have a precise locality within the world that would render the power of the hidden people as the being of democracy and thus the possibility of the truth of the political. In order to understand what we mean by the latter, it is vital to establish a clear framework in the relations between *potentia* and *actuality*.[1] It is not an easy task, and the path is splashed with landmines and booby traps, or, perhaps, the path itself is a booby trap. Our starting point then has to be Aristotle's *Metaphysics*; for it is there that the difference between both concepts becomes central for the philosophical history of metaphysics. Our excursus through Aristotle is not destined to cover every instance of his construction of metaphysics but only those aspects that can submit our proposition to strict scrutiny and in doing so clarify the viability of our proposal.

But our focus goes beyond a simple recuperation or setting afoot of the distinction between potentia and actuality. Our target is much more precise and demands the most accurate surgical tools to reach it in its remote location, to perforate through its thick bone and tissue while extracting the exact point where the actualization of difference is not only practicable but a full necessity of radical democracy. Furthermore, the fact that we can reach such a recondite point is synonymous with the being of democracy. Our wager, which will become clear in this excursus, is that within the metaphysical compound of the Aristotelian opus we can prove that the hidden people, as the being of democracy, are in fact pure actuality as *Energeia* or being-at-work. The latter affirmation will be fathomed through the understanding of actuality in complete accordance with the Aristotelian definition, which disavows a great part of the political philosophy of potentia from Spinoza to Deleuze and Negri while reinforcing some of its most powerful aspects. Although this proof will demand to veer in 'contrapelo' of Aristotle's politics, it will nonetheless be consistent with, and a product of, his metaphysics.

Potentia as a political and metaphysical concept has fuelled a rich and productive engagement in contemporary political philosophy. It has become a new and vivacious opening of the possibilities of political transformation from the bottom while escaping metaphysical essentialism and mystification. Within the maelstrom of controversies and interpretations that the concept awakens, there are two that stand out for their insightfulness and the possibilities they beget for radical democracy. I am referring to the work of Giorgio Agamben and of Antonio Negri, the latter through his most noted works[2] and as a co-author with Michael Hardt of the Empire trilogy. Both are *hegemonic* in the thought of radical democracy and constitute an immense landscape of speculation and praxis. In this respect, for them our proposal of the need to actualize difference is nothing short of a blasphemy. This is precisely why the steering of our theoretical vessel must navigate the waters that they have established with such fluidity and precision. Hence, our reading of Aristotle's *Metaphysics* will be done against their understanding of power as *simply* potential.

The quarrels with Agamben and Negri (sometimes with Hardt, though often alone) are distinct. Both share a common feature in the creation of their political philosophy: they shun away from *actuality* because they see in it the demise of politics. The common thread of the interpretation is that if potentia is actualized, contingency—as the possibility of the new and of the transformation of power—will thus be fulminated with it. The difference is that, in the face of the horror of *the actual* as potestas, they take different paths. Agamben seeks refuge in the poetic figure of the *passion of not being and not doing* incarnated in the figure of the scrivener who refuses to write and thus maintains potency through the suspension of wanting. On the other hand, although Negri as the Paulian reader of Spinoza sees the full blow of potestas as a reality which cannot just be wished away through impotence, he refuses to deal with actuality in order to maintain an immaculate meaning of potentia. To attain such purity of potentia as being, Negri reads Spinoza through a chain of suppositions that simply imply the withdrawal of potentia from politics and the sheer loss of the possibility of attaining a moment of the articulation of the political subject. As Mouffe has stated it, 'The problem with this immanentist ontology is its inability to give account of radical negativity' (Mouffe 2013, 78).

We will develop a criticism of Agamben in the present section and will defer our engagement with Negri to the following chapter. Nevertheless, it is vital to note that they are intimately connected. Hence, the critique and our own proposal will arise in its mutual composition and from the common core of Aristotle's *Metaphysics*.

ARISTOTLE'S SUBSTANCE

The great problem that traverses the work of Aristotle, and that Western thinking will inherit as the question of questions, is the one regarding substance. As Levi Bryant has stated recently, regarding the paramount relevance of substance for philosophy, 'While philosophers are quite right to reject the *traditional* concept of substance, the *problem* to which the concept of substance is designed to respond nonetheless persists' (Bryant 2011a, 272). Derrida puts all his chips in this quadrant of philosophy, to the extent that if the West as a concept, and as a historical and political force, has any identity, any one thing that marks it, it is, as we have seen, a metaphysics of presence. A metaphysics of presence means that the question of *what is it?* always points to a centre of a presence of something that at the same time unravels a principle that is absent, an *absconditus* principle which is not in the thing itself, but determines it as a thing. We can only talk of a thing when it is present as the absence of its principle.

To reach our goal it's fundamental to understand what Aristotle means by *substance* (Ousia[3]) since it resolves the question *what is being*. Substance is the fundamental particle of truth. The primary name of being and thus the constitution of any possibility to access to a single universal judgement of the objects that structure the world (Aristotle. Met. 1.981a). Aristotle's engagement of substance is complex and has perplexed scholars over millennia. Here lies the bedrock of the metaphysics of presence. The constitution of being for Western philosophy will always refer back to Aristotle's characterization of being through substance. Inside it, we may find not only a diagram that infuses all Western philosophy, but also the elemental distinctions that lead to the definition and sheer possibility of power, causality, logical necessity, ethics, existence, the dyads of being and becoming, final and efficient cause, possible and impossible, and time.

Aristotle treats substance from diverse views, but two are pivotal: his approximation from the *Categories*, on the one side, and from *Metaphysics*, on the other. Do they converge? Are they inconsistent with each other? Can they be made to mean a single and complex definition?[4] This crossroads offers special difficulty, and the aporia between both terms has marvelled and vexed thinkers to our day. Substance can be named and used from multiple perspectives that serve to achieve certain aims within a particular science. Hence, number, quality, form, modes, individuality, as part of the *Categories*, can define substance for these sciences in accordance to the definitions that they seek within their own boundaries. But when engaging metaphysics (as Aristotle names first philosophy), substance adheres to a new and mighty meaning that designates being in an absolute and final manner. Thus, substance in metaphysics is the name of being. Here we must remember Antonio Negri's beautiful scholium, 'Philosophy speaks because being is not mute' (Negri 2003, 36).

We are not holding that Aristotle designed two diverse conceptualizations of substance which are strange to each other, one from categories and the other from metaphysics. Rather, we hold simply that the categories aim at a certain trait of substance that is included as the stepping stone of his construction in metaphysics that thus takes substance to a new level. To speak of substance from categories is surely to already speak of substance in metaphysics. Nevertheless, the categories are concerned with one metaphysical aspect of substance: to signal out its individuality through quality, quantity, place, activity, passivity, etc. The other more compelling questions of the metaphysics (which categories alone cannot solve and that are the backbone of our inquiry) are: how are things generated and how do they remain as substance through change, how do substances come into existence and perish, and how do they remain substance through time and change (transitions). As we have just stated, these questions cannot be answered through the direct application of the categories but nonetheless, the categorical individualization is their basic starting point. Put on the head of a pin, the categories determine substance as individuality as the precondition to determine being from the *Metaphysics*.

DEFINITION OF SUBSTANCE

From the outset, we encounter the riddled definition: 'Being is said in many ways' (*pollachôs legomenon*). The phrase 'said in many ways' is Aristotle's flag on the peak of philosophy, the vortex of meaning, the putting forth of every philosophical endeavour. It offers the urgency of existence, a doubt, a tremor; it seems a warning from an old sorcerer, the signalling at the entrance of a labyrinth of vertigo; it drops you at high speed into the centre of the problem while the centre dilates until losing any reference to geometry. But, does it mean a natural tendency of being to be slippery or vaporous? And the natural incapacity of language to pin it down to meaning? No, it instead means that everything that is said in many and tumultuous ways must always refer to substance. It means that substance can share many names, positions, and modes, but it remains substance through and through, so the names are not the different names of one holy entity, but rather the countless possibilities for the spread of substance to remain the same. In a nutshell, being is not ambiguous; it is what is said of being that is ambiguous. In *Metaphysics*, Aristotle puts forward a definition of substance that arches between Categories and Metaphysics:

> Clearly then it is by reason of the substance that each of the things referred to exists. Hence that which is primarily, not in a qualified sense but absolutely, will be substance. Now *primary* has several meanings; but nevertheless substance is primary in all senses, both in definition and in knowledge and in time. For none of the other categories can exist separately, but substance alone; and it is primary also in definition, because in the formula of each thing the formula of substance must be inherent; and we assume that we know each particular thing most truly when we know what 'man' or 'fire' is. (Aristotle. Met. 7.1028a)

A first casting of the nature of substance is that substance is primary substance, and if this primary substance were not to exist then nothing else could exist (Aristotle. Cat. 2b6). But what are *primary substances*? According to the Categories, primary substances are individual objects (*that man* Socrates, *that horse* Bucephalus), so substances can be contrasted with everything else, that in relation to their individuality, are either secondary substances or accidents. Substance is thus all the predicates of individuality. Aristotle defines substance as 'that which is neither said of a subject nor in a subject' (Aristotle. Cat. 2a14-15). So we have before us our first concept of being as substance as that which is *not said of others* and is *not present in others*. This is the definition of primary substance from the categories. So primary substance is such because it is not predicable of, or attributable to, anything else. Substance begins to make up a certain corporeity before our understanding; it is determined by two kinds of predicables. One predicable is 'what is said of an object': man is said of Socrates. The other predicable is what is 'in' an object: Socrates the individual is not a predicate of anything else, so the property is in a thing as a 'subject'. When we run the definition through its possibilities, we encounter a sharper meaning of substance: the individual which is not accidental.

For Aristotle, substance is said in many ways, so in order to signal the specificity of substance he draws a division between primary and secondary substances. For example, Socrates is 'white', 'cultured', or 'tall', or Socrates is 'talking to Protagoras', 'sitting down', or 'In Callias' home'. The first conclusion of the categories is that primary substances are particulars which can be predicated to have secondary substances which are universals (Studtmann 2014). For example, Socrates has to be singled out among his kind (universal) which is humankind, but for Aristotle, such universals such as 'belonging to a kind' do not serve the concept of primary substance, because we could only find identity among kinds which only serve as a preliminary step to reach the individual (not the particular). Only an individual passes the litmus test of 'said of' and 'not present in'. Man is said of Socrates but only in a secondary way, 'white' is said of Socrates but only in an accidental way. White does not define Socrates and his whiteness does not define white which can have a life independent from being in Socrates. But Socrates, the individual, cannot be said of anything else, neither of 'man' nor of 'whiteness'. Another man named Socrates will only produce a transitory obstacle of 'homonymy' easily surpassed by referring 'the' Socrates to the formal categories (quantity, quality, relative, modes). Employing the categories, we can finally establish that the Socrates we are talking about is primary substance for he, as an individual, is not present in any other being, having the opposite side as truth, that is, Socrates as a name or a man cannot 'be' without his substance. Secondary substance, the genus, is an appendix of primary substance; it serves to approximate being, to single it out, but it does not form it.[5]

Aristotle defines subject as 'that of which everything else is predicated, while it is itself not predicated of anything else' (Aristotle. Met. 1028b36). There is then a twofold in the categories. The first definition, 'not said of' and 'not in', serves the purpose of identifying an individual as a subject, as a singularity. Hence, the example we are toying with would read: Socrates is not said of and is not in anything else but *that* Socrates. On the other hand, Aristotle divides 'things that are said of' into seven distinct kinds (quantity, quality, relatives, position, etc.) to establish 'what is said of' in relation to this classification. The list of categories[6] can be deemed a compass aiding the seeker to determine the location (a particular mode of standing in the world) of a substance within a vast geography. Thus the predicates: Socrates is 'white', 'cultured', 'talking with Protagoras', 'at noon', 'in Callias' home' are all independent predicates to the substance of their predication, that is, Socrates. But they are also predicates of Socrates that pin down the modes in which Socrates stands in the world in a particular time (actuality). So the movement between the first classification of 'what is said of' and 'not in' stand as a correlate to the classification of the seven modes and forms in a coalesced process that determines the individuality of being among its genus and before the world. We must bear in mind that individualities are not substantiated by genus (Socrates is a man) but that genus is an auxiliary (secondary) form of determining individuality (not all men are Socrates, nor is Socrates all men). In conclusion, kind, genus, quantity, quality, etc. always stand in relation to substance as primary being; they exist insofar as they are related to substance in a dependent way. The beings in the primary sense are substances; the beings in other senses are the qualities, quantities, etc., that belong to substances. Hence, you can take 'white' and the rest of the list and cross them off and you would still have Socrates as substance, just in a different *mode* of being. A vital aspect that we will work on later is that the categories give an account of time at different points, like snapshots, but not of time as a continual flux, that is, time as production of being.

To put it bluntly and maybe in a simplified way, what the categories intend to detract from a multi-universe of complex things, relations, and formations, is an individuality. Hence, the question of 'what is Socrates' is referred to the analysis of the categories that make Socrates a specific individual regardless of particular accidents (fat, cultured, tall) and the genera (man, biped). The categories allow a certain singling out of an individual.

For both categories and metaphysics, substance discloses the same meaning. The problem of categories addresses an epistemological problem—that is, how do we know substance, how can we identify that x is substance, or what is the substance of x. Furthermore, it determines the modes of the substance in a particular time, in a particular position, and in relation to other things that fashion the world (that is, how the individual stands towards the world). For metaphysics, it's a metaphysical question with all that is imbued in the term. The question here is twofold for Aristotle and stems from a unique concern. First, how does substance come about (generation) and perish? Second, how can an object persist in its substance (the thing that makes it what it is) through transformations of time and space? This is the terrain of potentia and actuality. However, we must first determine what substance is, regarding the questions posed in metaphysics, since it is here that being is defined *qua* being, as the constituent indivisible particle of what exists.

Categories become a kind of bracketing of the modes through which a thing is, its qualities, quantities, etc. For Aristotle, what maintains our understanding of the physical world in stability is not a framework. Rather, the factor that determines what a thing is regarding a given relation is made relevant only through the categories as a process of individualization, of singling out from within the immense array of combinations. It is thus not a necessity of coherence that the understanding stamps onto the world to make it feasible and to prevent the unknowable physical world from going haywire, but a means of recognition of a thing in itself through the suffering of the effects of the relations with other identifiable things. Properties depend on substances and not the other way around. A property is instantiated in substance; it marks a change of the relation that does not affect substance but lets us identify substance against its own backdrop. The identity of substances does not depend on a categorial definition of it: categories, remember, help us identify the substance in a certain mode of its being. Categories do not trace individuals back to an origin in which they may be identified by their belonging or not to the definition of the origin. Even if substance was independent of the modes of existence it would still be substance, no matter what the modes are.

Substance is then equivalent (and here it gains all the force of *ousia*) to a single meaning to which we always have to refer to. This not only means that any evocation of reality must name substance in order for reality to be, but a deeper thing is involved here: substance is the only and defining substratum of meaning.

Substance within the construction of the categories allows us to locate concrete identities—a particular man or thing as the primary substance. What makes Socrates *Socrates* in relation to other men and everything else. Being fat, six feet tall, cultured, pale, or smart are localizations of properties in regards to substance (Cohen, 2009, 200). On the other hand, metaphysics asks the question *what is the substance of such an individual*—what is preserved as substance not regarding the transformations it suffers during a lifetime, or the gaining or losing of accidental properties. In order to gain such a footing, we need to elevate the fundamental question: How does substance, in this pure metaphysical sense, come into being? The question of coming into being is encapsulated in the question of generation: How are substances generated? And how do they perish? This is the stone thrown into calm waters of ontology that ripples and builds the storm of philosophy. Contained in this apparently simple query lies the answer to such acute questions of this guise: How can we speak of an identity of an object if its properties are always being transformed through time?[7]

Substance is the primary concept of being. Every classification in the *categories* in Aristotle's system defines being, even being in motion but without the difficulty of transitions—that is, the transformation of time. Confronted with movement (not as physical motion but as transformation)— that is, with the problem of the continuum as change and becoming—the categories fail to ascribe being. While substance can describe being in its totality, it only does so on the condition of modes of being in a particular frozen frame of time. Nevertheless, substance becomes blurred and utterly unstable in transitions, in the unappealable becoming of time. The bug biting its way to the core of the Aristotelian description of being and substance is the transition, the unstoppable change that befalls things; in other words, the continuum; so, Aristotle must reach out with all his force to try to appease the unappeasable—movement, transformation, or, in a word, the transition.

For the metaphysics, substance is not a matter of change regarded only as motion. Motion as such is an exclusive endeavour of Aristotle's *Physics*, which in his regard is 'second philosophy', whereas *Metaphysics* is 'first philosophy'. In the latter, motion is not regarded as a simple change in position of a thing through time, but rather as something more complex: how a thing perseveres in its beingness despite the change befallen in its thingness. This is the crux of the matter for Aristotle. Change of the most unforeseeable ways can occur to a thing but a thing must remain as substance. Substance is thus the unchangeable character of a thing that makes a thing *the* thing. Therefore, change can occur to its qualities without fettering the 'thingness' of a thing. Whatever defines substance is present at every time of the existence of a thing. The substance of a thing is present at all times and places. In categories, substance is simply the individual but only through the 'metaphysics' can we grasp the centrality of substance in the construction of being. Even more relevant for our enterprise, the central question is, how does substance come to be? The question of the becoming of being is where the division line is drawn between potentia and actuality. This latter question swings and defines the core relations of metaphysics as first philosophy; it defines the threshold of the possible and the impossible, the necessary and the contingent, and the dividing line (if such a line exists) between potentia and act. Being as a possibility, becoming as a necessity, and transforming as a capacity, are all burning questions in the heart of potentia and actuality. We can begin to throw ever more burning questions into the bonfire of metaphysics: is *becoming* an integral part of power? Is *to be* a relation of power? What can the body do (Deleuze 2001)? Are things determined by their 'capacity' to change *in* themselves, or in other things *qua* themselves?

For Aristotle, the principle of substance is not what lies mysteriously in the nest of the *arché*, extending its hands from obscurity to baptize the substance of a thing with something other than the thing. Rather, the principle of substance is plainly what a thing is and/or what it may become. Change deemed not as simple physical motion but as the property of generation and transition can be the irruption of contingency, chaos, and indiscernibility; transitions are the seed of possibility for being.

That there is a *thing* that we can signal as a proof of presence demands the demonstration that the thing persists in time. That is, there is something about that thing that remains stable regardless of change, which concurrently demands that we seize both the generation (coming to be) of that thing and its perishability. Substance is what is said to remain the same notwithstanding the brutal changes that can occur to an object during its being an object.

But before diving into the waters of potentia and actuality a prior step must be taken, a step that determines the relation between generation and transitions. How things are generated and how they remain themselves through transitions already supposes a relation between the potential required for generation and its actuality. In this respect, Aristotle opens up a new line of inquiry heading all efforts to define generation and transition where the categories are insufficient; in consequence, a new conceptualization must take place. Before opening this line, let us think of exemplifications to survey the kind of troubled waters we will be crossing. Think of a house, a statue, a song, a movie, a plum cake (Alice's in *Through the Looking Glass*), a man (Socrates again), a people, a shredded carrot, yellow wings breaking from a cocoon, an arrow in flight, a dog about to bark, the death of a galaxy, the birth of a cell, a kettle heating water and the vapour that it produces, a foal splashing in the mud after falling from the womb, the first stroke on a mural by Siqueiros (and the wall before it), a rocking chair, ashes to ashes, a person operating a blowtorch welding two metal parts together, Wittgenstein's red slab. Think of all these things from the perspective of generation and transitions: when can we say that the thing is authentically the thing, and when is it potentially the thing? Are we standing on the brink of virtuality and possibility? On the edge of logical possibility? How can we ascribe meaning to an event? The answer to all of these questions is not simply a logical matter but instead chains all the dimensions of what we call *being* and henceforth of all we can call *power*; it defines the possibility of existence.

As we have stated earlier, our hunger is defined by the complex intersection of power—that is, of potentiality and actuality—so we will proceed by simplifying some logical links in Aristotle's thinking. We have already determined that substance is the individual; now we need to know what the being of an individual is. How is it generated and how does it persist through transitions?

In *Metaphysics* book seven (Book Z), Aristotle advances new arguments in order to rule out essence, universals, and genus as the constituent of being. In a gesture analogous to the categories, he arrives at the subject as the being of substance (Aristotle. Met. 7. 1028a–1041b). However, the question, through generation and transitions, becomes, *what is a subject? What determines the existence of a subject as substance?* Hence, it is no longer viable to single it out through the categories, for now we need to establish further the cognition of generation and permanence.

According to Aristotle, *matter, form*, and the *composite* of both (hylomorphism) all seem strong candidates to fulfil the substance of a subject—of its generation, continuity, stability, permanence, and perishability. In his words, 'By matter I mean, for instance, bronze; by form, the arrangement of the form; and by the combination of the two, the concrete thing: the statue' (Aristotle. Met. 7.1029a).

The first candidate, matter, is discarded by Aristotle, because not only does it not advance anything beyond the definition of substance as headed by the categories, but it also makes the definition circular.

We have now stated in outline the nature of substance—that it is not that which is predicated of a subject, but that of which the other things are predicated. But we must not merely define it so, for it is not enough. Not only is the statement itself obscure, but also it makes matter substance; for if matter is not substance, it is beyond our power to say what else is. (Aristotle. Met. 7.1029a)

Bronze does not make the statue, wood is not the substance of a table or a guitar, bones and flesh are not the substance of Socrates. Clearly, as has been established, substance must meet a constituent standard: it must be separable (*chôriston*) and a *this something* (*tode ti*). Substance must be a determinate individual that is capable of existing on its own 'for it is accepted that separability and individuality belong especially to substance' (Aristotle. Met. 7.1029a). Of course, we can argue that matter is separable from substance and that it survives on its own, but as we will soon discover, it cannot meet both requirements at the same time regarding substance.

A piece of wood can be in a guitar, in a table, or in a house, but as matter it does not constitute the substance of the guitar, the table, or the house. All we can say about it, as far as we can go, is to say that such things are *wooden*. Effectively wood can exist separate from and maintain its individuality thereof from the guitar, the table, and the house but therefore it would not even be part of the substances called guitar, table, or house. Thus, in those particular cases of the predication of substance wood is not a matter of the substances referred to it. Separate from form, matter fails to be *a this* of substance. A piece of wood is individual on its own but when composed into something other than in itself it becomes a part of substance only if it is attached in a certain matter and given a specific form. So matter cannot be simultaneously separable and individual. Matter is discarded as substance.

Another problem perceived by Aristotle is that if matter were to count as substance, matter would have to enter the thing of substance totally unchanged. Therefore, we would have to imagine that the statue of David by Michelangelo is identical to a block of marble, which in turn would be identical to the vein cut and this to the quarry and therefore, finally, to earth, ultimately establishing the absurdity that the substance of David is earth. Moreover, along the same line of argumentative proof, there could not be a distinction between Michelangelo's David and Trajan's column (neither of time or space) since both are made from the same matter. Henceforth, if matter were to fashion substance, we would always stand on the verge of identifying a further matter of which the matter we name is composed—and, thus, we would be forced into an inevitable chain of regress. But even if we succeed in identifying the Alpha matter, by itself it lacks any power to distribute itself so as to create a composition of elements beyond itself. So according to Aristotle, something else, an excess, is needed in order to define substance, something that organizes matter into a certain *this*.

Let us structure this point about matter and its claim to substance from another perspective, bearing in mind that the target of substance in metaphysics is to identify the generation of substance (its possibility, modes, potentialities, actualities) and its capacity to remain the same through transitions.[8] The aforementioned would then suggest that the true meaning of substance is to be found in the *composite* of form and matter, which is true for Aristotle in his *Physics* (Aristotle. Phys. 195a6–8) but not so from a metaphysical examination (Beere 2006). Hylomorphism (the name of the compound) has a strong claim for substance, but also succumbs to the sword of metaphysics. Consider the following; 'It is obvious, then, from what we have said, that the thing in the sense of form or essence is not generated, whereas the concrete whole which is called after it is generated; and that in everything that is generated matter is present, and one part is matter and the other form' (Aristotle. Met. 7.1033b).

Let us commence from a logical highland: A composite—in order to be a composite—demands the pre-existence of whatever it is made of. Consequently, if it is made of form and matter, both must pre-exist, for if one of them were to be created *in* the composite, the whole logic of composite as substance would be self-defeating. Standing before a bronze sphere, we know that it is not the sphere *as such* that has been generated—that is, it is not *the concept* of sphere that has been generated before us—but rather that some matter called bronze has been turned into a bronze sphere. This allows Aristotle to hint strongly at the composite in this way: 'But if the essence of sphere in general is generated, something must be generated from something; for that which is generated will always have to be divisible, and be partly one thing and partly another; I mean partly matter and partly form' (Aristotle. Met. 7.1033b). Remember the trait of substance is that it is not a predicate of anything else, and it is not *in* anything else. Therefore, it would be necessary, in order to keep the said definition intact, that whatever creates substance must pre-exist substance for it to be a composite. Henceforth, if we are talking about a bronzed sphere as a composite of form and matter, bronze must pre-exist the composite; but in the same logic, *form* (the sphere) must also pre-exist the composite. Aristotle then asks a fundamental question: is there some sphere besides the particular spheres? What he is pointing out is the resolution of the following question: does whoever makes a *bronzed sphere* thereby make the bronze and the sphere? Or does he rather create a sphere that is bronzed—that is, does he give form to matter? Just as Michelangelo did not create the matter but the form in the David, so he did not create it out of a pre-existing form. Nevertheless, we can stretch Aristotle's logic further. It is not the nature of bronze to be sphered—if it were, in this particular case, then the form would surely pre-exist the composite. Since it is not the *substance* of bronze (matter) to be sphered, we cannot hold that form pre-exists the composite. Seen in another way, it was not bronze that came to be in the sphere, although bronze surely pre-exists the bronzed sphere: we do not call it simply *bronze* as we do not call the David simply *marble*. Therefore, the concept of composite also begins to crack at its seams within the test of substance. Of course, we can respond that if the David was made out of butter it would not be *this* David, so marble is a constituent part of that specific substance. The point would be well taken: marble is part of the composition, but not the substance. Michelangelo did not create marble in creating the David, but instead generated the form (a certain *this*) *from* the matter, which is not the same as to hold that matter was created *in* the David.

Consider that letters are matter and syllables a composite (Aristotle. Phys. 195a16). Take two sets of syllables: *on* and *no*. They share the same matter but their disposition, as distribution of their components, is completely diverse. There is always the other thing that has to be presupposed in a syllable: not just the sum of letters but the structure, a particular tonality, a field of attraction between the parts, the excess of the structure that they denote. This supposes a form, and form as the assembly that binds the parts together as an organized whole, or as something in itself beyond an erratic flux of matter or a piling up of stuff. Form is then for Aristotle the principle of organization of the structure that is substance: it is the rule of the formalization of matter. It is a principle of organization insofar as matter is caught up in a process of becoming something other than itself. Matter must become substance under the organization of the form.[9] Form is what is ultimately generated, whether naturally or artificially, and thus form is substance.

POTENTIA AND ACTUALITY, THE THRESHOLD OF DEMOCRACY

The crucial advantage that form possesses over the rest of the claimants is that it brings a precise sense of organization to the definition of substance, which is not, as it were, a mere random piling up of elements but rather a perfectly definable unity. Nevertheless, unity becomes a highly complex notion when considered in the light of temporality. We have been emphatic in demonstrating that the categories are the compass for determining the location of a substance in a given time. But the problem boils over when we try to capture substance not in the stillness of a given time but as the product of change, as immersed in the permanent production involved in time. Again we are confronted with a perplexing question: what exactly is form, and how is it caused? Or, rather, how is form a cause of substance and of being? Such an answer can only be given within the formulation of potentiality and actuality, of the virtual and the possible, of power itself: power as generation, maintenance, and destruction. The problem of generation and transitions is impenetrable from the categories alone unless a further differentiation is introduced between potentia and actuality.

As a first approximation, we may grant the dyad of potentia and actuality a basic finality: to define what is possible, what may be possible, and what is not possible at all. Surely, to attempt to formulate the precise meaning of the dichotomy between actuality and potentiality is to reckon with the question of the source of change and thus the origin of a thing. The question of whether form can be construed as being hinges on the definition of potentiality and actuality.

In order to better grasp the inseparable relation between form, substance, and time through its determination in the dyad of potentiality and actuality (from now on simply *the dyad*), consider the thought experiment which I call *the spinning wheel of Teruel*. This particular spinning wheel can create any and all things in the universe, with only one exception: it cannot produce itself. Nevertheless, if the spinning wheel can create any and every thing, couldn't it create the materials of the spinning wheel separately? (The maidens, the flyers, the tension knob, etc.) But if so, how would the wheel itself be assembled? The coming together of the parts would demand a certain ordered motion, a coordinated placing-together of separate parts that would render the unity a functional whole. So the question is whether the spinning wheel can bring about the putting together of the parts. Thus, if it cannot create itself, can it order time and space to create another self? This returns us to the question of generation. As a first and shaky approximation of form, generation seems to be movement; but, if this is so, can our spinning wheel create the motion of its production? Or, since the wheel may produce anything in the world but itself, would such motion only beget the production of a second spinning wheel? This would suggest that generation does not come about simply by motion but rather through a very precise meaning of motion as an organization of time and space, creating a certain organization of things. This is our first glance of power. As I said, this is simply a heuristic exercise, but it is one that allows us to grip what's at play here. Motion and repose, beginning and end, authentic and copy all are imbedded within the central question of the dyad (potentia/actuality), which defines its outcome and possibility.

Nevertheless, the central operation of the dyad is the ever-problematic relation between being and non-being. Non-being—the negative, the vacuum, the lack—is essential to the construction of ontology as first philosophy but is also its breaking point. Non-being is the extreme and unaccountable force that can destroy any certainty and predictability when confronting being; it is the precipice of being, its utter contingency and the most extreme meaning of probability. Being is always besieged by the possibility of its negative, non-being. It is the limit of the pendular movement of Western thinking and praxis as well as the ghostly shadow behind its very movement. Non-being is *the* site of struggle, of redemption and sin, of power and exclusion, of violence and creativity. The dyad is the coming-to-terms of being and non-being, the profound engineering of the possibility of being. It is what announces being as a possibility—that is, being as becoming, being as the origin, the source, and the cause of itself and the world. Becoming is thus turned into the index of the neutralization of non-being; it forestalls the menace that threatens to throw the obscure blanket of nothingness over being. Thus Aristotle, through the dyad, is the great conjurer of the explosivity of becoming. While Parmenides derives unicity from the absence of being as the contrary of being, and Plato turns to non-being as a form of ideal alterity, Aristotle resolves the paradox by adding a form of non-being that is conditioned by being: potentia (Mendez-Hincapie 2015b, 129). Potentia is the solution of the enigma of non-being as the possibility of the becoming being. The dyad brings a precise account of becoming, where in every being there is what the being already is and how it became to be as such in a straightforward and unbreakable relation.

Aristotle saw correctly in the problem of transition and the continuum the loose cannon of logics and metaphysics, the ticking bomb inside being which could demolish any attempt at stability and certainty in the blink of an eye. The outcome of ontology, logic, and metaphysics rests on the cleavage between potentia and actuality as the defining system of transitions and the continuum, of generation and perishability. The dichotomy of potentia and actuality tries to avert the abyss between the thing, the possibilities of the generation of the thing, and the change imbued in the process. But beyond the very conditions of the possible and the impossible, what is at stake in any transition is the determination of necessity and contingency, the order of cause and effect, and of being and nothingness. The dyad is thus set out to bridge and give ground to the problem of origin and the principle of change.

The dyad defines several terms which are central to being and becoming. Change can be contingent or necessary, or it can be possible or impossible. Contingent refers to what can happen without it being necessary that it happens. Necessary refers to that for which it is impossible not to happen. Impossible is that which cannot, under any circumstance happen—that is, the impossibility of being. Following Quentin Meillasoux, we are concerned with two kinds of contingency. One is a *relative* contingency, which we can designate as a perishability 'that is bound to be realized sooner or later. This book, this fruit, this man, this tar, are all bound to perish sooner or later' (Meillasoux 2008, 104). On the other hand, *absolute* contingency refers to the fact that the only necessary thing is contingency; all becoming is contingent, so contingency is thus the only necessity.

The possible is always contained in potentia, but the outcome is always circumvented by actuality. What is at stake in the split between contingency and necessity is the possibility of the future, the consistency of time, the infinity of human action, the possibility to transform the world. As we can begin to sense, the dyad is deeply immersed in the definition of power as the possibility to affect reality and to order time and space in a certain fashion. It traverses all of the cardinal points of power, and it is the cornerstone of piercing questions such as, who has the power? Who can use power? According to which modalities of change? What are the limits of power? If there are such limits, how are they to be established? Is power pure contingency? If it is not, how can the necessity of power be established?

To the extent that the dyad decides the possibility of being, then it is obvious that it stands as the gatekeeper of the principle of non-contradiction (PNC). We can postulate this principle as follows: 'The same attribute cannot at the same time belong and not belong to the same subject and in the same respect'.[10] Or, in Aristotle's own words, 'It is impossible that the same thing belong and not belong to the same thing at the same time and in the same respect' (Aristotle. Met. 1005b). The principle of non-contradiction has been the bedrock of Western logic since Aristotle. The true power of the principle is that to not observe it would negate the possibility of meaning. As such, Aristotle formulated it as an *anhypothetical principle*, which means it is a fundamental proposition that is not deducible from any other proposition. It is the proposition that determines the viability of any other proposition and, as such, is the axiomatic definition of principle, the archetype of principles. For it to be anhypothetical means that to even try to contradict it would be to suppose its use. To state that the principle of non-contradiction does not exist would be to presuppose that it does exist as the possibility of formulating of said negation. A famous phrase sometimes attributed to Avicenna brutally reads, 'Anyone who denies the law of non-contradiction should be beaten and burned until he admits that to be beaten is not the same as not to be beaten, and to be burned is not the same as not to be burned'.

Book Nine (Theta) of the *Metaphysics* begins

We have treated of that which is primarily and to which all the other categories of being are referred—i.e. of substance. For it is in virtue of the concept of substance that the others also are said to be—quantity and quality and the like; for all will be found to involve the concept of substance, as we said in the first part of our work. And since 'being' is in one way divided into individual thing, quality, and quantity, and is in another way distinguished in respect of potency and complete reality, and of function, let us now add a discussion of potency and complete reality. (Aristotle. Met. 9.1045b)

As is the case with Aristotle, potentia and actuality are said in many ways and in many types of multifaceted relations. The very words offer resistance and have been the subjects of constant temporal transplants and revisions. He uses one word to describe potentia—*dunamis* (δύναμις)—while he uses two to describe actuality: *Energeia* (ενέργεια) and *Entelecheia* (ἐντελέχεια). As we will see, this second division is not to be taken lightly. Both terms (Energeia and Entelecheia) are far from being transposable to each other; they mark a deep contrast that will be central to our endeavour of actualizing difference.

Dunamis involves many meanings at once. It can be said of faculty, capacity, strength, or possibility. Because the concept is the substratum of our construction of the meaning of power, we will use the word *potentia* in all cases. The use of this one term across a variety of cases, though, does not collapse its meaning into singularity, for there is no such thing as a *universal* actuality or potentiality; there is no prototype of actuality. The dyad is drawn up to explain change and motion while still enabling what change brings on to substance to be understood in its stillness. As such, the conditions under which a thing exists actually will not be uniform, since their actuality relates only to the precise form of potentiality that has resided within them; it is only in this relation of relations that we can point directly to the presence of either actuality or potentiality.

Let us think of our examples in order to grasp the importance of the distinction. At what exact time does a certain bunch of bricks, cement, nails, and beams become a house? What is it that is potentially a song, a horse, a choir, a cake, a mural, a metallic alloy, a state, or the people? What is the actuality of an arrow in flight? Is cold, tepid water potentially vapour? Potentiality and actuality is the chief distinction between things that do not exist and things that do exist. It is not only the passage from one to another but the index of its possibility: it gives the point of discernibility between being and coming to being, and the exact determination of its possibility in time. Thus, a thing that exists potentially does not exist, although the potentiality as such does exist. As I write this book, each word that I write stands as more actuality and less potential of writing. One key question is whether every written word exhausts the potential to write. In one sense it does, for the word already written exhausts the potentiality of writing *that* word. The potentiality of *writing*, considered in itself, however, is not exhausted with the addition of a word. So, in a very specific manner, potentia witnesses that which is absent in an act while also determining the act as a certain something, which is Aristotle's definition of substance. The point that has to be captured is that a *certain something* exists only insofar as it is the actualization of a potency.

Aristotle explains that although potentiality *can* have several senses, those that are equivocal may be dismissed. However, 'the potentialities which conform to the same type are all principles, and derive their meaning from one primary sense of potency, which is the source of change in some other thing, or in the same thing *qua* other' (Aristotle. Met. 9.1046a).

So we have gathered enough information to pose potentia in one meaning that integrates its different openings. Potentia is first and foremost a source of movement or change which is in another thing than the thing moved or in the same thing *qua* other (Aristotle. Met. 1046a). As we can observe, here a fundamental distinction can be drawn: there are some things that possess potentia in themselves, while others require an external agent to execute the change. According to Aristotle, a boy has the potential to become a man, but also has the potential to become a great pianist. In the first case, the potential belongs naturally to him, and will be actualized if nothing external hinders it; the potential is immersed in his nature, hence, actuality is the natural deployment of that potential. In the second case, actuality depends on a possession of a *rational formula* and can only be possessed through a transformation of the thing *qua* other; in the case of our example, the development of the ability to dominate the art of playing the piano. We thus have a first and provisional division of potentia between natural and acquired. In the first sense, potentiality is tied to progression, natural development, an installing of a constancy that is already determined in its cause. Here, change is associated directly with movement (*kinêsis*), and such a movement deemed in some kind of a straight line where the actuality is already lodged in the potential that is already determined in its cause: a tadpole becomes a young frog, which quickly becomes an adult frog. It is the second sense which is tricky and offers the complexities we are looking for. In the second sense, potentia is tied directly to actuality more than to movement. Hence, it does not depend on a natural progression or a coming to be that is encapsulated in some sort of natural womb and would then extend its becoming as its extension. In this second type of potentia, the intervention of an exterior cause is fundamental. A rational formula organizes the potential in a certain something whose cause is to a certain extent a pre-given material. The type of potentia which Aristotle defines as *acquired* can only be possessed when it has been previously exercised or obtained by a rational formula. Now, imagine that the boy becomes a virtuoso of the piano (actualizes the potential to learn). How do we recognize his potential to play the piano? According to the second definition, he has acquired the ability to perform the piano by practice and the learning of a rational formula, so he possesses the potential to play the piano precisely at those times when he is not playing the piano (just as he possesses the potential to see when his eyes are closed).

These two constructions of potentia are problematic if taken alone, for they cross each other at different coordinates where it is difficult to establish a strict dividing line. All the same, they grant us a direct approximation of the elements of the dyad. Every non-existing thing must exist potentially, and things do not exist to the extent that they have not come to complete reality (Aristotle. Met. 9.1047b). Consequently, the difference between potentia and actuality is the frontier between being and non-being. However, the limitation of the construction lies in the stabilization of the relation, its mutual gridlock, where contingency is defined only as the possibility of a thing to be actualized. What the latter creates in turn is a neutralization between contingency and necessity, in the sense that non-being is ordered entirely as a consequence of being: it is tied to it in every possibility of becoming. Accordingly, when being comes to be, it is *necessary* that it came to be from a given potentiality. While what is now potential reflects the contingency of its becoming, the contingency of the future is captured in the necessity of what is presently actual. Nonetheless, it is not that potentia is contingent; what is contingent is the coming to be of what is potential: what is in potentia may come to be or it may not. Contingency is reduced to this precise operation within the dyad. A seed may blossom into a flower (becoming a flower is contingent), but when the seed comes to be *this* flower, actuality is necessary as a retrospection from actuality to potentia. Potentia and actuality are not separable: they are the concise extremes of reality, neither of which could be described as an independent concept, and it is only from analogy that we can gain a grip on their meanings. They suppose each other to the extent that what is actual comes necessarily from potentia, and contingency only refers to the possibility of a potentia to be actualized. Contingency thus functions not as a causal force but as merely the possibility of the becoming of what is already programmed within potentia.

But here a further question remains to be dealt with. It seems that the definition of potentia and actuality depends ultimately on a linguistic attribution of the predicates that are at play. The arrow in flight is in a potential fall but also in an actuality of flight. At what moment exactly does a boy become a man, or a woman, or a third or fourth term? Aristotle acknowledges the difficulty and tries to cauterize it in various ways. The first is to explain potentia as a kind of privation, and the second is the structuring of the primacy of actuality in regards to potentiality through a theory of causes. The latter is where we will find the vanishing point of power as the actuality of difference. Let us begin with potentiality as privation to prepare our final assault on the dyad.

POTENTIA AS PRIVATION

Within the division of potentia between natural and acquired (or rational) formula, there is a second division that is pivotal in Aristotle's body of work. Potentia is composed of an active and a passive part. In his rant against the Megarian school, who hold that a builder is not a builder unless he is building, Aristotle answers that such an affirmation is absurd because we call a builder not only he who is building but also—and with the same meaning—he who has the capacity of building. To be a builder is to have the capacity to build. Therefore, to possess an art is to have acquired the potency to execute such art, and as such, the potentia is not lost in its passivity but preserved in its fullest sense. If the opposite were to be true, a man holding his breath would not have the potency to breathe and would be, by this definition, dead many times a day. Henceforth, privation applies to both natural and to acquired potency. But while natural potentia is only capable of deploying itself, *acquired potentia is capable of both itself and its contrary*. The flame is capable only of burning but the medical arts can produce both disease and health. The reason is that science is a rational formula, and the same rational formula explains a thing and its privation.

Now let us think of the dyad in relation to modal statements and the principle of non-contradiction. Regarding the negation of a modal statement, potentia as passivity in relation to actuality can deny the mode but not the dictum. Therefore, the negation of 'it is possible to be' is 'it is impossible to be', but in terms of potentia the affirmation and the negation do not exclude each other as in the claim: 'It is possible for its being to be either possible or impossible'. *What is potent is not always in act*: he who walks exercises his potency not walking, and he who builds exercises his potency not building. The privation is always a potential of *not* exercising, of not actualizing, which implies the capacity to *do* or *be*.[11] We are seemingly before an extraordinary force of potentia to erode the sacrosanct principle of non-contradiction and thus to bring about contingency as its mark. This mere possibility upsets the order of the whole edifice of logics, physics and ingrains the need to reshape metaphysics.

Contingency is the sign of transformation, of revolution, the promise of new eras and fresh beginnings. It is the irruption of the utterly unexpected that shatters anything that is parasitically bonded to reality through the supposition of necessity. Contingency is pure becoming where the outcome is unpredictable and hence razes knowledge out of its prefixed and smooth rotation. It is the limit where possible and impossible are yet to be decided, it is the point where time folds upon itself opening any and every possibility. Contingency is therefore the constant and undisruptive aptitude of becoming, the crushing of any truth value, the incalculable and volatile force that interrupts repetition, while it collapses the system of representation as the power to represent anything other than pure presence. Furthermore, contingency is the clogging of the machines of certainty: it is the event that sets truth apart from knowledge. Contingency erases the limitrophe of the camp and the city, as it explodes the formalized statute of language as norm and obedience from its inside as a bomb lodged in its bowels. In its most precise sense, it is the inrush of the Real that the symbolic cannot inscribe and thus forces the reconstruction of the symbolic from scratch. It is thus pure immanence and freedom as positive infinity. Contingency is, in a phrase, pure possibility.[12]

Henceforth, the fundamental question that contingency forces upon philosophy becomes: what can we see in the future through contingency that is different from that which is seen in the present and the past? The answer is that we can see the same, but lacking any names.

As stated before, the contingency implied in the Aristotelian construction is a relative contingency, meaning that the entity that comes to be from potentia is necessary. Hence, contingency is reduced to the co-relation of potentia and actuality, where actuality defines potentia. Consequently, contingency is said of a thing that might or might not become actual (a seed might become a plant, a boy might become a man). But there is nothing necessary in it being a seed, nor is it a necessary outcome for it to become a full-grown tree (as it is contingent that the cub becomes a bear, a boy a man). Nonetheless, and this is the acute point, the existence of a tree *necessarily* determines the retrospective existence of the potentia of the seed. Notwithstanding, if this relation is dislocated—if the umbilical cord between potentia and actuality is severed—what appears behind it is absolute contingency, meaning that the only necessity for a being to exist is pure contingency, so every being would necessarily be contingent (Meillasoux 2008, 119). As we will see later, Aristotle conflates potentia and actuality only to give pre-eminence to the latter and thus neutralizes the power of the contingent.

On the other side of the possible, necessity is the frustration of the new, the blockage of time and denial of the future outside of a monotonous and planned becoming. Necessity filches the self from self-determination. It turns a certain violence into a certain power as necessity, and supposes the self-destruction of being in structures that pervade ontology as truth. Necessity is the mirror of what simply *is the fact* that gains the stature of truth as inert stuff that cannot be acted upon, that cannot be moved or changed.

What authors like Antonio Negri and Giorgio Agamben see in the actualization of potentia is the irremediable loss of contingency and with it the forfeiture of the opportunity of the new, of creation from the *nihil*. They see the death of politics as the becoming of the new at the hands of actuality. As Negri states, 'Contingency is the future, it is the indefinite that human praxis as potentia integrates into the positive infinity' (Negri 2003, 103). It is a sign of the times: once we come to see the great beast of persistent horror, the solution is to lock oneself up in the dream of immanence, in sheer immobility, as the beast can sniff out any twitch of divergence. In order to maintain potentia as an everlasting contingency, these authors submit potentia to therapeutic hibernation so that it does not burn out in the blaze of actuality.

The first measure of potentia is a capacity to produce effects, and thus we can perceive its impression in power. Nevertheless, the kind of effects it produces is already determined by actuality. As stated by Agamben, Aristotle opposes and at the same time joins potentia (*dunamis*) to act as the basis of both his physics and his metaphysics (Agamben 2015, 243). So potentia as such is at the basis of the question of what a thing can do and what it can become. The original problem of potentia is announced in the question 'What does it mean to have a faculty? In what way something with a faculty exists?' (Agamben 2015, 245). *Dunamis* means potentia as well as possibility, or, basically, that the possibility of something actual is connected inextricably to its potential to be. The term *faculty* expresses the mode in which a certain activity is separated from itself and attributed to a subject, a vital praxis of who lives. So according to Agamben, the Aristotelian doctrine of potentia contains an archaeology of subjectivity.

Incapacity is the privation contrary to *capacity*. Hence, every capacity has a contrary incapacity for producing the same result in respect to the same subject. It is clear that to have a faculty, to have a potential, is to have a privation. This is why a sensation does not feel itself, just as a combustible does not burn by itself. The key term for Agamben is *Steresis*, privation. The question is, does the exercise of potentia neutralize the potentia *not to*? (Agamben 2015, 252).

Potentia is always spiking the thin line of the principle of non-contradiction. Its dependence on actuality means that whereas that which is incapable of happening cannot happen to anything, everything which is capable may fail to be actualized. Therefore, that which is capable of being may both be and not be. In that same line of thinking, the same thing is capable, in potentia, both of being and of not being. This is a property of potentia that traverses a great portion of the principle of non-contradiction. Granted, by the very nature of potentia, the possibilities *to be* and *not to be* never arise together in time (primordial condition of the PNC). The power *not* to be or to act does not fit fully with the principle of non-contradiction, hence, it is always a modal relation subtracted from the *same time*, which is the central demand of the principle.

THE PASSION OF IMPOTENCE IN AGAMBEN

From the preceding discussion, we may conclude that it is possible—and this is what is important to Agamben—for a being to be and not be under the condition that she remains in potentia and does not pass into the act. In this precise sense, potentia is below the radar of the PNC. So the sophisticated answer that Agamben gives in order to preserve the full power of potency and

thus of contingency is as follows: 'If a potency of not being belongs originally to all potentia, the truly potent will be only those who, in the moment
of the passage to the act do not annul their potency of not being' (Agamben
2015, 253).[13] Agamben thinks of a potentia detached from a subject, a property in its own right, so when a potential is exercised it is exhausted in the
act. To prevent the exhaustion of potentia, Agamben fixes its force, its true
powerful gesture in passivity, in the *passion of impotence*. Such a way of
understanding potency, Agamben tells us, is the secret thread of the Aristotelian doctrine of potentia (Agamben 2015, 99). If there is a power *not to*, it
is because it is possible according to the principle of non-contradiction and
thus all the power of contingency is preserved. Nevertheless, this preservation
comes at an excessive cost, the impossibility of action, the utter shutdown of
being inside an inexpungable barrier of inaction where any possibility of the
political is banned from the start.

True potentia is the potentia that shall *can* itself by not passing into the
act. Avicenna, Agamben tells us, is faithful to the Aristotelian intent when
he calls it *perfect potentia*, and exemplifies it in the figure of a scribe in the
moment he is not writing. Where potentia is held in relation to the act in the
form of a suspension, it shall *can* its own act by not realizing it, and through
it sovereignly achieves its own impotence (Agamben 2015, 45). However,
under this perspective, how can we think the passage to the act? If every
potency of being or doing is originally the potency of not being or not doing,
necessity is thrown to its opposite shore; hence to remain in *power*, power
must not come to actuality.

Agamben resorts to *De Anima* to explain potentia as an essential relation to
auto-affection. Sensation is in potency, not in act; in the absence of external
objects there is no sensation of our own senses. We see darkness blindfolded
and hear silence in the vacuum precisely because senses are in potentia. To
see implies the potency of not seeing: it is not a simple absence but something existent and defined; it is a privation (Agamben 2015, 248). Potentiality is thus always the constitutive ability *not to* be something. Capability is
always understood then primarily as the capacity not to act: 'The being that
is properly whatever is able to not-be is always capable of its own impotence'
(Agamben 2015, 249).

Agamben's lush poetic fantasy of the flesh of potency is the image of how
the Suda describes Aristotle as the philosopher who wets his pen in thought;
it is Melville's Bartleby the scrivener as the modern holder of power, as
he is capable but does not want (Agamben 2011). In this sense, potentiality is achieved and preserved only in not being, in preserving its instance
permanently as a passion of not being. The measure of potentia thus lies in
permanent suspension of acting and in the extreme lust of thought in itself.
According to Agamben, impotency (adynamia) is a privation contrary to

potentia (dynameí), where every potency is impotency of the same in relation to the same. Impotency does not mean the absence of potency, but the *potency of not* passing to the act. Agamben calls this *potency of not* the fundamental passion, where all human potency is co-originally impotence. Hence, for Agamben, every potency of doing something is always a potency of not doing. If this was not the case, potentia would transcend itself in the act(uality) and would be jumbled with it, thus potentia and actuality would become indiscernible.

In his study of Melville's "Bartleby", Agamben (2011) is trying to establish that the scrivener's repeated phrase, 'I would prefer not to', is the perfect archetype of potentia. Since in Aristotle the act of writing is the passage between pure potency and act, thinking is the purest sense of potentia. The blank board or the empty titillating screen have the potency of being written on or not being written on. Agamben's model, however, is a wax tablet. An indentation, a caress, or a subtle stroke wounding the surface of the wax tablet would render potentia actual and therefore the *passion of not* would be lost forever; unlike the board or the screen, erasure is never total for wax. Nevertheless, if thinking is pure potentia that can become or not become writing, how can we think of a potency of not thinking (Agamben 2015, 105)? What would it mean for a potency of not thinking to pass to the act? And if the nature of thought consists in being in potentia, what would *thought* think?

The aporia consists in the fact that supreme thinking cannot not think *nothing,* nor think something, nor remain in pure potency, nor to transcend to the act. Aristotle escapes the aporia with his famous thesis of the thought that thinks itself, a thought that just thinks in the pure potency of thinking and not thinking. But as Agamben warns us, the aporia is resuscitated as soon as it is solved, for how is it possible to think a pure potency from the actual? How can a thought that cannot be thought think? What this refers us to directly, without any buffer, is the zone of absolute nothingness. As Nina Power puts it, arguing brilliantly against Agamben's view, 'To fetishize inactivity as some kind of minimal excess that preserves the individual from his or her total immersion in activity is a nostalgic dream; far better to begin, as if for the first time, with the raw material of human life and the vampiric way in which it gets periodically drained' (Power 2010, 7).

Agamben's thesis of true potentia, as the one that refuses the passage unto actuality, would be a fertile ground of combat to prove, as Nina Power suggests, that such a reduction of power to the power *of not* does not produce any possibility for the transformation of power. Or, as we have held, it would forswear the possibility of asserting the power of the people as the immanence of difference. Nevertheless, I believe that the true problem is elsewhere, not in the definition of potentia but of actuality. Agamben reduces it to the potency of *not-to,* or what he wrongly calls *impotence.* What we are committed to demonstrate is that Agamben and Negri as paradigmatic thinkers of our time are shooting their ammunition in the wrong direction. Their target is misplaced; in lieu of the end of contingency that actualization would bring about, they race to lock power in the panic room of potency. Their argument, in short, is that if potentia is dominated by actuality, the actualization of potentia is the obliteration of contingency and therefore the impossibility of the new. As we will come to prove, they are identifying actuality with *one* of its forms and neglecting the other.

If impotence, as Agamben holds, is a defining feature of potentia, it would mean to equate impotence with incapacity, and thus that which has not happened to the incapacity of happening, and that which has not come to be, as necessarily incapable of coming to be. If to be in power over something is tantamount to not exercising said power, power becomes the severance of power through its immobility. The only form of power resides in not actualizing it, and power thus becomes impotent. As we will see further, Agamben falls into the pit of a performative fallacy (a poetic one, but nonetheless a fallacy) that is symptomatic of much contemporary philosophy. To think the adverse of the cruel and devastating power expressed in the liege of capital and state, these philosophers deem it necessary to reduce power to inaction, to bring it to a total overhaul. What this accomplishes is to deadbolt the power of any possible transformation within its own impotence. It is the lobotomy of the social brain or general intellect, and it is the burial ground of revolution. On the other hand, if we place impotence in actuality, contingency would recover its power of transformation. This latter project is our endeavour.

The splitting point from Agamben comes as Aristotle grants actuality priority over potentia through a theory of causes that is elevated to a first principle. Let us explain this as briefly as we can, as one of said divisions of causes is our point of departure to prove the necessity of actualizing difference.

For Aristotle matter exists potentially, so only when it attains a form may we speak of actuality. Matter is actual only when it becomes form. Every potentiality is always produced by a thing that exists actually, so actuality is previous in time to potentiality. 'Man begets man', and the seed is not produced by an instantaneous miracle but comes from an actual existing tree. Consequently, even if it is true that the potency of the seed precedes *a certain tree* that can come to be (or not), the seed itself proceeds from an existing actuality that is actual as a species. As Aristotle puts it, 'The actual which is identical in species though not in number with a potentially existing thing is prior to it' (Aristotle. Met. 1049b18–19). Nevertheless, such priority is not only possessed by natural things but also by things that come about through a rational formula. Let us go back to Michelangelo and his block of marble. First, we can only gain knowledge of the *potential* of the block when it is transformed and a form is given to it. So the block could be left to decay slowly on its own, but once it is transformed, it becomes *a certain something*, and only then can we point to it and assert that it possessed a potentiality to become this certain this. Only within a retrospective manoeuver can we hold that marble had the potency to become the David. Potentia can only be named from actuality: only in actuality can we predicate the potential of something as actuality. When it was a simple block of marble, it was holding on to a potentia to be anything that could be made out of marble but lost it when it became the David. Hence, the potential could only be named from an actuality that dominates the present. To think the inverse would be to hold that form is a derivative of matter, but remember here that matter designates only a possibility, and form is the true meaning of substance. In this precise sense, Aristotle demonstrates that actuality is the primacy of the present; the present measures the possibilities, and hence the existent is given priority over the inexistent, which is possible only if it reaches existence. As Aristotle puts it:

> That actuality is prior in formula is evident; for it is because it can be actualized that the potential, in the primary sense, is potential, I mean, e.g., that the potentially constructive is that which can construct, the potentially seeing that which can see, and the potentially visible that which can be seen. The same principle holds in all other cases too, so that the formula and knowledge of the actual must precede the knowledge of the potential. (Aristotle. Met. 1050a)

Potential is potential only because it leads to actuality: there would be no potentia without actuality, and thus potentiality is only verified in actuality. Through this line of thinking Aristotle proves that actuality is prior not only in time but in logos to potentiality, so actuality is the material, formal, and efficient cause of potentiality.[14]

THE TWO ACTUALITIES OF POWER IN ARISTOTLE: ENERGEIA AND ENTELECHEIA

Nevertheless, in the theory of causes Aristotle gives priority to one particular cause over the rest as the defining element of the superiority of actuality over potentia, as the definition of what is actual in reality: the *final* cause. Aristotle characterizes the final cause as the end *(telos)* for which a thing is done. The cause that inclines the balance in favour of actuality is that things propend to an end. Achieving such an end is pure actuality and thus the perfection of substance and of being. The relation between potentia and actuality, then, is enclosed in this circle as pure logical necessity. This is where Agamben et al. recognize the obliteration of potentia. Aristotle describes his teleology as the cornerstone of his metaphysical edifice:

But (actuality) is also prior in substantiality; (a) because things which are pos-
terior in generation are prior in form and substantiality; e.g., adult is prior to
child, and man to semen, because the one already possesses the form, but the
other does not; and (b) because everything which is generated moves towards a
principle, i.e. its end. For the object of a thing is its principle; and generation has
as its object the end. And the *actuality is the end, and it is for the sake of this that
the potentiality is acquired;* for animals do not see in order that they may have
sight, but have sight in order that they may see. Similarly men possess the art
of building in order that they may build, and the power of speculation that they
may speculate; they do not speculate in order that they may have the power of
speculation—except those who are learning by practice; and they do not really
speculate, but only in a limited sense, or about a subject about which they have
no desire to speculate.[15] (Aristotle. Met. 9.1050a)

It is in the final causes (telos) where the Aristotelean *Big Bang* bursts. It is
the concept that distillates and orders the rest of the metaphysical constructions, and it is the constituent particle of the reality of being. All the risks and
abysses of change, motion, metamorphosis, transitions, and the might of time
come down to this proposition. Matter can be recognized as a potential state
only insofar as it can come to *form*, and only in the sense that it already tends
to the finality of the actualization of form. With the latter construction, potentia is demoted to a mere physical property and equated to motion, motion that
can survive *only if* it fulfils what is already programmed in actuality, which
thus becomes a normative statute by which potentia is compelled to abide.

Nevertheless, a crucial distinction is made at this point. What is the difference between the finality of something natural (the boy that became a
man, the marble remaining a rock) and finality as a rational formula (the
piano virtuoso having executed his potentia to play the piano)? Let us recall
that Aristotle called actuality both Entelecheia (ἐντελέχεια) and Energeia
(ενέργεια). We have already held that such a division is not fortuitous and
the terms cannot not be unified as a single whole belonging to one and only
meaning. Its difference cuts deeply and definitively into the Aristotelian corpus and it is the exact point that enables us to actualize difference without
losing contingency as the feature of power; indeed, it allows us to intensify
it to a new dimension.

The principal dimension of the Aristotelian move is that perfect actuality
is equated to finality. What is actual is what has achieved its finality, but this
mushrooms into a new domain of complexities, for how are we to recognize
that something has achieved its end? For example, how can we determine that
a painting, a symphony, a mural, a revolution, or a boy have accomplished
actuality? Bearing in mind that *finality* is the point of contraction of all
metaphysics and thus the supposed crystalline determination of being, such a
question unravels the very question of the substance of politics.

The first complication of the dual definition of actuality is that actuality does not merely involve *what is happening right now* but also comprises a striving towards permanence within changing conditions and thus it faces in the direction of perishability. As explained by Joe Sachs, within the works of Aristotle the terms Energeia and Entelecheia, often translated as actuality, differ from what is merely actual because they specifically presuppose that all things have a proper kind of activity or work which, if achieved, would be their proper end (Sachs 2005). The problem comes when both terms are translated simply as actuality.

The first term is *Energeia* whose root is *ergonó,* which can be translated as activity, action, and operation, from which derives the adjective *energon,* meaning active or working. The etymological compound brings us *energeia,* from *en* (in, within) + *ergon* (work).[16] In this first approximation, we have a first meaning not only of actuality but a very specific finality of actuality which is the work required to maintain the state of a substance through the *being-at-work* of the substance. Aristotle would call this the *nutritional principle*. This is what Joe Sachs has defined by a very precise composite as the 'being-at-work of some definite, specific something' (Sachs 2005). Potentiality thus relates to the continuing effort of a condition to the full completeness of the actual, where actual will be what has been the exercise of the continuing effort of the condition. The being-at-work that is the result of a precise capacity implies directly that the capacity qualifies the work and the work the capacity, not as a tautology but as a necessity. It is a specific way of being in motion, a change programmed from within the full result. Potentia is thus set retrospectively from actuality, and only what becomes actual in the strict sense of the continuing effort of the condition can be deemed to have fulfilled its potency.

Let us now define the second meaning of actuality as finality. We must be attentive to this definition because it is the parting of waters of the sea of being. It is where the particle *telos* becomes the nuclear device of actuality and therefore entails the clear and concise split with Energeia. Aristotle, Sachs tells us, invents the word Entelecheia, by combining entelēs (ἐντελής, 'complete, full-grown') with echein (hexis) which means to be a certain way by the continuing effort of holding on to that condition. But a third and defining block of significance is put into the composite when Aristotle plays with the more usual word endelecheia (ἐντελέχεια, 'persistence') by inserting *telos* (τέλος, completion) as the definite component of the concept (Sachs 2005). Etymologically, Entelecheia is thus composed of *en* (within) + *telos* (end, perfection) + *ekhein* (to be in a certain state).[17]

There is, then, a fundamental addition in the construction of Entelecheia, something that is well beyond Energeia and that announces that which can only become when it is perfected. Hence, preservation is no longer the finality but something which, while being outside of work, defines what work must strive for: completion. This is the subtle, almost invisible ingredient that launches substance and being on the hunt of an ideal of perfection. *Telos* is thus introduced as the fulcrum between *en-telēs* (being within), and *echein* (hexis), turning the plain meaning of *holding on to* into a more qualified *being in possession of an end*.[18] The crucial point is that perfection and completion are one—indeed, the etymological root of perfection (*perficere*) means *to be complete*.

We are thus faced with a fundamental split within actuality, a split anchored in teleology. Natural final causes pose no problem, for they are involved directly in Energeia: it is the being-at-work to preserve substance that defines being. Energeia is a circular movement within the natural substance. There the principle of action is at the same time its end, in which we can identify no intentionality. Accordingly, the butterfly striving to survive *is* survival: its internal principle of change is its own form. The nutritional principle means that natural beings absorb energy from their environment in order to transform it into life. For natural things, formal, efficient, and final cause are one and the same: the actualization of being *qua* being. Actuality thus means to reproduce forms already actualized in themselves and to preserve substance, enduring the passing of time and interventions of others.

As Aristotle states:

> Thus in all cases where the result is something other than the exercise of the faculty, the actuality resides in the thing produced: e.g., the act of building in the thing built, the act of weaving in the thing woven, and so on; and in general the motion resides in the thing moved. But where there is no other result besides the actualization, the actualization resides in the subject: e.g., seeing in the seer, and speculation in the speculator, and life in the soul. (Aristotle. Met. 9.1050a)

The first part of this passage is devoted to actuality as finality in a rational formula, while the second part is devoted to nature. Thus, while the potentia of a rational formula includes the possibility of its contrary (the potential of the *pharmakon* to produce either health or illness), this is not a possibility regarding natural potentialities that can only produce themselves as survival or continuation of the species. In the latter case, the principle of generation is already included; hence, 'One thing is potentially another when, if nothing external hinders it, it will of itself become the other' (Aristotle. Met. 1049a). Being a butterfly, a piece of wood, or a neutrino possesses no negation of itself, or of being a certain something contrary to what it is; there is no *qualification* of its actuality.

In *Energeia*, perfection (as a final cause, a telos) is already constitutive of being: it is its substance by the fact that it lives and strives to survive. It is thus a natural, self-defined perfection. The horse reaches actuality by living and feeding, by simply being a horse with no additional qualifications. Hence, it needs not any further virtue or prerequisite but life itself. As Negri states, '[A] composite individual can be affected in many ways and still preserve its nature. The whole of nature is one individual, whose parts, all bodies, vary in infinite ways, without any change of the whole individual' (Negri 2003, 13). The *Energeia* is an *at work* to a telos; it forms a continuity of completeness, as the perfection of activity is life itself. As Joe Sachs puts it, 'The thinghood of living things consists in organized unity, maintained through effort, at work in a variety of activities characteristic of each species' (Sachs 2005). *Energeia*, then, refers directly to an organized state that persists in time through work. Hence, Energeia is not concerned with what a body can do beyond itself, beyond the conditions of the continuum of life, but—and this is the core of the connection—it does set the fundamental conditions in which such a thing can be asked. This is our key point, for if what we are seeking is the meaning of politics and the composition of the body politic, we are thus asking the question of who belongs to it and under what conditions. The answer, through radical non-liberal democracy, is *everyone* and *everything*, with no further condition than life itself and no exception that can be imposed beyond the production of *difference*. Furthermore, if we can muster an understanding of work beyond the potestas of capitalism and understand it instead as *living labour*, we move one phase closer to the actuality of difference. It is here that it is fundamental to understand Energeia through what Joe Sachs has termed 'being-at-work-staying-the-same'.

To be is to exist with no further specification of the modes in which being is defined as being, once the end of being is already part of being. Nature is already a final form, a source of a being that is self-sufficient and cannot be a predicate of anything else. Now a crucial and inevitable question arises. Is not Energeia in this configuration equivalent to Spinoza's conatus, where 'each thing, as far as it can by its own power, strives to persevere in its being' (Spinoza 2002, E3p6)? As will become clearer further on, this is the root of the misreading of power in Negri and Agamben. When we say their target is astray it is because they are shooting at actuality *only* as *Entelecheia* and with it they destroy the mark of actuality as *Energeia*. In this misfire, they ignore the fact that Energeia is there staring them dead in their eyes, with the result that they remain trapped in potentia, failing to put the political question in actuality where it can provide a praxis as well as an ontology of the political subject. In Energeia, contingency is not absent but is rather the constitutive element. But let us first get closer to our target.

The question of *what can a being do* beyond its beingness is the question not of Energeia but of Entelecheia. Nevertheless, it can only be answered when Energeia is set as the fundamental requirement of being. What a scientist can accomplish or what an artist may create are questions that are limitless on their own, but the fundamental precondition is that existence is the nucleus of their being. Only when all life is considered as politically viable and the force of belonging appertains to a polity with no particular condition can those questions be answered. They are not political questions, but they do depend on the definition of politics as the fashioning of the common.

In Entelecheia, actuality is defined by an element that is beyond actuality, as a power to persevere in beingness. The key is that potency engaged as *Entelecheia* is capable of its contrary and, thus, it is defined by privation (as Agamben correctly maintains). The fundamental feature is this: insofar as rational potentia can produce effects contrary to its finality, then it follows that to be a true actuality it must produce those effects *well*. The pharmacist must mix the matter in a certain proportion if it is to achieve health; otherwise, he will produce the contrary effects. As we have shown, natural potentiality (irrational potency) is actualized directly in its generation and perseverance, while rational potentialities must not only produce a given effect but also produce it well. Let us escape an apparent circularity. He who possesses a technique (the boy who is a piano virtuoso) does not suffer any transformation: the technique is potent from a *privation*. What he produces, however—the sounds and tones which come from a pattern of hitting the keys at a certain speed, strength and harmony—is dominated by the necessity of doing such a thing in accordance with a principle in order for his execution to be deemed the actualization of a telos. All rational potentialities are so called because they do so *well*: they demand a certain technique, a definite know-how. Hence, the fundamental concatenation is this: if the very definition of politics depends on Entelecheia, life as its precondition logically becomes a qualified life and thus politics is denied at its core. Politics would depend solely on a condition and thus democracy would become impossible.

AGAINST AGAMBEN'S IMPOTENCE, ENERGEIA AS THE ORDER OF THE ACTUALITY OF POWER

The question raised at the border between being and non-being is whether we can think potentia as necessarily related to will—and, thus, to freedom. As Agamben explains (Agamben 2015, 251), for the Greeks the concept of freedom defines a status or a social condition and not something that pivots on the experience or the will of a subject. In other words, *hexis* is defined beforehand as a capacity to do something: it is a precondition of the execution of a certain something, and such a capacity determines the exercise of potentia. In classical Greek terms, to be free corresponds to an already existing qualification of life, a split within forms of life where some are welcomed into politics and some are excluded according to said qualification. There is no direct passage from potentia to a generic form of freedom: the freedom to do anything (possible or not) is qualified from the beginning. Hence, we confront a strong mediation, a hinge between potentia and freedom, which is precisely the quality with which the subject is endowed as a property and as a disposition that defines the act in potentia. In this sense, freedom is confined and predefined by the specific faculty awarded by a specific know-how. Potentia is thus directly related to a *techné,* a disposition, and not to the exercise of conscience or any other quality. Only he who knows how to do x, that is, who has trained and thus suffered first a transformation in his faculties, can *not do* x as the full exercise of his potentia. Of course I, who only has had training in performing *air guitar* while listening to '*the Who*', can approximate a *real* guitar and play. But according to Aristotle, I lack the true potentia to do so, since only a person who has a true disposition, an authentic expertise may exercise the potentia of not playing the guitar. Only within the realm of such a disposition can potentia be attributed to a subject. Hence potentia is not a right or a property, but a power to affect. Said power to affect, though, is qualified in terms of precision; it is qualified by the actual. In what sense? How can we know that X subject has a potential, a power to affect? The only answer is actuality as Entelecheia, that is, the accomplishment of a *telos*. It is clear, then, that freedom has little or nothing to do with potentia, and the term that fits the Aristotelian definition is *hexis*, a disposition that defines a property, which is not in itself a property but the breeding ground of the execution, of the possibility of the act. Hexis cannot be read in the modern sense of freedom as self-consciousness, as a reflective unfolding of a will, but only as the withholding of power to affect in a certain qualified way.[19] For Aristotle, human potentia is knitted into *techné*, to a very detailed know-how that requires preparation, that is, a very specific kind of knowledge and expertise. So if politics is defined from this perspective, politics as the exercise of a singular plural being in common is already denied at its foundations.

According to Aristotle, the human animal is lands apart from the rest of the living things. The latter only possess a natural potentia in becoming something out of their own natural cocoon, to become what is inscribed in their natural code. The seed that becomes the flower and the cub that becomes the bear suffer a transformation which is necessarily imbedded in their own nature. Necessity, in these cases, is dependent on the undisturbed passage of time. Take, for example, chance. In natural teleology, chance is the occurring of external causes that disrupt the principle of natural finality. Nevertheless, in artificial teleology, the principle is always external to nature: it is, very simply, *artificial,* and it is defined as the possibility to actualize a form that is different from the materials. The nature of wood is not to become a chair, a table, or a bed, it is just a matter that can be actualized through a certain technique, a certain procedure. Hence, the form that it may attain is regulated by the requirement of the finality—that is, that the form is not an aleatory joining of parts but a determinate form that defines the actuality of a chair, a table, or a bed.

We could here further elaborate on the problematic construction of finality as Entelecheia, but our aim is different. Our aim is to prove that Agamben (and Negri, for that matter) takes to heart a connection between Entelecheia and power, and thus establishes a prohibitive barrier to actuality, because he identifies it *only* with potestas and domination. Agamben and Negri are partially right; if we build the meaning of politics through Entelecheia (as is at the core of coloniality), we would have to equate politics to a doing well, to the exercise of a certain *techné*. Only those who acquire the possession of a certain know-how could be part of the political. In Entelecheia, the condition of actualizing a rational potentia is already qualified, a condition that comes about from the transformation of a subject to a *qualified* subject who dominates a rational science. Spinoza will universalize and disqualify the hexis, turning it into a generic right over the world. But our point is that we do not need to go so far as to equate men with God, which also consigns the rest of life to dependence on our species. The problem is if the definition of the political falls under a rational telos (Entelecheia) or an Energeia as a *being-at-work*. This is the vortex of politics as ontology; it is the definition of the political which tilts any balance of power and of beingness.

What would the telos of a polity be according to Aristotle? The answer is not given in the *Metaphysics* but in the *Nicomachean Ethics*: virtue is the telos of a polity, the one that defines whether it has achieved the finality of actuality and thus beingness. Virtue (the doing well of politics) is the fulfillment of the perfect exercise of reason, men's distinctive and highest feature. Just as the virtuoso of the piano only achieves actuality by executing the piano with a certain technique, so politics is only rendered actual when it is actualized by virtue as the *doing well* of a polity. Hence, the traditional interpretations that run through the infected veins of the West, in line with Aristotle, consider that politics follows Entelecheia, and so Plato's virtue (areté) and Aristotle's *Eudaimonia* demand that politics be defined as a question of refinement, perfection, excellence. The perfect polity is as such because it has achieved an actuality through virtue as a telos. Thus, Agamben rightfully understands that the aforementioned qualifies life into a *certain* life (zoe tis), as the *rational* actualization of potentia. Politics, then, can only be determined as such by a certain finality that involves a stringent qualification of life: a division between the rational and irrational, the virtuous and the vile, of the *oikos* and the *politikos* and of life (bios) and bare life (zoe).

According to Agamben, Aristotle defines happiness as the being-at-work of the soul according to virtue (Agamben 2015, 320). This is what defines the essence of the political and thus the immemorial split of Western political ontology that coloniality blissfully picks up on and passes on to posterity. The actuality of the political is defined as a praxis of the soul bestowed to logos, where praxis means 'every act according to its proper virtue'—that is, in pursuit of its perfection (Aristotle. Nic. 1098 a 7–18). The passage from potentia to actuality in Aristotle, then, is defined by perfection, by a qualification of potentia in the *final* result of the work. So to safeguard potentia, Agamben withdraws labour to passive potentia, and, moreover, to impotence.

Accordingly, ethics and politics will be defined for men through their participation in such an operation according to virtue. But curiously enough, for Plato and Aristotle, the belonging to politics is defined by natural conditions. Remember that for Plato it is natural that the strong govern the weak, the wise the ignorant, etc. And for Aristotle, the quality demanded for politics is a natural virtue. Politics is defined by a doing well, but the very confines of the description of doing well can only be posited by those who are already inside politics! Politics is thus reduced to the level of a techné: if to play the harp is to play it to perfection, then to live means to live to perfection according to a logos. But the logos cannot define an abstract, a priori and universal property of perfection, and thus the power to define perfection is deferred to those already belonging to the political body. This is the key condition that Agamben finds between to live (zen) and to live well (eu zen). To live a full life becomes not the purpose of politics but its line of demarcation, its legal qualification and stringent limit. Only those who live in virtue, who have dominated the techné of life, are allowed to be called into the political. This is the primordial encryption of politics and the machine of democracy's mutilation. The work of man as his essence, its *operability*, is a *certain life*. As Agamben makes clear, this is *biopolitics*, but though that description shines by its own philosophical richness, nonetheless, the answer does not solve the conundrum but instead deepens it.

Agamben is absolutely right to reject the parallelism between politics and Entelecheia: as he states, 'Politics, as the work of man qua man, is extracted from the living being through the exclusion of his vital activity as a-political' (2015, 324). Politics as the qualification of life immediately becomes potestas. Hence, destiny, fate, or a universal reason becomes the metaphysical necessity of a *work* of men as telos, a destiny programmed in a hidden finality that is always imposed retroactively from a given potestas. Concepts such as class, nation, patriotism or the free market are constructed on this basic division. Wherever there is a finality of politics beyond itself, we will always find power as domination: a power that is always held as a remote *arché* that determines the development of politics as a necessary becoming of destiny.

The question of this pseudo-politics that defines power as potestas can be reduced to the question of who defines the finality. Whoever stands in the place of the decision is, by definition, the sovereign. Power in its natural plasticity congeals into the power to define the finality of the polity even before the polity comes into being. We are thus in the land of a false constituent power, and so the simulacrum thickens. The final cause becomes the rule, the norm of action. Efficient cause becomes mere tributary to the final cause. In the tension between politics (the political) and the simulacrum of politics, encryption snatches language as the first common. The fundamental rejection of politics as finality is that what *finality* denies is the very possibility of a relation of power. Terms such as consensus, opposition, and representation become a technology of administration. The encryption of the political becomes, as it were, the *proper finality* of politics. This is where the *savage anomaly* of Spinoza will appear, affirming the final cause as potentia itself. This is another key to understanding the actualization of difference: what is external and contradictory to potentia is the definition of potestas, not of actuality. Doing things for their own sake is the definition of difference as potentia, and when this potentia is predicated on a common *for its own sake*, it becomes its own source of preservation as a common. Here we touch upon a proximity with Negri's reading of Spinoza: 'Not the final cause, then, but the efficient cause constitutes the ethical being: *conatus-appetitus-cupiditas* forms the agent by means of which the tension spreads from essence to existence' (Negri 2003, 103).

We therefore have before us two limits of power oscillating in the tense cord of actuality. On the one side, we have *Energeia* as a permanent being-at-work of substance to persevere in its organization. On the other extreme, we find that actuality can only be defined when a telos is put forth as its defining concept, so only perfection can bring about actuality. The vital question becomes, then, in what part of the cord is politics to be found? The biting question is: what is power when considered as politics? And, lastly, is politics rational?

In answering these questions, we are not assuming a naturalist conception of politics or calling for a return to some sort of a lost paradise: we are only describing the rational formula of politics. Politics can only be considered when every being that makes a difference is considered as the condition of the existence of politics, *with no further qualification*. Hence, the ontological condition of politics is *Energeia*.

We either read *work* as telos, as finality, and convert it to reason, where historical destiny and all its horrors are but a stone's throw away (homology, unity, race, nation). Or we read work as living labour, as the social brain (Mendez-Hincapie 2015a), as the exposure of difference by means of a power relation as the defining essence of actuality, as property of the self.

Why not simply understand the ontological tissue of politics as potentia? Simply because potestas exists! It is a whole disposition of power that already divides the people as its constituent disposition. The people are already its creation as its hidden component of operability. Hence, confronting potestas, potentia would be impotent on its own. Instead, the power of the hidden people must be actualized if the division of the people in the simulacrum of democracy is ever to be overturned. Consequently, what we call facticity, reality, or actuality, both in political terms and regarding the possibilities of language, is nothing but a world already divided brutally by power as potestas. It is a world of exclusion and asymmetries sanctioned by law, where equality before the law means inequality before structures of power in a solid state. Facticity is thus the omnipotence of potestas. There is no point zero from which to garner an ideal of pure and immaculate potential; rather, the point zero is *already there*: it is the thin peel from which we observe the spectacle of mass destruction. We already speak from a divided and atomized world of potestas, of the rule of the law of the few over the many. We can only speak of the possibilities of the world, of its transformation, once we acknowledge that we inhabit a world already defined by extraordinary powers that have divided life, not as secondary or collateral effect of politics, but as its core value, as its own property and substance. As Malcolm X would have it, 'We didn't land on Plymouth rock; Plymouth rock landed on us'. Coloniality names the division between potestas and potentia; it is the constituent element of reality, the refractory and precise place of power in a solid state. To deny this, or to intend to go beyond its limits, is to speak of a power that is not only not actual but impotent. It is to speak of democracy as a form of government or an organization of power as a simulacrum. In coloniality, the *corruption* of forms of power *is* the point zero. We cannot even name politics when its meaning is not available to be created by all. True democracy is where politics can be named as a *certain something* rather than everything. It is the possibility of meaning within an infinitude of difference, and this infinitude of difference is a *being-at-work to preserve itself.*

Agamben is stuck on the Aristotelian idea of form as the accomplishment of labour (work) where the finished work would define retrospectively a vocation and thus a prefigured nature of humanity, a finished work defining a nature. But defined from Energeia, humanity's work is to relate power to power; it is before all synergy, it means to communicate. The prime matter is a technical aspect standing between potentia and actuality that remains forever contingent within the relation. The work (labour) of man that decides his essence is political, and only when it is first political can we push away life marked by teleology, by historical faith. Agamben destroys labour, confusing it with destiny. He denies its constitutive breadth of the production of time. Actuality will fall irremediably into potestas when the actuality of politics is equated to Entelecheia, but not if what the actualization of potency avoids is the possibility of power to be actualized in a particular subject through a particular disposition or qualification. The Energeia of the people means a distribution of power necessarily only on equal bases, where equality is taken not as a legal standard created from within, but instead as the logical result of difference (equality as grounded in difference's production of difference). Politics is not a precondition of differences: difference is the precondition of politics. Hence, the distribution of power is the actuality of the people. Power can only be actual when it is in a strict relation to the power of all. This is what makes potestas impotent.

Nevertheless, Agamben's impotence is a recrudescence and ultimately a mirage of power, a split on a different angle of the same exclusion. Before potestas and its utter pervasiveness the only answer is *not to be*—it is, as Chantal Mouffe has defined it, *a politics of withdrawal* (Mouffe 2013, 66). The withdrawal, Agamben's privation, becomes a negative presupposition of representation, a metaphysical cliché. To enforce this impossibility upon potentia is to ensure that it never becomes actual and to render it impotent and utterly powerless. This is also to impose the reality of exclusion, to assert the asymmetrical structures of power as an immovable facticity and so as the sole condition of language. In the passion of impotence there is no escape, nowhere to hide from the industrial line of subjectivity that is capitalism. Agamben moves potentia to coincide with Plato's *idea,* accepting that the state of exception is the unchanged given, the anaesthesia of power.

Agamben has fallen into the pit of indistinction: he confuses history with ontology and then goes on to endorse the official history as the only history. First, the classic Greek definition of politics as qualification (telos) is but the *historical fact* that runs untrammelled through the construction of the West and that coloniality simply intensifies and globalizes; but that politics can only ensue when there is an infinite opening for difference is *the ontological definition of politics.* Second, that power as potestas is the official history of Western thought impedes him to see the alternative: the hidden people as the permanent strife of difference against unity, a definable and definite articulation of power as actuality, and actuality as an ordered legality. Hence, the fracture at the fantastical origin of Western politics between life and a certain life is picked up by Agamben as the only viable narration of politics, a universal history of politics that of course can only be opposed by the fantasy of impotence. Agamben adheres pacifically to the idea that potentia and potestas run in parallel, untouched vectors of reality. His prognosis of the division of life between bare and full life is an adequate and precise historical account of the qualification of life that defines Western politics. The account certainly narrates what has been the trajectory of power as domination, but it misses the constituent grain of political ontology. In other words, life as an arbitrary division has been the definition of potestas, but only in so far it has been a systematic denial of democracy as the only order of politics; it is but the descent into the longest night of the simulacrum. Nevertheless, failing to see the true composition of politics as Energeia and not Entelecheia, Agamben designs yet another prison to evade potestas; he shreds and shutters being in the oblivion of *not doing*. When we establish that the only order of politics is democracy as the actuality of difference, we are turning the narration completely upside down. The division of life and its further qualifications is the utter rejection of politics, not its unmovable truth value; hence, the Western narration of power and all its ill-conceived extensions of legality, legitimacy, and justice function as the greatest simulacrum known to humankind. What Agamben fails to denounce is that the history of Western politics depends on the absolute annulment of democracy, and is thus bare power as domination, sheer violence.

Agamben leaves us two possibilities which are a repetition of the same gesture. The first would be to define *work* by the final end of work, which means an irreconcilable split of life and the perseverance of all the Western tradition of exploitation according to some hidden logos (a hidden telos as arché) that dictates and justifies any and every kind of hierarchy as natural. The second would be to glorify the passion of the potency of never becoming. This would assume the actuality of politics as a necessary split produced by the pre-eminence of the *finality* of actuality. It mandates a potentiality that can never become actual because doing so actualizes the split between life and a *certain way of life* according to the necessity of achieving a finality.

Is there a third possibility? Not only do I believe that there is, but I maintain that in this third possibility is a displacement of the traditional understanding of the Aristotelian split of Entelecheia and Energeia which will render a brand new construction of the subject of politics and of the taxonomy of politics itself. We are tracking the conditions under which we may actualize difference, and therefore we are met with two conditions: (1) that actuality is not seen as a finality, as the *end* of being-at-work, but simply as being-at-work, where all finality beyond constituting politics is severed from the commencement; and (2) that the creation of the common language of politics does not function as privation. This is where our interpretation of Energeia breaks the dead matter of politics. *Staying the same through work* brings a necessary redundancy to politics wherein whatever changes, changes into that into which it changes; this means the possibility of transitions of power and the possibility of overcoming the thick and decrepit cluster of potestas, and it means that contingency is at the heart of power. This is the only meaningful and consistent way to understand substance in Aristotle.

The argument favouring privation as the root of the legitimate exercise of a technique falls apart when we define politics through no particular virtue. It does not imply a naturalization of politics, but understanding the very simple fact that life (and *only* life) is the very condition of politics. Politics—if understood not as a qualified exercise but as being under the condition of being a common—leads us directly to work not as qualified work, but as work producing the conditions of life on its own (living labour), with life understood as an integration of difference through difference. Or, as Antonio Negri would have it, 'It is not possible to say being, except in terms of production' (Negri 2003, 143). Henceforth, if potentia is a relation of differences, labour is not tied syllogistically to actuality, but to the actualization of potentia as difference. Being only becomes being in its power to be—this is living labour. It is true that Aristotle joined technique and politics, but this is a fault in his definition of politics, not in the relation between potentia and actuality that defines a precise ontology. Work to preserve in itself as a common is the work of difference. It is the space of deployment of *ipseity*, the cornerstone of the possibility to name politics and its confines through the naming of oneself as the source of difference, where the *one* and the *common* belong in an assembly of difference. In the words of Jacques Derrida, 'By ipseity I thus wish to suggest some "I can", or at the very least the power that gives itself its own law, its force of law, its self-representation, the sovereign and re-appropriating gathering of self in the simultaneity of an assemblage or assembly, being together, or "living together", as we say' (Derrida 2005, 14). The point, which before any other consideration is logical, is that the question of the *one* of difference and of politics can only be made from actuality as Energeia. The latter does not imply a utopian end of politics. On the contrary, actuality as the possibility of democracy is the only beginning of politics as conflict, as the overriding of the simulacrum of liberal law which in turn means the negation of politics through the neutralization of the political. Here we can define violence as precisely that force which renders impossible conflict *within* the law.

With the actualization of difference through Energeia, we come across a paradoxically rich meaning of community. The first sense is of an operative community that resists the onslaught of unity and identity through difference, an unfixed community where power as difference relates to everything (the order of politics as conflict). The community is, thus, open to every being that communicates difference. But the community may never be closed and thus it is also inoperative in a second and derivative sense: once difference is never fully actualized but is a becoming, the precedence of a *certain way of life* disappears and with it the pre-eminence of the telos of the final form. Community is always a remainder of the possibility of the external as the core basis of the internal. The internal is always incomplete and endangered, the bond of the community is thus always open, always retracted to a point of revision by the potentia of the hidden people. A frontier guarded not by the police but reversed from its inside. As Illan Wall marvellously concludes, 'Community is possible only because we are without an absolute' (Wall 2012, 113).

In the present book, we have established a fundamental line of reasoning between politics and democracy. First, we have proven that conflict is the dimension of undecidability and contingency of every order (Mouffe 2013, 131). The latter means that politics can only exist when conflict is its constituent concept and that democracy is the only order of politics, since it is the only form of distribution of power where conflict has not been decided and hence its outcome is always contingent. This means, second, that potestas is the negation of politics, because conflict has already been decided as an attribution of (solid) power to certain particularities that are naturally meant to govern the rest. Given this, democracy as the only possible form to define politics also means that the language through which we define conflict and deal with its appropriation must be available to all (it must be decrypted). No particular may have a hierarchical hold on language or its use. The latter not only means that language is the first common of the being-in-common of politics, but also that any denial of this principle is an upsurge of power as potestas. As we have also proven, the people *as hidden people* are created as a precise historical subject through a primordial exclusion from the body of politics, whereas the people *as such* are the resistance of difference to the overwhelming power of a fictitious totality under whose name potestas crouches. Potestas is the programmed drainage of the power (being-at-work) of the people.

The aim of the *hidden* people is to break open the gates of politics. Energeia is the pivot of the common being of politics. It is its very condition of possibility as existence, the point where language becomes nameable through language under the condition that it remains open to an infinity of difference. Whatever human beings can achieve through intelligence and imagination is only granted when the base, the condition *sine qua non*, is the being in common of work. Think of it in this way: the mere possibility of agreement on the concept of *Eudaimonia* depends on the constitution of a polity as Energeia. Actuality is *at work,* is actually happening: it is the permanent resistance of the people to inclusion in a state of exception. It is a striving to keep difference from being absorbed by unity and identity, and it is what inhibits potestas from taking it over, thus converting living labour into exchange value.

The solution to the problem of the continuum regarding substance is solved by Aristotle by identifying substance precisely with the continuum. The hidden of the people are form as substance determined by a violent act of potestas. The people are the element of difference as a continuum that determines the transition through a certain ordered motion of its power. The multitude, as we will demonstrate, is the spinning wheel of Teruel: a reflection of impotence, it can create an image of motion but it cannot act and produce the transition and the motion as the organization of time and space. Potestas is the fact of power that is not necessary, but that necessarily has deprived potentia. The first natural common interrupted and encrypted by potestas is the very possibility of power.

What is cast in Energeia is composition as perfection, with no further qualification, transcendence or finalism than the composition of the common of politics. And what would this composition look like? As an open infinity, an open constitution of being where every difference is included as its own topic of enunciation. A decrypted space of language where language means the utter necessity of the common, furthermore, where the common and language become one and the same thing. In short, Energeia means that the future is yet to be decided.

One thing must be crystal clear; we are not defending the thesis that power in itself is an actuality; this would be a physical impossibility. The nuclear thesis is that the *people* of the hidden people are the actuality, as the very condition for their power to always remain in potentia. Power is always opaque, modal, diffuse; it cannot be an object of direct knowledge. The only thing we can bring down to knowledge are its practices (Deleuze 2014, 68). When power ceases to be a practice, the only thing that reminds is reverence towards power, that is, the necessity of potestas as the divinity of power. It is precisely because potestas is based on an illicit intent to solidify power that power can only be a flux and circulate when it is placed in an actuality as an ever open actuality Where it can propagate freely. In other words, as a colophon of our demonstration, power can only be potential when it is placed in Energeia. Actuality, then, must be understood not as a superior form of reality that precedes potentia both in time and logics (Aristotle), or as a plane of immanence incommunicable with the great outside due to its monadic substance (Deleuze), or as the power of impotence (Agamben), but as the space where potentia becomes the necessary and consistent origin of language. The final work only makes sense by virtue of being a product of the work of difference, of a relation that is inexhaustible. Energeia is the primal mover of ontology; it is the opening of politics to difference. It is power jumping out of its prison of totality and into actuality, as the world recovers its poetic mystery.

NOTES

1. Just as a reminder that we are not reviving some piece of bygone vestige of dead language, consider the specificity of Heisenberg's claim in the following paragraph:

> One might perhaps call it an objective tendency or possibility, a 'potentia' in the sense of Aristotelian philosophy. In fact, I believe that the language actually used by physicists when they speak about atomic events produces in their minds similar notions as the concept 'potentia'. So the physicists have gradually become accustomed to considering the electronic orbits, etc., not as reality but rather as a kind of 'potentia'. (1958, 124)

2. Especially *The Savage Anomaly: The Power of Spinoza's Metaphysics and Politics* (Minneapolis: University of Minnesota Press, 2003) and *Insurgencies: Constituent Power and the Modern State* (Minneapolis: University of Minnesota Press, 1999).

3. Marc Cohen helps us understand the complex historic—linguistic relation of the terms substance and the original Ousia.

'Substance', the conventional English rendering of Aristotle's word ousia, is in fact misleading, suggesting as it does a kind of stuff. The English term 'substance' entered the philosophical vernacular as a translation of the Latin substantia, which was itself an inadequate attempt to translate Aristotle. What 'substance' and substantia both miss is the connection of the word ousia to the verb 'to be' (einai). A better rendition might be 'reality' or 'fundamental being', but 'substance' is deeply entrenched in the philosophical literature and will be used here. A good gloss would be to say that ousiai are the 'ontologically basic entities'. (Cohen, 2009 p. 196)

4. For a very novel take on the aporia between the categories and substance described in *Metaphysics* Book Z, see Wedin 2000.

5. In Cohen's words:

The idea here seems to be that what makes species and genera secondary is that they are just kinds or collections. A species is just a collection of individuals, and a genus is just a wider collection of the individual members of the species that fall under it. Without those individuals, there would be no species, and without the species there would be no genera. (Cohen, 2009, p. 199)

6. The number of the categories varies according to Aristotle's different works; there are ten in *Categories* 1b25 a, seven in the *Physics* (225b5) and *Metaphysics* (Met. 11.1068a). In *Metaphysics*, he states, 'Now since the categories are distinguished as substance, quality, place, activity or passivity, relation and quantity'.

7. Put in familiar terms: is Theseus' ship still Theseus' ship if it is dismounted piece by piece and then replaced in the same order by different pieces?

8. If substance is an organization of elements as a coordinated whole, and matter by itself is inert in relation to substance, what would the matter-as-substance of Socrates be? Mitochondrial membranes? Chains of DNA? Carbon? Flesh and bones?

9. In all of these argumentative patterns, the reader must bear in mind that our final destiny is the crossroads of potentia and actuality, where matter plays the pivotal role.

10. For a sophisticated attempt to destabilize the principle, see Priest, G., and T. Smiley, 1993, "Can Contradictions be True?", *Proceedings of the Aristotelian Society*, 68 (Supplement): 17–54.

11. 'and as we call even a man who is not studying "a scholar" if he is capable of studying. That which is present in the opposite sense to this is present actually so is that which is awake to that which is asleep; and that which is seeing to that which has the eyes shut, but has the power of sight; and that which is differentiated out of matter to the matter; and the finished article to the raw material. Let actuality be defined by one member of this antithesis, and the potential by the other' (Aristotle. Met. 9.1047b–48b).

12. Contingency is not chance. Take, for example, the throwing of two dice. Although we do not know the sum of the dice that will result (the highest probability being seven), we do know the impossibility of the sum being 0, 1, or greater than 12. Where there is a determination of the impossible there is necessity. As Quentin Meillasoux explains, 'Thus chance always presupposes some form of physical invariance—far from permitting us to think the contingency of physical laws, chance itself is nothing other than a certain type of physical law—one that is "indeterministic"' (Meillasoux 2008, 160).

13. The text is in Portuguese; the English version is a free translation made by the author.

14. We are not interested here in conducting an extensive inquiry of the theory of causes in Aristotle since we are only interested in the one of them that leads us to understand the fear of actuality in contemporary thinking. The causes can be identified as (1) Material: 'That out of which a thing comes to be, and which persists' (Aristotle. Physics. 194b24). (2) Formal: As we have seen before, it deals with the identification of substance as form. (3) Efficient: the primary source of change or rest, determined by the cause of motion and rest. (4) Final, which we will analyse in detail. For a detailed account, I recommend, among others, Joe Sachs, 'Aristotle: Motion and its Place in Nature', (2005) at http://www.iep.utm.edu/aris-mot/#H2, retrieved August 14, 2015.

15. Italics are mine.

16. http://www.oxforddictionaries.com/us/definition/american_english/energy. Retrieved August 3 2015.

17. http://www.oxforddictionaries.com/us/definition/american_english/entelechy.

18. For more specialized discussions on the difference between Echein and Hexis, see 'Alexander of Aphrodisias: On Aristotle Metaphysics 5', translated by William E. Dooley, Bloomsbury, London 2013. We will follow Agamben in using the term Hexis since his work is our target of decryption.

19. In a final stroke of the occultation of power as potential, Agamben turns the people into a finality, against the core of his own theses. He quotes Dante, saying, 'It is not the work that exists regarding essence, but essence exists regarding work'. Here the key is the Latin *operatio* as equivalent to ergon. Agamben draws potential back to intellect as an encumbered form of logos, in the form of Dante's multitude as the unicity of a possible intellect (Agamben 2015, 328). The multitude is the generic form of the existence of potentia, which is always on the verge of actuality. Here the multitude is the thaten, Aristotle's primordial material, the raw material. Hence the question that arises can be formulated as such: Would the *work* of the people be an *operari ex nihilo* or a *facere de materia*? The theological monotheistic answer is that *nothingness* is God itself in potentia. But here it gets tricky, as Agamben affirms, for if God possessed a *potency of being*, it would follow that God possesses a *potency of not being* which would contradict eternality as God's first principle of existence. It would further follow that it would be possible that God could not want to *not be*, for that would negate creation as act, and nothingness could very well be the only potentia which God exercises. The monotheistic response is that God descends to the abyss of nothingness and creates, not *from* nothingness (that would be a limited

potentia of some kind), but by *annihilating* nothingness (Agamben 2015, 110). For the hidden people, however, nothingness stands as a queerer paradox, a materially defined geography of flesh and bone, walls and statutes, prohibitions and exceptions. The nothingness of the people is the state of exception where it must remain for sovereignty to operate and the simulacrum to function. The liberal God has created the creatures and the oceans, carving them out of the same nothingness to which the hidden people are condemned. Hence, on the one hand, we have the material geography of the market, finances, human rights, constitutions, a unity of things and concepts that refer to things themselves as a whole; on the other, we have at its origin a Basilean act of creating from scratch. The sovereign legislator of reason or the cogito, then, is necessarily tied to the nothingness of the people. Agamben, therefore, has just tied politics to Entelecheia, to a primordial qualification for the order of language.

Chapter 5

The Phantom Pain of Civilization

Against Negri's Understanding of Spinoza

There are two basic and insuperable hindrances for Negri's project of building power as absolute potentia. First, in order for Negri to maintain pure potentia, he logically needs to eradicate mediation. His strategy is to move mediation further and further from absolute potentia, as if he were moving the radius inside the circle hoping that it magically changed names by the mere execution of the feat. Such an exploit ultimately fails, as mediation is necessarily reintroduced at some point or another in order to explain either the passage from substance to attributes in Spinoza, or in his building of the idea of the *multitude*. Mediation, as we will prove, is ultimately the key problem that any analytics of power must face and that Negri denies, as it would blemish his project of pure immanence. The second hindrance is that to the extent that he identifies actuality with potestas, he must build a meaning of potentia that never comes across actuality and thus constructs potentia necessarily through a series of *as if's*. Power (potestas) is subordinated to power as potentia, *as if* in our composition of reality, the relations of production were subordinated to the productive force of the multitude. He deems Potentia as the generic right to the world of the multitude *as if* potestas did not already order the world through a strong mediation of hidden principles and constitutive zones of exclusion. In other words, the preservation of potentia in Negri implies the ultimate sacrifice of politics in its own name. It implies the construction of an impossible subjectivity, the multitude, through a weightless principle, potentia.

Power is before all action. Negri neglects the necessary *point of friction of power*—precisely the element that makes power an *action*. Power as action is unimaginable without friction; it is its physical trait. Pure potentia eschews conflict: it is unable to perforate the dense scab of an already existing diffusion of power as exclusion and oppression. What Negri misses is the necessity of a point of transition from potestas to potentia as the fundamental political act. Along these lines, he also neglects the fact that the (hidden) people, far from being a unit of hegemony, are a dispersion of difference that is kept silenced so that power as domination may reign freely. In structuring the multitude, I am afraid Negri feels the phantom pain of the loss of civilization, an Eden tainted by state and sovereignty.

As soon as we begin to descend into Negri's reading of Spinoza, we will be able to strongly identify with our understanding of actuality. Insofar as we are not engaging Negri in his reading of power and substance in the Spinozian Ethics, we share his construction which we deem fundamental for understanding power. However, there is a limit to this strong parallelism. Our wager is that reading power in the key of actuality as *Energeia* (chapter 4) and not as the potency of an absolute substance garners the former a definite insurgent point of unblocking power from potestas and thus opening politics to an articulation of ontology and democracy. In short, what our gesture makes viable is politics qualified only as the order of the common, which is what is exactly missed in Negri's reading of potentia as absolute substance. The problem with Negri is that as long as he refuses to engage actuality—and, thus, a point where a decision must be taken—he finds himself in need of constantly moving the line of mediation. Mediation pervades the edifice of absolute potentia: it cannot be done away with, for as soon as it is deactivated in one part it reappears in another with even more corruptive power.

Negri's refusal to recognize a necessary point of transition will lead him to a path of no return. Ironically enough, we will see him ultimately build a stronger condition for the qualification of politics than the ones presented by Plato and Aristotle. As he traces the route of escape, Negri will turn to the ancient concept of *pietas*, and through it he will build a new and unexpected form of transcendence through a strong version of qualification for the exercise of politics. In the end, Negri will open a sinister backdoor for everything he rejects.

In the last stretch of the chapter, our aim, in engaging Hardt and Negri, is to dispute not only their construction of multitude, but also more precisely what they deem the *biopolitical* possibility of an *information society* (as the trademark of our times of post-Fordism) to transcend capitalism without any further condition. This is to be a revolution that will stem only from the bliss of the flow of communication in a binary-number fest of love. As we will prove, what they call the information society is still a highly encrypted physics of power as it replicates, with the same stamina, the principles of domination. The wondrous machines of technology and communication are programmed in highly sophisticated languages and in extremely elitist environments that are instrumental for the domination of capital at its best. Even though we are connected irremediably in a network of ever-extending information, as a

General Intellect, the cultural language of the machine remains encrypted: its flows and commands are still dependent on the hunger of the market, and its core intellect remains a highly scarce material. Hence, information can only become democratic when the machine—as a point of absorption of power-knowledge—is itself decrypted and politically liberated. We will engage Marx's concept of the machine as an ideal apparatus of power and follow his insight according to which the machine, being more than merely a mechanical dispositif of power, is its material core. Certainly the machine will play a key role in liberation—just imagine all the immaterial knowledge freed from the yoke of capital and feeding the common; it will be a new dawn of humanity. Nevertheless, while the dice fall as they do and the political rules remain encrypted, every language, cybernetic or not, remains occluded as a sign of political prostration. Hence, pretending that the information society possesses the intrinsic tools to liberate itself is as farfetched as pretending that the machines will liberate themselves and us in the same process. Our point is that we are certain that the information society brings about a completely new reconsideration of power and communication. But we are also certain that the potentialities of what Marx denoted as a *social brain* can only begin to be liberated in a purely political act, an act of transition that meets the standard of the actuality of power.

NEGRI'S 'SAVAGE ANOMALY'

There is an incongruity in the legalized history of Western philosophy, a bloated point in the perfect regularity of the configuration of being, a metaphysical abnormality that causes tremors in the conceptual stability of the edifice of power. It is the *savage anomaly*, a term minted by Antonio Negri to denote the queer place of Spinoza's philosophy in the trajectory of modernity that bifurcates its path irremediably and opens a novel and vibrant line of reflection and production regarding ontology and ethics. Specifically, Spinoza's ethics reach a point of no return for the liberty and autonomy of humankind. In the time of the totalitarian love of power and the glacial fear of becoming other than the model, a return to Spinoza offers a new and seemingly uncharted region where the construction of power and freedom correspond to pure immanence. Pure immanence signals the extinction of the need for remote principles and the measuring of power through the pedestal of transcendence. Immanence supposes the absolute correspondence of body and mind, as well as the primordial place of ethics as an integratable construction of a collective and infinite political subject that meets no match in its supreme power while it includes all multiplicity at its atomic composition. Thinking and becoming in the world through this newfangled consideration of power and philosophy defeat all the traits adjoined to power as submission and servitude, of the fetish of its symbols, and of adoration of anything that incarnates power as glory, elevation, and domination. Spinoza is thus the architect of the machine of revolution, a machine that is made of human flesh and mind welded as one by love and liberation. This machine subverts the debauchery of the fascination of power for its own sake and transforms it into the garb of emancipation. Spinoza has thus built the machine that produces pure positivity excavating the land of negativity out of its nook of transcendence. *Good riddance to transcendence* is the motto of this particular machine of immanence.

If we could simply juxtapose Spinoza with traditional philosophy of power, we could state that while for the latter power is a property of the one or the unity of the few, for the former, power is not a property but the immanent substance of the *all*. While the latter is a sinkhole that flushes down the drain of transcendence every vestige of common creation through a strong mediation, the former is the construction of the world only as a result of the action of the common.

The great gesture of Spinoza is to flatten—in one single and formidable stroke—metaphysics, God, men, and nature, turning them all into a unique substance that corresponds to the power of men to create and sustain the life of the common. As lucidly stated by Negri, 'Spinoza is a philosopher of being who immediately effects the inversion of the totality of the transcendent imputation of causality by posing the productive, immanent, transparent and direct constitution of the world, the great theoretical thesis of Spinozism: a single substance having an infinity of attributes, *Deus sive Natura*' (Negri 2003, 10). In the Hobbesian and Kantian tradition of being and power, all the terms (God, men, nature) are necessarily disjointed, deployed as nodes and marks that fabricate being as independent but interconnected parts of a transcendent machine. Power always descends from a hidden exteriority to bring the mission of humankind into conformity, yielding a creature whose task becomes simply an adaptation of her capacities into the ruling model of power. The creature thus always confronts an already existing reality that defines it, and to which it must pay the reverence of obedience. Power as transcendence is always exterior to subjectivity; it is a deafening order that must be observed at all costs for it determines the unity of subject and world. Transcendence, the emperor of the metaphysical underworld of determinism, is neither an object nor a subject, but rather the field of the thunderous emergence of the command. It offers no possibility of interlocution because all the combinations of language are already prefigured in its deployment, retained in its invisibility. In this bizarre assembly line, morality is the unattainable voice that dictates all the compositions of the modes of power. It is this definition of power imbedded in morality and transcendence that is confronted by Spinoza. In the words of Deleuze, 'This is why, Ethics, which is to say, a typology of immanent modes of existence, replaces Morality, which always refers existence to transcendent values. Morality is the judgment of God, the *system of Judgment*. But Ethics overthrows the system of judgement' (Deleuze 1988a, 23).

The shock of Spinozian metaphysics commences with the definition of substance, though it is a fairly conventional style of definition for its time. 'By substance I mean that which is in itself and is conceived through itself; that is, that the conception of which does not require the conception of another thing from which it has to be formed' (Spinoza. *Ethics*. I D 3). But beyond the orthodox definition, what unravels the whole system and gives it its revolutionary acumen is the equation of God, nature, and men in terms of substance and thus in terms of power. As Connelly expresses, firstly, Spinoza 'posits a self-caused something (substance) which is the cause of all things this is its essence, which follows from its properties (infinity, immutability, capacity to know, etc.). Spinoza calls this something "God"' (Connelly 2015). This is where we find the key to the treasure of the Spinozian revolution. In his definition, the cause of substance is neither a remote material cause nor an efficient cause that pulls the lever from an exteriority. Rather, substance is *cause* of *itself*. The circle of causality closes upon being. Cause is not said in any other meaning but cause of itself. Substance, then, is not a diminished and derivative product of anything, but only cause of itself. Being begets being in immanence. As the archetype of all causality, substance becomes the complete meaning of cause. If substance and cause are one, if nature and God are one, and if men share the meaning of a self-caused substance, this amounts to an astonishing feat of philosophy: creation and production are immanent, and hence there is no room in them for transcendence or mediation. Substance is thus the factory of being and all of its creations, without reference to any higher externality and with no need of a dialectical mediator. In the words of Deleuze, 'Thus God is the cause of all things; and every existing finite thing refers to another finite thing as to the cause that makes it exist and act' (Deleuze 1988a, 53).

Spinoza seems to fuse the swords of reason and theology in a conciliatory act that deposits their thrust under the force of ethics. He then goes on to dismember them in a revolutionary act that turns metaphysics and politics onto ethics as the order of things. Against the prevailing Cartesian split of body and mind, Spinoza equates God to nature, nature to man, and body to mind. As a result of the primal metaphysical flattening, body and mind are understood not as two separate substances but rather as mere expressions of one unique thing.

Regarding the relation of nature to God, the flattening achieves a similar transformation. God ceases to be an *absconditus*, a force that guides life through an inscrutable will and becomes identical to nature. In the words of

Deleuze, 'God does not possess the perfections implied by the "creatures" in a form different from that which these perfections have in the creatures themselves' (Deleuze 1988a, 52). Everything that flows from the power of God flows through the power of nature and of men. God possesses infinite attributes and thus nature and men are equal expressions of said attributes. As Spinoza explains, 'By God I understand a being absolutely infinite, i.e., a substance consisting of an infinity of attributes, of which each one expresses an eternal and infinite essence' (Spinoza. *Ethics*. 1 D 6). Although the attributes of God are infinite as is her essence, men express such attributes through a *limited* set of their own attributes, that is, body and mind. The body as extension and the mind as thought are the human attributes that express the infinite primordial substance. The latter does not mean that the attributes of men are inferior to those of nature and thus a derivative. On the contrary, as Deleuze explains, substance corresponds to each attribute qualitatively and not numerically (Deleuze 1988a, 52). It is therefore not an arithmetic relation of number to number, as if men possessed a limited capacity of informing infinite substance; rather, through the extending body and the thinking mind, the infinity of the attributes of God is expressed absolutely. The connection of men and God (nature) is accomplished through a plane of immanence as a joining of the attributes in one single expression of substance. Thus, Spinoza proceeds in defining the attributes of men: 'By attribute I mean that which the intellect perceives of substance as constituting its essence' (Spinoza. *Ethics*. 1 D 4). As men, we can only know and possess two attributes, but that is all that we need to become one with God and nature. We express God's infinite intellect in our mind as we express God's infinite extension in the extension of our body, and yet through this precise mechanics, we know there is an infinity of attributes. If an equation was possible it would read as follows: the two attributes of men express the infinity of the attributes of God (nature) at every instance of the expression of the said attributes; they are one and the same and reverberate at unison. As Deleuze puts it, 'We know only two because we can only conceive as infinite those qualities that we involve in our essence: thought and extension, inasmuch as we are mind and body' (Deleuze 1988a, 52). Through our attributes we know, in the exact moment we express, the infinity of the attributes of God.

The plane of immanence is thus built as an impenetrable fortress. The world stands on its own ground and no negativity or mediation may frustrate its construction or deployment. The acid storm of transcendence—'a specifically European disease' (Deleuze and Guatarri 1987, 18)—is banished forthright. As a result, immanence means that every relation among singularities ceases to refer to external and recondite principles that determine the grades and intensities, and, more importantly, transcendence cannot condition the legality of their encounter.

The circle closes in on the idea that grasps God and nature as one and the same. There are, according to Spinoza, two sides to nature. In the first, we encounter its active aspect, the infinite production of everything that we may call the world in its dynamics of renewal and transformation. It is what Spinoza denotes as *Natura naturans*, the naturing nature, expressed through the infinite attributes of God and recognized as the self-causing and infinite activity of nature. The second is what is sustained by the active aspect, *Natura naturata*, natured nature. In Spinoza's words, it means 'whatever follows from the necessity of God's nature, *or from God*'s attributes, that is, all the modes of God's attributes insofar as they are considered as things which are in God, and can neither be nor be conceived without God' (Spinoza. *Ethics*. P I, Pr. 29). In short, *natura naturata* is what nature is, as created by God. As Deleuze clarifies, 'Natura naturans (as substance and cause) and Natura naturata (as effect and mode) are interconnected through a mutual immanence: on one hand, the cause remains in itself in order to produce; on the other hand, the effect or product remains in the cause' (Deleuze 1988a, 92).

The fundamental flattening of God and nature and the definition of the attributes mean one essential swerve from the reign of transcendence. Nature in its productive or created essence does not seek to fulfil any purpose: there are no final causes imbedded in its genetic code, and it does not pursue to emulate any principle that would dictate its composition. Precisely because the principle is internal and equal to existence, immanence is the only way to grip its *quiddity* or distinctive essence.

The chain continues to expand as we consider the signification of the right and law of nature. In the plane of immanence, we find a conclusive meaning of both. The Tractatus Politicus (TP) defines the right of nature in the following manner:

> By the right of Nature, then, I understand the laws or rules of Nature in accordance with which all things come to be, that is, the very power of Nature. So the natural right of Nature as a whole, and consequently the natural right of every individual, is coextensive with its power [potentia]. Consequently, whatever each man does from the laws of his own nature, he does by the sovereign right of Nature, and he has as much right over Nature as his power extends [quantum potentia valet]. (Spinoza. TP. Ch II. 4)

Along with transcendence, any prince-like figure is expatriated from nature: there is no dictator governing nature to ensure compliance with any specific order or destination. God is not a legislative intellect ordering facts and events in accordance to a will detached from her creation. Creation, God, and nature are one single substance expanding its power as one. Power is the power of nature to be and to become that which is shared immanently by men, not as an imitative act but coextensive to existence. Power, thus, is a generic right to the world, unhindered and unmediated by anything else. Power is right. However, all the tenets of this edifice are sustained by the deep cut between potentia and potestas.

POTENTIA AND POTESTAS:
THE FUNDAMENTAL SPLIT OF POWER

There is a shortcoming in the English language's ability to express the diversity of power as expressed in Latin between potentia and potestas. Although both refer to the concept of power, their mutual difference parts the waters for the comprehension, not only of power, but also of its meaning as the organizing principle of the world. Potentia is the immanent expression of men's substance onto the world: it is the exact space and instant where power and right become one and the same thing. As Emilia Giancotti puts it, 'The division between power and potentia reveals a pivotal binding between metaphysics and ontology' (in Negri 2000, 15). To exercise potentia is to exercise power infinitely by the right of nature; therefore, potentia is a generic right to the world of every singularity that expresses God's infinite substance. When we exercise potentia, we do not do so to conform to pre-given laws of nature or any other transcendent entity but we do it as the deployment of our existence. To have a right to the world is defined by the power to exist. Potentia is, then, the creative power of substance, God's power by which she and all things are and act as their own essential self. Potentia is then defined when we grasp that every natural thing has as much right as it has the power to exist (Goetschel 2004, 69). Natural right becomes equal with nature and power, all coexisting in a straight surface of immanence.

On the other hand, potestas is the art of splitting apart, of annexing right and power. It is the power contrary to potentia, whose movement is to frustrate potentia by alienating the right to nature, converting the right of all into a particular power. In short, it is power as domination and exclusion that subverts the equation of immanence. Potestas is a deviation of power and of right. It is recognizable when a particular hinders the potentia of another's singularity to extract power as its own. The anomaly in the plane of power, then, is potestas, a sort of inversion of the principle where particulars conquer the definition of nature as power and dissolve potentia within an aberrant actuality. As we will come to understand, potestas is a negative affection: it is where the generic *right* to the world becomes the particular *might over* it. Potestas is power in a solid state.

Nevertheless, we must take the definitions and their interaction a step further and place the problem in the location where it becomes problematic and where all of its characteristics resonate with the very possibility of being: coexistence. Coexistence pushes the plane of immanence to the harshest test of its endurance. It snips the umbilical cord of substance. Assessing its demands, we should be able to establish whether the plane of immanence and the flattening of metaphysics are capable of overcoming the test of multiple singularities sharing space and time, affecting each other permanently and thus generating friction within minds and bodies. It shall also aid in the even more exigent task of establishing how potentia stands to potestas when the latter is not simply expressed in singularities but in determinate structures of power—that is, power in a solid state. Coexistence is the coming forth of the social and the litmus test of the political. Two Spinozian concepts are then fundamental to exercise the test of coexistence, *conatus* and the transformation of *affections*.

Here we come to another axis of the definition of power and right: conatus, which is defined as that 'by which (things) endeavor to persevere in their state' (Spinoza. *Ethics*. Ch. 6). It is immediately revealing that the definition shares an intimate proximity with Aristotle's definition of Energeia. This is our springboard to set both terms apart and thus maintain the imperative necessity of actualizing difference, so we must proceed with caution. According to Leibniz, Deleuze tells us, conatus has two senses: physically it designates a body's tendency towards movement; metaphysically, it is the tendency of an essence towards existence (Deleuze 1992, 230). For Spinoza, Deleuze continues, nothing could be further from the truth, for there is no *tendency* in the body to possibly persevere in life. The dynamic characteristics are linked to the mechanical ones, not in a determined position of a line of movement but through a corrugated space where affections clash against each other in correlations and variations of degrees of power. The Spinozian modes of a single substance exclude all finality, so the endeavour to persevere is always in a tight and multiplied relation to other equally power-packed conatus. It is the mutual affections, the interchange of power, that determine the capacity to express power and, through it, to make a stake in the world. Nevertheless, to reach the boiling point we are seeking, we must heat the coil even more. For our quest is to determine what happens when the intersection of potestas and potentia is arranged not in a plane of singularities but when potestas is instead the formidable machine of sovereignty, biopower, subjugation, market, and state as intimate features of coloniality that cannot simply be wished away by the fairy dust of immanence.

In order to continue our elucidation of the Spinozian edifice, it is vital to clarify the interplay of the concepts imbedded in it. For Deleuze, 'The complete modal triad may be presented thus: a modal essence expresses itself in a characteristic relation; this relation expresses a capacity to be affected; this capacity is exercised by changing affections, just as the relation is effected by parts which are renewed' (Deleuze 1992, 233). In summary, for Spinoza, there is no ultimate correspondence, no hierarchical organization of beings, no predetermination of an outcome: everything in nature is physical. The variations of power are entrenched in the relations of the modes; they cannot be classified outside a quanta of power, where every quanta affects as well as is affected by other relations of power. There is, then, no preformed stability and there is no finality ingrained in the relations. Substance as self-caused essence means that, within the production of affections, the only cast, the only frame, is the relation in itself. This is why *conatus*, in a second determination, is a tendency to maintain and maximize the ability to be affected (Deleuze 1992, 99). In the flattening process, nature is not the complete and final form of symbolization of all that there is, but an open and incomplete process where the multiple affections of singularities install their own conatus simultaneously and permanently. Power is not coined as a finality or the source of the production of solitary and well-defined beings, but it is instead immersed in an undying flux of quanta of power. There is no clear and distinct ordering of being without power. Conatus allocates the existential function of essence, and it is the affirmation of essence in a mode of existence. In conclusion, conatus is the existential mode of essence.

Affections and conatus open the geography of power wide open. We are constantly in a struggle; we are acting and thus affecting other singularities, and being acted upon by the quanta of power of other singularities. As a result, there is always a degree of inclination in our mental or physical capacities. This is the key to power for Spinoza: affections determine our capacity to persevere in being; they are the thin line between life and death. We are always in between a bombardment of positive affections that augment our power or negative encounters that diminish it.

When we cross our concepts, we then discover that the aim of potentia is to increase the power of singularities, to multiply power through the social body. The aim of potestas is to reduce it to immobility or sheer disappearance and hence to coagulate power in a single body, in a solid state.

We stand at the junction of power. Through the intersection of conatus, modes, affections, and attributes, we must determine if power rendered in this way presupposes mediation and thus transcendence. That is, we must show whether the blends are by themselves enough to garner an authentic definition of power, democracy, and liberation, which could warrant difference as the order of being and the fundamental openness of an ontologically founded politics.

At a later stage, we will also test Antonio Negri's effort to conciliate the disparity and imbalance in the definition of democracy and multitude in Spinoza's oeuvre. This will involve taking on the latter's inclination to define democracy as a form of government in both the Tractatus Politicus (TP) and the *Tractatus Theologico-Politicus* (TTP), in sharp opposition to the defini-tion of potentia in his *Ethics*. I will expound and push to the limits the con-tradictions discovered in Negri's difficult labour of trying to demonstrate how the Political Treatise 'conquers metaphysics from the inside' (Negri 2000, 43). As we will find, this is a very difficult pill to swallow. But first, we must concentrate our efforts in the construction of the attributes.

THE ATTRIBUTES OF GOD AND THE SLIPPAGE
OF THE MACHINE OF IMMANENCE

Spinoza defines the central piece of the attributes as follows: 'By attribute I understand what the intellect perceives of a substance, as constituting its essence' (Spinoza. *Ethics*. ID4). As we have stated, men possess two attributes—extension and thought—which express the infinity of God's own attributes. As stated by Negri, 'A constitutive ontology founded on the spontaneity of needs and organized by the collective imagination: this is the Spinozian rationality' (Negri 2003, 10). The pressing question is whether in moving from God's attributes to men's attributes there is any kind of slippage or mediation that would confront the idea of pure immanence; or, if this is not the case, how can we attain the said passage within a plane of immanence?

The theory of the attributes is vital to establish the passage from the imma-nence of God to the multitude. Spinoza's and Negri's stake is that immanence transfers itself without folding back into transcendence, a clean-cut passage without any type of mediation. Such a passage would not only unveil the epistemological question of how to know being, but also more profoundly, the ontological definition of how potentia marks the x of being.

The vexing question is the form in which to grasp the true meaning of the attributes as the expression of immanence. In other words, how can we distinguish between acts of potentia and potestas in our own acts? This is no irrelevant question, for if we were simply plugged in naturally to God's attri-butes this would imply that potestas (domination) is a natural impossibility, which is absurd. Nonetheless, if there is a further step required to obtain such a fundamental connection, it could very well mean the need of mediation and thus a monumental crack in the structure of immanence.

According to Spinoza, 'A true idea means nothing other than knowing a thing perfectly, or in the best way' (Spinoza. *Ethics*. IIp43s). The passage thus involves grabbing a thing's causal connections as they are structured and permanently happening. That is, not only the connections between singu-larities and their own quanta of power, but in the same tract the connections to the attributes of God and hence to the laws of nature. This is the reason why Spinoza categorically states that 'The order and connection of ideas is the same as the order and connection of things' (Spinoza. *Ethics*. II, p 7). Without the adequate idea of the expression of an attribute, we could gain no distinction between the myriad of singularities and their interactions. More importantly, we would have no proper access to God or nature as the cause of substance; hence, they would descend to a pure state of indiscernibility, and potentia and potestas would also be indistinguishable. The corollary of this depiction is that within the connection of the attributes a *tertium* is necessary. This further step is expressed by Spinoza as the connection of the attributes through that which the mind captures through reason: 'But this necessity of things is the very necessity of God's eternal nature. Therefore, it is of the nature of Reason to regard things under this species of eternity' (Spinoza. *Ethics*. II, p 44). Of course, reason must not be understood here as judgement, but rather as correlation of affections, a notion of the commonality of affections that compose reality. Only here can we gain access to the full expansion of the definition of the attribute as 'what the intellect perceives of substance, as constituting its essence' (Spinoza. *Ethics*. I, d 4).

In the words of Stephen Connelly, 'The constant refolding of consciousness inherent in being the subject of God or Nature's immanent power grants to the modern subject the absolute power of synthesizing consciousness, and so of constantly moving to reorder its own will, its own immanent command' (Connelly 2015). Immanent natural right supposes consciousness not as a depository of God's substance but as the creator of its own consciousness, as the creator of its own actuality. Consciousness as a form of knowledge cannot grasp God by itself in stillness, but only through the affections of others, in an enduring fluidity of communication with other singularities. This is the thesis of the identity of the attributes in substance, what enables them to be unified while remaining truly distinct (Macherey 1997, 88). Hence, again it is the proposition 'The order and connection of ideas is the same as the order and connection of things' that brings unity and congruity to the relation of substance and the attributes. Consciousness becomes the awareness of the passage from the modes of potency to their exponential growth through the social body. It is what, for the likes of Negri and Deleuze, closes the circle of immanence.

The attributes are not an external exposure, a catheter through which substance injects reality into our lives from a secluded region where it lay soundless. Hence, it is not the physical representation, through a second kind of symbolization of substance; rather, the attributes signify the absolute unity of intellect and substance. There is nothing outside the intellect except substances. The intellect is the capacity to understand and position our own substance, not within a marked temporal or spatial relation, but as eternity. We thus see the necessary eternity of all things in nature. This is why Negri understands that it is through the attributes that the infinite propagates itself (Negri 2003, 41).

AGAINST NEGRI, THE SPINOZIAN

Up to this point, we have revealed the reasons why Spinoza's point of departure from modern philosophy fits into a long tradition of rebelliousness to a metaphysics of presence that includes Marx, Nietzsche, Deleuze, Derrida, and Negri. Nevertheless, our main interest is Negri's interpretation of Spinoza, not only because there is an ample constellation of intellectual and political praxis around it, but also because of the predominance that it has acquired as a paradigmatic account of the complexities of ethics and power stemming from the division of potestas and potentia. In Negri, we find not only piercing intellectual refinement, but also the prominent handbook of power and liberation of our times.

There is a panoply of heavy criticism on the work of Negri stemming from the likes of Mouffe, Rasch, Laclau, Meiksins-Wood, and Žižek which usually reads that his theories shy away from conflict and thus miss the point of political articulation. While I agree in the main with his critics and bear their partial influence, my aim is to demonstrate that they are still superficial in the sense that they do not fully give an account of the conditions of possibility of his theoretical armour, which I believe is connected directly with his interpretation of Spinoza.

The core of Negri's interpretation of Spinoza is an unbending quest to preserve the immanence of power at all costs. Immanence construed in a stark opposition with transcendence means liberation and an equally distributed power among all singularities. It means that metaphysics is not the perseverance of an occult divine source but a construction of the world as common ethical ground. Hence, the imagination of a multiplicity means that thought is the foundation of ethics. Immanence as the factory of being means that subjectivity is not subjugated in her becoming to any externality other than its natural power to persevere and positively affect others. Immanence means that the expansion of power within the social body is infinite and only finds its point of integration as a refusal to coincide with any mediating or foundational status or diagram of power.

The multitude, which is Negri's bet for the axiomatic subject of ethics, is the ever-intensifying force that overthrows the maleficent need for sovereignty and state. The multitude stands for the positivity of being while the *people* stand as its hideous negativity, the denial of being and of political ontology. The multitude is, then, the radical immanence of potentia, the constitutive and unyielding process of the creation of the political through the carnival of love that washes away law and its pretension of hierarchies and classifications of subjects. Meanwhile, *the people* are the cunning of potestas, the poison at the heart of political ontology. In conclusion, for Negri, mediation, sovereignty, the state, and the people stand in a singular position to power as potentia; they are its absolute denial.

The case against these interpretations is quite simple but has far-reaching implications that descend to the very possibility of an ontology of democracy. What if we were instead to execute a simple inversion, one that is not capricious, but correlative to our decolonial enterprise, and, indeed, is at the heart of our decolonial manoeuvre. As we shall try to demonstrate, the true order of the world, the funnel of being, is not potentia but potestas. There is a monumental blind spot that impairs Negri's vision utterly: he cannot see coloniality as the true order of being, and where he is able to perceive its invasive spill into the world, he integrates it quickly into the majestic wall of civilization. As we have previously stated, in structuring the multitude as the subject of immanent potentia, what Negri feels is a phantom pain of the loss of civilization. Yet again, against the ferocious outbreak of power as domination, the immanentist carefully imagines the sanctuary, the absolute interior in an inverted architectural logic to power. But we know all too well that the beast of potestas can claw its way into any shelter no matter how deep the well is dug. As we will prove, his construction of *imagination* cannot absolve mediation, which becomes the paper cut in the eye of pure immanence.

SPINOZA THROUGH THE LENS OF COLONIALITY

As good brothers of Spinoza, the optician, we shall see the scratched world through the lens of coloniality, and the aberration this supposes upon reality will compose an absolute branching of the paths to be followed. We will polish this lens from the concavity of our labyrinthine *ghetto* and not from the panoptic of legal philosophy. Coloniality is not a metaphor of power, or a sore expanding in the smooth skin of civilization: it is *the* matrix of power and of being. Coloniality is not an accident among others, an element clutched in a gridlock of signification, but is the very definition of reality and the very possibility of meaning. If we were to take coloniality out of the equation of power, we would fall directly into the pit of a metaphysics of presence, of power irremediably tied to power as domination.

Negri's *positive ontological process* disregards true historical events and the pervasive geography of power that coloniality bears as its defining feature, and hence its balance and real compositions become a mere drop of water in an ocean of power. In fixing being as an ever-intensifying and unlimited potentia, he constructs its becoming as if there were no barriers, no oppositions, no forms of friction beyond simple opposing singularities. He proceeds as if, against the backdrop of a paradisiac ethical expansion of consciousness, there was no ongoing destruction of bodies and isolation of minds. This strain of positive ontology becomes a form of poetic hysteria, a denial of the plundering force of well-defined structures of power. What we are calling for is to take seriously the composition of power and to focus on a counter-potestas that stands as the nuclear force of the composition of reality. This composition is present and pervades the very real processes of capital under the wing of coloniality, where force and violence counteract and define this being not as the pure ecstasy of becoming, but as a subaltern subject (Guha 2000, 7): walled, wretched, inferior, a permanent error of being.

In order for the composition of potentia to work as the factory of subjectivity—as the immanent production of being—many suppositions must be made, and thus its operability must be surrounded by many *as ifs*. Potentia is the *infinity* of being—*as if* potestas had not already sanctioned it as a *totality*. Potentia is the generic right to the world of the multitude—*as if* potestas did not already order the world from the inside as division and subjugation. The catastrophic clash between potentia and potestas that horrifies Negri and makes him retreat into a pure potentia makes this very retreat a logical impossibility because the said potentia is already tainted and crossed by potestas. It can only find itself and its infinity through a confrontation which supposes a necessary point of actuality and decision, of transition and departure. As we will see, Negri builds on a concept of ethics that is deprived of politics and thus creates ontology in an absolute vacuum of power.

For Negri, the constitution of productive forces and relations of production occur inside the void, with no point of friction, because he fails to see that power as potestas has effectively ordered the world into a *certain something*. Although it is absolutely true that 'Productive force emanates from the infinity of being' (Negri 2003, 242), it is nonetheless also true that in order to concretize those immanent forces, there are two things that they must confront. The first is the spurious constitution of being through coloniality that builds the world and assigns being a precise location and function within a structure. The second is the means to actualize the infinity of being, which does not mean a simple return to the institutionalization of power but to supersede the power that has created the exclusion. The exaltation and joy of being, as Negri refers to the absolute potentia of a multitude, must first confront the barrier of potestas. Potentia and potestas are not in a relation of incommensurability but of contradiction; if it were not like this, potentia as a productive force of being could only extend upon its own void.

If a constitutive ontology of a free subject is to be deemed ontological, then the passage to politics is absolutely necessary. Spinoza's political theory is a theory of the ethical composition of subjectivity, *as if* the true composition of the legal order was not already carved out of potestas.

According to Negri, 'Antagonism becomes the key to greater ontological perfection and greater ethical freedom' (Negri 2003, 153). Henceforth, our main point of departure will be that although Negri recognizes conflict and struggle, and his philosophy is a philosophy of liberation, he fails to see in potestas the constitutive factory of the subjectivity of power. Antagonism, for Negri, is always between singularities; it is never posed as the opposition of agency against structure that is constitutive of truth and power. In his frantic escape from any point of mediation and of power in a solid state, Negri proceeds with a beautiful and penetrating style to sort out the imbalance of power and potentia, but in doing so he will finally find a wall of mediation which he must leap over with grace. The wall remains, and the leap thus becomes the mediator he was trying desperately to banish.

Since antagonism occurs, for him, only in a plane of singularities (measured in fairly meaningless asymmetries of quantum of power), and not between defined and subaltern subjects of difference facing enormous machines of potestas, the immediate effect of the leap is that he awards potentia a sort of magical mechanical property. According to Negri, potentia as positivity of being is in an ever-expanding mode. Hence, when it comes up against the obstacle of potestas (which is also a singularity), *cupiditas*—as the expression of potentia—converts potestas, immediately and with no obstruction, to potentia. The weightless plane of potentia by itself supposes that there are forces on a collision course: on the one side, potentia as the fundamental expression of absolute substance, on the other, potestas as the denial of absolute substance. When the elements collide, the result is settled in favour of the former as it will simply transfigure the sad passions of potestas into the joy of the synthesis of the absolute (as if potestas were a discrete and malleable chemical reactor which just needs to be in a simple interaction in order to transform itself). Conatus is transformed to cupiditas, an omnipotent act of love, *as if* the encounter between singularities was done among equal quanta of power in a timeless space, and on an equivalent footing granted by natural equality. All the aforementioned *as if* potestas were a piece of supple clay and possessed a mere natural disposition to be transformed.

Negri's thesis resembles a domino effect. Potentia being the first piece to fall sets off a chain reaction that turns potestas into potentia, as if they were pieces of the same assembly, as if all there was was pure expansion without any transitions or points of resistance. Put another way, for Negri potentia is a stone thrown from above a body of water which ripples, creating circular waves that come to conquer the whole body of water. What he does not realize is that the water, the falling motion, and the stone are all already a fabrication of potestas. In this same line of inquiry, we will find that the multitude, as the product of imagination, can describe the process of taking consciousness of a determinate political situation of oppression and submission; but this, however, would be a *political act without politics* because it fails to recognize itself in potestas.

For Negri, the absolute affirmative power of cupiditas does not recognize that the real point of antagonism is a structure of *people as totality*, which is an already stratified form of power in a solid state which creates the hidden people as its excrement and condition of existence. The multitude would then not be the protagonist of the transformation of politics but its passive product. The hidden people, on the other hand, are both the creation and the definition of difference, precisely because the concept, as political action, crosses the lines of antagonism. Consequently, the hidden people are the overpowering of people as totality by people as infinity.

Negri fails to see 'the blessed history against the damned' as he calls it (Negri 2003, 7). And when he does see the damned, which is not often, he is thinking of those who are immersed in a relationship of capitalist production that creates an evenness of the relation through a transparent opposition of forces. On the one side is the capitalist who extracts surplus from labour, on the other is the worker who enslaves his labour power so that it can be extracted smoothly. The spirit of *operarismo* is deployed without missing a beat in Negri. Potentia would then be the sea breaking the levy, the worker taking the helm of capitalist production in a single and swift act. He does not see the initial excision of the colonized that holds the appearance of the building together. There is a previous and more definite division, one that not only extracts the surplus of labour but also legitimizes it in a legal body of exclusion of necessary partitions of race, nationality, religious beliefs, and gender, which we, of course, call coloniality.

My thesis may be found indefensible if it is taken to be a simple transposition of a line from potentia to actuality, as if it were simply moving the stakes of ontology from contingency to necessity or renaming potentia as actuality. But this is not the case. We are making one simple but fundamental observation and tracing its consequences. Potentia in itself, as the motor of the possible, does not possess enough political charge—either to explain power in the world that is stabilized as a dividing wall, or to overcome power that is solidly fixed as the building columns of law and subjectivity. We are confronting a whole different kind of animal. Power in a solid state is the brute fact, not one that can be measured by a knowledge that springs out spontaneously from modes and attributes interacting in a state of things that are free from the tendency to solidify power. *As if* potency created a meta-language beyond potestas; *as if* that or any kind of measurement was exempt from the ideology that furbished the interplay of singularities. Our main wager is that politics can only exist first in antagonism. And *only if* we perforate the wall of potestas may we construe power as an actuality, immune to any qualification and any telos that serves as an accounting method of exclusion and the principle of invisibility.

Two reasons guide our affirmation. First, the formidable power of potestas as a defined architecture of the world already constitutes the field of language and values and thus the production of subjectivity is captured rigidly in the walls of this simulacrum, where to know or to assign meaning is already mediated by encryption. Second, only actuality, as a logical opposition to the actuality of potestas, can offer a point of transition and dissemination that stems from the full recognition of the antagonism that defines the topography of power. Otherwise, there would be room neither for the sacrifice of the father as the inceptor of the law and the origin of the community nor for the preparation of the surprise of revolution. We would all be located in a smooth surface where the true anomaly—the other, the woman, the rogue, the indigenous—is suppressed as normality. Potentia within the Gargantuan bulwarks of potestas loses all its texture, all its breadth, and draws back to being Agamben's empty wax tablet, a surface and nothing but a surface, decomposing in space and time. As stated by Oscar Guardiola-Rivera:

> In every place where human activity is interrupted, where there is a blind spot, a crevasse in our carefully reasoned intellectual grids and mental maps, archaic objects and inhuman things crouch huddled threatening to throw into disarray the entire order of things. Spinoza saw the black rebel standing in the entrance to one of such interstices, and it horrified him. (Guardiola-Rivera 2009, 168)

Power in a solid state is composed of the necessity of law and state sanctioning the contingency of a market that is always in the process of reinventing itself. Hence, affections and modes never remain the same: they are always dislodged from themselves and they traverse the dimensions of potentia and potestas with the same intensity. Hence, pretending to leap over potestas means taking power for granted, which is the full-blown naturalization of coloniality.

Potestas is the hegemonic and self-referential act within language. The fact of power in coloniality is that potestas is the order of representation. If so, this means that subjectivity is always determined to act in a certain preordained manner, where the link between subjectivity and potentia is severed as the condition for the existence of potestas as language and command. Nevertheless, there is always a gap between the impossible command and the wholeness to which it refers. The excrement, the lack, the incompleteness does not wither but is transferred and substituted in a complex lacing of objects where the totality of the world is withdrawn and is created at one and the same instant as simulacrum. Any potential of any subject is determined by this interplay of commands and desire, of totality and the gap. Reality becomes a derivative, where all the partialities and traces of the operation build the conduits to complete reality. We are speaking of the twilight zone of art and revolution, of subversive writing and resistant bodies. Subjectivity is always crossing the lines of potentia and potestas, tainting, bristling, and disrupting the conditions of language; it is never at the same time one or another. Beside—or, rather, between—the sheer destruction of the dimension of representation or holding it together through partial objectifications lays a third option: the sublimation of power. It is only in this deranged niche of possibilities of language that an alternative to pure potestas can be construed. In other words, only inside the entrails of the beast of sovereignty and state can we break free from it. The specific wager here is that in its intent of total-izing symbolization, potestas inevitably leaves a gap, a hole, which we will discover is all that is needed as a starting point to overcome it utterly: the very point of the articulation of the political.

Through this new stance we can describe our critical engagement with Negri's Spinoza in the following summary which we will then develop thoroughly:

1. Actuality as Energeia offers a theory of transitions that is equipped to confront the imprint of coloniality as the order of the world. Sovereignty, state, and the legal conception of the people thereby fashion a stringent facticity that simply cannot be wished away; any form of liberation must confront them in order to overcome them.
2. The dyad of potestas and potentia is not an opposition of singularities but of agencies of difference and gigantic structures of unity. The colonial matrix of power is the order of the condition of politics; the world, as it is, is built over potestas.
3. The concept of the hidden people does not only offer a strategic advantage over the multitude: it offers the ontological truth of democracy and poli-tics. Rather than shying away from conflict, it takes it to its ultimate limits in order to overcome the totality as the blockage of power.
4. The hidden people are the actual being of difference and thus the agent of change; the multitude is an insubstantial chimera that lacks any power to face the monumental grids of potestas. Democracy, then, is not an appen-dix of time and history but the true legal dimension of difference, and thus it is the only order of possibility of politics. The eternal clash between unity and identity on the one side and difference and commonality on the other is incarnated in the current clash between capital and democracy. Only the hidden people as the actual agent of difference can dethrone capitalism as the order of its negation.
5. Sovereignty and the state of exception are the supreme paradox of power. There is no path of liberation that can go around or behind it. All their repulsive connections of transcendence and violence, of rule and excep-tion, can only be defeated by looking the beast dead in the eyes. Far from being the congealment of potentia within the prison of the state that we are

forced to walk away from, they offer a unique political opportunity for a burst of difference from the inside.
6. The hidden people have ingrained in their genetic code the blueprints to decrypt the ideal machine of potestas that encrypts knowledge and supersedes labour as the defining feature of capitalism.

IMAGINATION AND POWER

Our first line of inquiry will be to determine the consistency that the role of imagination has as the constitutive force that unites God's (and nature's) substance to the singularities in Negri's interpretation. Or, in other words, we shall here inquire into how the absolute may remain absolute in its passage through the intellect, knowing that such passage is the very condition of immanence.

Let us begin with Spinoza's definition: 'The affections of the human body whose ideas present external bodies as present in us, we shall call images of things. . . . And when the mind regards bodies in this way, we shall say that it imagines' (Spinoza. *Ethics*. II, p 5). For Negri, 'Imagination is the channel through which beings associate as a new being' (Negri 2003, 35), where everything is *surface*. In the same act that the imagination captures the essence of substance, it creates the conditions for a *multitude* to arise as the subject of ethics, the vessel and ground of a collective being. As we have already seen, God (or nature) as substance consists of infinite attributes, each of which expresses eternal and infinite essence. For Negri, imagination is the point of capture of God's power (potentia) by which she and all things are and act; it is her essence as such. 'The attribute is the same thing as substance, and yet its difference is stated in relation to the intellect' (Negri 2003, 57). It is at this point that imagination joins conatus with consciousness and explodes in all directions to constitute the world. The intellect pertains to *natura naturata* not to *natura naturans*—that is, in capturing substance, imagination is not yet a creative apparatus.

Negri's answer is that the attribute appertains to substance and possesses an ontological identity with it. Substance as an infinity of attributes means that there is no formal reciprocity between them, no differentiation of quanta of power between the creature's attributes and those of God. The attribute is thus not an opening in or of the substance but simply a means of participation in the versatility of the total being. Attributes do not organize the expansion of being but only reveal it. Attributes, as functions of the mediation of the spontaneity of being between substance and mode, have been reabsorbed on a horizontal field of surfaces (Negri 2003, 47). They no longer represent agents of organization reduced to a linear horizon where only singularities emerge; they simply pose themselves in an immediate relationship of the production of substance. In short, the attributes simply put power in relation without ordering it. Negri is again at pains to demonstrate that the attributes are not normative, that they do not impose an *ought to be*, a revelation of the substance in the finite intellect.

Let us describe in detail Negri's interpretation. The unification of the attributes creates a dimension of the world that is not hierarchical but flat, equally versatile and equivalent. The idea of power, as univocal power, and as the dissolution of the very idea of mediation and abstraction, leaps to centre stage. Negri solves the conundrum of potentia and potestas in favour of the former within an ethical and not metaphysical plane. He breaks free the logics of subordination in the process of production of politics. As he draws an equivalency between Spinoza's account of the potentia of the absolute (God) and the potency of the multitude; they become one and the same thing in an infinite plane of immanence. The power to be and to act become absolute. The variance that can be brought into the modes and attributes of being and power would only grant us a degree of differentiation in our coming to know them, but this is an external action of knowledge that does not affect the wholeness of the ontological edifice. Natural right, then, is freed from any transcendental or physical constraint to become the expression of potentia as the construction of liberty. What is thus achieved is the exclusion of any mediator, any third term that would govern the relation from a transcendental space. There is no transfer of right or power from singularities to the unity of the sovereign but instead an infinite production of power with no limits beside its own immanent exercise. Hence, power is not subordinated to a particular sovereign but is the multiplication *ad infinitum* of the power of the multitude which becomes a fertile and inexhaustible womb for the creation of being. The upshot for Negri is that Spinoza's political thinking 'traverses natural law to deny its two fundamental principles: the individual and contractual principle' (Negri 2000, 52).

The *conatus*, when it is determined to do this or that, is so determined by an affection *(affectio)* that occurs to it (Deleuze 1988a, 60). These affections that determine the *conatus* are a cause of consciousness: the *conatus*, having become conscious of itself under this or that affect, is called desire, and desire always means a desire for something (Spinoza. *Ethics*. III). There is, then, a profound linking of the chain between cupiditas, conatus, and imagination which functions as the constitutive principle of human praxis. Such linkage commits to the limit of immanence and accumulates power—that is, it is always a constitution. The constitutive praxis becomes the extent of our relationship with existence (Negri 2003, 180). As Negri writes, 'Politics is the metaphysics of the imagination, the metaphysics of the human constitution of reality, the world' (Negri 2003, 97). Even more revealingly, 'The process of civilization', he writes, 'is an accumulation of productive capacity. It is the destruction of the necessity that is not liberated, and therefore the destruction of contingency and therefore the destruction of non-being' (Negri 2003, 143).

The phantom pain of civilization is presented as double-fold. There is a natural deployment of the potentia of the multitude, pure positivity of being that extends from its own bosom, an avalanche of power as potentia that is meant to master the world. Nevertheless, there seems to be an anomaly in its path, something archaic that contradicts this civilization of pure positivity of being: potestas as negativity. Consequently, non-being is presented by Negri as the negation of civilization. In so doing, he has presented potestas as an anomaly, and equated the invisible and subaltern subject with power as domination. Here his beautifully crafted ethics of liberation drowns in its own pool of impotence because of a failure to see the productive aspect of potestas. Negri thus duplicates the gesture of coloniality: he unites potestas with negativity and, in doing so, immobilizes the main product of potestas, the hidden people. The hidden people are paralysed in negativity. These are the nuts and bolts of power as domination: the hidden people re-emerge, as W.E.B. Du Bois and Lewis Gordon remind us, as problem people. Whether from the vantage of the colonial machine or from the vantage of Negri's valourization of the multitude, the colonized appear as mere negativity that must be overcome.

But the problem is both deeper and subtler. According to Negri, the passage from the attributes to substance demands the presence of intellect, a 'moment of logical emanation' (Negri 2003, 57). But doesn't this suggest that he is admitting the need of a mediator and of *eminence*? Negri tries to present it as a necessary slippage, a tiny drop of oil leaking from the grand machine of immanence. But that slippage is the necessary passage of mediation, the articulation point between organization and spontaneity. Without it, the absolute would remain silent, incomprehensible, locked in its own mute and drab truth. It would thus be the transcendental, the *arché* that lurks in darkness, that determines being through its telekinetic power. For substance to remain immanent it requires this drop of oil, the tiny hole in its belly where the intellect may peek inside to gain insight into the mystery of the absolute.

The attribute, then, begets the problem of revelation, of hypostasis. Following Negri, 'In the objectivist interpretation the attribute acts as the agent of the absolute, but only in the centrifugal direction' (Negri 2003, 44). But then again, we have absolutely no way of knowing (other than to have a mediator not determined by the relation) if from the creation of this majestic potentia a centrifugal force follows, one that would spill out of itself and affect the world as a whole. What determines that we are not inside a self-fulfilling prophecy (Merton 1948)? What if this force is also centripetal? What if the fact of the creation of power was on the side of potestas and not potentia, or in the plane of politics and not in a self-preserved and automated plane of ethics? It would mean the following chain of contradictions. First, assume the utter lack of mediation: there is nothing to mediate between, since substance is one and the same immanent being. But second, given the unity of substance and being, the intellect would not be needed to conceive the absolute. What follows is determinism in its purest sense. If the intellect exists, it means a mediation between two things. But if there is such mediation between two things, this has to mean that the absolute is not an absolute, for it provokes a movement to come forth from itself. The passage implies two kinds of beings, and neither could be absolute. We have thus two logical possibilities:

1. Movement from x (absolute) to y (consciousness) equals one and the same, so the mediation of the intellect is irrelevant to grasp and partake of the absolute. This would amount to absolute determinism. The human intellect plugged entirely into God's attributes, where intellect is just another way of saying that it is fully determined to act according to a superior form of thought (superior because from its configuration it does not have a capacity to act in any other way than the one programmed by substance).
2. Movement from x (absolute) to y (consciousness) equals a mediation. The absolute, through mediation, becomes something different to itself: it is interpreted and destabilized from its slot by an action other that itself, and hence it would not be absolute anymore, which by its own presence would violate the plane of immanence. The absolute thus either becomes an emanative principle or it makes room for an ulterior form of interaction, a necessary intervention by something else that it cannot hold within its essence.

The problem gains an unsuspected acuteness when we invert the order of production of power. In an ethical plane that meets no point of friction and no contraries, potentia would effectively be an unstoppable strength that transforms all proceedings of reality. But if potentia is confronted with a major contradiction—one that not only stands in a symmetrical opposition to it, but is itself the uterus for the production of subjectivity and the determinant point of the use of language—we find ourselves dealing with the incapacity of potentia to create an articulate version of power, if any version at all.

Negri's interpretation puts us head first before two very difficult connections.

First, his construction of an intellect that is an expression of the absolute is an ethical plenitude that does not recognize politics. It is ethics in its own vacuum, a precious construction that pretends to build its own planet of ever-lasting love outside the orbit of politics as antagonism. This version denies that the root of what we call the social is political, containing a major and irreparable consequence: it oversteps the fact that language has been blocked and encrypted from the beginning of the social bond. Furthermore, encryption is the very condition of the social bond, so what the intellect finds is always corrupted by potestas and its violent forms of distributing power. The eye of the beholder is already encrypted and casts the shadow of a foreign aesthesis. Intellect is already enmeshed in a language that is not its own, and this presents us with a reality where intellect is always an expression of a grammar of power as domination where every utterance of meaning presupposes an encrypted structure. Hence, once politics shows its fangs—represented as a full-throttle potestas, that is, the actuality of the architecture of power— Negri's ethics shrug, unable to bring forth any possibility of organizing a political transition. If potestas is not a mere opposition to potentia, but the very place where language is organized and hierarchized, where strata are fabricated and subjectivities are granted or denied, then potentia on its own (as the passage from the absolute to singularities) becomes a docile expression of power annexed completely to potestas. Potentia ultimately becomes the expression (as simulacrum) of potestas. Negri sees the negative product of power as potestas (non-being), but fails to see the *producer* of that negativity (the structure), as well as the fact that this negativity is created as an excrement (the hidden people) of power in a solid state. Even more crucially, he misses that the world is a *certain this* (oppressed, ruled, hidden) and not a *certain that* (an extension of virtue to the intensity of being).

Second—and here we can even afford to do away with a political argument and simply focus on the ontological argument—any passage from substance to intellect necessarily implies a mediation, a construction that is beyond substance; otherwise, pure determinism would take the place of pure immanence. If the power to create is in the imagination, then this power disrupts and collapses the totality which is the base of substance and existence. Therefore, collapsing the presuppositions of imagination would thus vanquish its very possibility. If this is true, then why even presuppose the absolute? Because it is the plane of immanence: not supposing the absolute would mean that potentia falls apart and is transformed into potestas. Therefore, the power of the imagination to create would erase its very possibility of being immanent. That the imagination can divide means that it can separate itself from substance and therefore from immanence. Finally, if we connect both arguments, the result is a catastrophic legitimation of power as potestas, the naturalization of a world of domination and exclusion. The zone of demarcation is then that substance, through this operation, becomes a model.

Negri's operation reminds me of Garcia-Marquez's *Chronicle of a Death Foretold*. A mother (Plácida Linero) looks out from a long corridor through the open door of her house and sees two men, knives in hands, running in the street towards her house. She knows they are doing so in order to murder her son, Santiago Nasar. She believes her son is inside the house, but what she does not see, due to a blind spot produced by the angle she is standing in, is that her son is also in the street rushing to the door to evade his attackers. The mother dashes to save her son, and at the minute her son is about to make a safe entrance she shuts the huge door closed, leaving him outside to be stabbed to death by the Vicario brothers. Negri locks the door of ethics to politics and shutters any possibility of the articulation of conflict. This is his blind spot, the angle that impairs his view of coloniality. Rejecting negativity, he forsakes the fact that the hidden people are created and hidden precisely in negativity. The worst part of this is that he serves up the political subject on a silver platter for potestas to carve up and devour.

The operation between substance and intellect always supposes a composition. In the combination of arguments, we can behold how substance becomes an exteriority, a model; hence, it is not presented as an infinite order accessible to a pure intellect. To gain access to substance, something other than its essence must be imagined: something that complements it and that makes possible understanding, judgement, or praxis. Hence, to see substance in its bare nakedness is impossible—indeed, the best disguise for reality is nakedness. In that order of ideas, to see is to compose; seeing is not a simple function but a gathering, an organization mediated by language. If, then, substance becomes a model, the role of singularities is either demoted to the status of a mere copy of the model, or it is potentiated to create a zone of reality that stands against the model; that, my friends, is politics. Our wager is, of course, to exploit the infinitesimal opening that a structure allows when trying to shut itself upon its own configuration, and, through it, to pull out the arsenal of politics.

Negri's ethical immanence transforms substance into a model, because when he holds that there can be no mediation, the lack of mediation truly applies to the relation between intellect and potestas. When he tries to revere absolute substance, he misses the basic point that potestas stands in its place as the modern Proteus, defeating the eye at its own game. Following Deleuze, in order to understand the relation of substance as ground and the singularity that claims to pertain to such ground, we may distinguish between the *ground* (or ideal essence) and the *grounded*. The grounded always takes the form of claimant or claim to said ground, and that upon which the claim bears. In other words, if substance becomes a model, it means that the grounded possesses an identity which is primary and the claimant will possess secondarily, assuming that its claim is well grounded (Deleuze 2004, 341–42). The operation of grounding renders the claimant similar to the ground, endowing it with resemblance from within and thereby allowing it to participate in the quality or object which it claims. Within this game of mirrors and copies, resemblance is always hierarchical: it is always said first of the model and then of the singularity as a consequence. As stated by Deleuze, 'Each well-grounded

image or claim is called representation (icone), the first in the order of claimants is second in itself in relation to the foundation; the rebellious images
which lack resemblance (simulacra) are eliminated, rejected as false claimants' (Deleuze 2004, 342). In denying a central aspect of potestas—its serving as the factory of language and subjectivity—we are thrown back to the
world of representation and mediation. Conversely, dislodging potestas and
potentia and granting each their space in the universe of power amounts to a
prohibition on thinking of an immaculate origin of words, where they were
clean from the human blemish of politics and an untainted gift of the Gods.
Awarding potestas its proper dimension forces us to think of the function of
words in the history of the composition of power—history as resistance, in
transplants and rhizomes, in intersections and divergences; history as that
which has maintained a common structure of gathering, of bringing together
against the monumental blockage of power as simulacra.

Finally, we see that imagination has to interact. It has to make a stake in
the world through language that is other than a mere repetition of what now
is recognized as the representation of a model. To bring forth is never a pain-
less act: it is not an act of appearance from darkness to light; it is a motion,
an unscrambling that cannot be captured in one single stroke, for this stroke
would be a sense of the flow. Hence, the perspective is always distorted,
never in line with the motion, always too late or too early; it is an anticipation
of motion, a rendering of the body as a space that can only see the afterglow
of movement. It always implies a transition, a modality between the subject
(at pains to make truth) and the coming forth. The space is a fold in between
that can only have sense precisely in that *in-between*. Thus, if imagination is
reduced to an effort to conform to an external substance, it becomes as fruitless as trying to identify what salt is in a desert of salt. To *make sense of*, as
an epistemological endeavour, must become the political act of becoming
other than itself through the recognition of the stuffed dimensions of power as
potestas. Meaning is not an aggregate of existing language or the completion
of the command, but is rather the coming to terms with the physical conditions of potestas.

We understand that Negri sees potestas and a world shredded by violence
or negative passions. Our point is that his framing falls short of the true statute of potestas. Potestas is not merely a fact among others surmountable by
the mere interaction with potentia: potestas is the fact of the world, it is the
given of power. If we accept the disconnection of the two strains of subjectivity—on the one side, the political subject as a simulacrum of hegemony
furnished in consensus and dispositifs of biopower, and on the other, a subject
of immanence as absolute substance—the ethical and the political will never
cross paths. And, therefore, power as potestas will remain unfettered. As we
have stated emphatically, maybe even repetitively, Negri does recognize the

dimension of conflict and of submission. The problem is that in order to safe-guard immanence as the *holy grail* of civilization, he evicts potestas as the defining structure of power and of subjectivity from the equation. The result is that he inevitably falls into a profound contradiction. As Spinoza recognizes, 'There is no singular thing in nature than which there is not another more powerful and stronger. Whatever one is given, there is another more powerful by which the first can be destroyed' (Spinoza. *Ethics*. IV, ax). And, further, 'This axiom concerns singular things insofar as they are considered in relation to a certain time and place' (Spinoza. *Ethics*. V, 37, sc.). Negri is only thinking of the relation of potestas and potentia in a plane of singularities, *as if* the relation were *vis-à-vis*. But what happens when potestas accumulates all powers—the power to express, to affect, to define modes? We are not talking about a Cartesian *Deus deceptor* that would have taken the place of a true God, but the fact that we are sons of a lesser God, that we are in fact the offspring of potestas, that potestas overlaps and overshadows every instance of reality. Hence, the only way to upset and overturn *power in a solid state* is to conceive the political as something deeply imbedded in its roots and forms of distribution.

IMAGINATION AS THE NEGATION OF DIFFERENCE: THE POWER OF THE HIDDEN PEOPLE IN RESISTANCE

Though our inquiry thus far has posed many problems for Negri, we must now return to a central, underlying problematic—namely, that he is neglect-ing the existence of the hidden people. Equating absolute substance with potentia disregards the primordial role of potestas, and equating the hidden people with negativity amounts ultimately to a dismissal of politics itself. In sacking potestas, Negri forsakes the fact that the hidden people are the stub-born truth of politics that refuses being reduced to some epiphenomenon of potestas. The hidden people are the permanent act of resistance against unity and identity, and thus are the basic fabric of ontology. The hidden people are not a multitude *to come* in some remote and messianic future; they are (already) the concrete struggle in the flesh against potestas. Insofar as this is the case, resistance defines the truth of the world of politics. It draws its actual dimensions from a permanent confrontation between difference and unity.

Democracy is not incarcerated in a perpetual postponement of the divine moment. Democracy is not the Promised Land that twinkles beyond the desert of a captive and remote reality. Democracy is the consistent reality of everything in the world that opposes domination. Democracy is actuality in constant motion; democracy is the resistance of the difference to the brute force of the rule of unity and identity. In short, democracy has always been present sternly in resistance, an unpostponable *today and now* that designates its own destiny. Resistance—far from being a historically fragmented and sporadic event—is the permanent exercise of difference, the vital contraposition of *being in common* to every simulacrum that imposes itself as the domination of unity and identity. In his drive to preserve potentia inside the vault of immanence, Negri expels resistance from politics and politics from power.

Democracy is an idea, but as idea it manifests as a quotidian practice of resistance that is present in every exercise of opposition to the homogenizing violence of liberal capitalism. The *we* of the hidden people is the resistance of difference, and, therefore, as a phenomenon of being in common, it already possesses an autonomous legal structure, as well as an intimate history from which it extends. When the relation of potentia is calibrated with potestas as the breeding ground of power, we begin to understand that the hidden people carries with it the implicit power to name itself, but also the power to delineate its legality as the general boundary of language. But even beyond the explicit—beyond being a particular legality in resistance—democracy is also the means of transformation (emancipation), and to that extent is the method that announces the democracy to come, which is none other than *being all a singular plural*, becoming the totality that alienates the gap (people as totality/hidden people) that created the exclusion in the first place. This is precisely what is thrown overboard by Negri's construction of the negativity of substance.

In Negri's composition, forsaken potestas rises again as a stringent form of morality undetected by politics, and thus action becomes mere obedience. This is what Nietzsche denounces: 'Morality is preceded by compulsion, indeed it is for a time itself still compulsion, to which one accommodates oneself for the avoidance of what one regards as unpleasurable. Later it becomes custom, later still voluntary obedience, finally almost instinct: then, like all that has for a long time been habitual and natural, it is associated with pleasure—and is now called virtue' (1996, 53). If we do not understand democracy as the power of the people to resist, in this gesture we are forcing the people's dependence on a transcendent model that becomes invisible through the construction of immanence outside of potestas. In doing so, we come to a profound contradiction of democracy: potestas, in the form of law, would have to authorize resistance. The latter would impose the absurd need for a validation, through law, of the requisites to exercise the power of the people. If resistance requires a transcendent authorization, it ceases to be resistance and simply becomes obedience. Obedience, as Douzinas clearly tells us, is the cause and effect of the sovereign (Douzinas 2013, 110).

The act of resistance is, in and of itself, the act of the community, and its strength and essence is to universalize the community that has been simulated and denied by liberalism. At the same time, resistance seeks to restore the hidden people as the missing species of the community, as its universality. At this point, the gap that separates the community with its true meaning is curtailed.

The traumatic encounter between the false totality and the excluded (who are the missing part of the totality) becomes the intimate mechanics of resistance and is the name of *being in common* that opposes the simulacrum of the eclipse of all possible origins. This is the vanishing point where the difference between inside and outside disappears, and the people as the constituent of politics acquires its shape. The people—as the unnamable, as the constitutive exclusion of the impossible totality—are the foundation of the emergence of a new truth that emerges from what is essentially absent.

POTESTAS AS THE TRUE ARCHITECTURE OF POWER

Negri's obsessive focus on potentia denies potestas and the whole possibility of politics along with it. Negri is distinctly a member of the European intelligentsia, and serves as an example that they are not looking for a theory after the crisis of Marxism; rather, they are looking for a benevolent father. They convert philosophy into jurisprudence. It is a search for a man-begotten father, as they fall into the trap of the need for totems. While capitalism is a fatherless flux, a rebel against its own cause, the left seeks to reconcile itself in the bosom of a protective Moloch. As Lambert puts it in interpreting Deleuze, 'After everything is said and done we find that the classical philosopher is after all nothing but a narrator of legal fictions *(les romans policiers)* whose only problem was phrasing a proposition in such a way that it provided an adequate discernment of the principles that would rule the final disposition of each case' (Lambert 2002, 19). Negri is more worried with the reconstruction of a narrative and the process by which it has to be ordained as such and hence confuses politics with jurisprudence and diminishes ethics to a queer form of theodicy.

In our case, potestas determines the capacity of being affected from above, which supposes a deep change in strategies, of connections and refusals. We need to account for a scheme: the incessant tendency of power to oppose identity and unity, a power that bestows a radical alteration in the plane of the encounter. What we are trying to put forth is that we are not only before a case of a Heideggerian *thrownness* but rather the inevitable existence of power in a solid state as facticity which cannot be eluded.

Sovereignty, the state, the law, and the market are all concrete scenarios of this facticity. They are all jam-packed with their own logics of power and production of subjectivity. A different strategy than that of unleashing the ethical is needed to cut across and oppose power as potestas. Potestas, left to be mere appendix of potentia, would be understood as a bad inclination, an error in the function of capturing the modes of substance, an aberration that has to do only with a bizarre and anomalous form of understanding. Nevertheless, potestas is not a mere opposition to potentia (its negative side, as it were) but the constitutive space of the possibility of language and subjectivity, which not only opposes potentia, but, to a great degree, defines its limits and possibilities.

The facticity of the colonial matrix and the hegemony of severe forms of power are the minimal organization of representation. They determine concrete forms of perception, not as a necessary and unbreakable truth, but as the describable, as the conditions of what can be said and under which circumstances, and in so doing they determine the conditions of language. The facticity of power is not a fact among others: it is the order of the world and the limits of how we know it. We are not only holding that Negri eludes power as potestas as an element that is necessarily a part of certain reality, but that potestas is the constitutive power of grounding reality. Politics does not come from blankness but from very precise allocations of power through power. As the limit of objectivity, the fact that there is a world becomes the limit of the possible only when we can fathom the limits of such objectivity through objectivity itself. What facticity holds together is not only material forms of power and its exercise but also the impossibility of the totality, the unfeasibility of a system to shutter upon its own congested confines. It means that the facticity of power always leaves open the fantasy of being: it is the gap of negativity and the incompleteness of being. On the other hand, Negri's refusal to acknowledge diehard facticity would have to suppose the need for building ethics as an automated scheme away from politics and its foundational conflict—in short, an act of escapism from reality. To borrow from another discussion that intersects with ours, Quentin Meillasoux contends that pretending to ignore facticity

> is self-refuting, because it assumes an absoluteness of facticity in the *act* of thinking while simultaneously denying it in the content of this same thought. Accordingly, facticity cannot be thought of as another fact in the world—it is not a fact that things are factual, just as it is not a fact that factual things exist. I cannot think facticity *merely* as the possibility that existing things could not exist, *or* that non-existing things could exist—the persistence of the two realms of existence and non-existence provides the very condition for the conceivability of facticity. (Meillasoux 2008, 121)

Potentia is, indeed, in this case, dreaming the impossible as the dream itself. Substance and language as the arch-fossil become the '*stuff that dreams are made of*'. To substantiate the dream of substance, waking up in the middle of potentia is waking up to the void, a freefall of language. Hence, where would the language of this absolute potentia come from? How can reality be sustained without it, and with what means beyond its elaborate shutdown? Is there a point of transition? To dream the dream of potentia is to dream of a meta-language free of all toxicity of potestas. But how can power be uttered in a non-language? Potentia, in order to be more than a mere concatenation of singularities, would have to understand ethics as a type of arch-fossil, to use Meillasoux's term: an ancestral reality that precedes language and its mere possibility of being enunciated, a givenness of being anterior to beingness (Meillasoux 2008, 25). It would suppose the possibility of language before the need to communicate, even before the need to fight for its meaning. After the ontological thinning performed by Negri, we do have *the world*, yes; but with no mediation, it would be just the repetition of a pre-ontological obviousness ('*the world is the world*') *where* nothing is added or subtracted from potestas and thus essence as power to exist would be a mute and senseless statement, indistinguishable when uttered in serfdom.

Potestas is far beyond being a simple negation of potentia: it is the structuring of the fantasy of being. It is the closing of identity and sameness, the referring to transcendental sources of power, the retreating and polarizing force of subjectivity, the dispositive of homology and fake consensual politics. Yes, potestas is the disgraceful frame of the world, but, nonetheless, it is *the* frame.

Potentia unleashed from the facticity of potestas becomes the Kantian noumenal. Causality as a plane of immanence operates only within potentia, so when confronted with a plane of transcendence of potestas it must lose its grip on immanent causality and absolute substance. The noumenal here is understood as 'a dimension that suspends the inclusion of man in the phenomenal network of natural causality' (Žižek 2001, 48). *Accordingly,* though as phenomenal entities we could not escape the causal connections that determine us, our freedom as moral subjects, according to Kant, arises in the noumenal dimension. There is no freedom whatsoever in the phenomenal world, whereas the noumenal is the realization of freedom. Following this line of reasoning, for Negri, potentia without the structure of potestas becomes an entirely noumenal entity which is phenomenologically impenetrable. Nonetheless (and here is the breaking point), that very same noumenal realm is the origin of any and every phenomenon; it is the excising point of logical derivation of cause and effect. Hence, it becomes a transcendent law that suspends the phenomena from the outside while erecting itself as the primary cause.

What we are shooting at is the fact that potestas can never become a fully sustained and automated structure of power. There is always a fissure that separates its own symbolization and the production of subjectivity, a leaking point that hinders any possibility of the structure closing in upon itself. As stated by Žižek, 'A thing can only accomplish its ontological statute through a minimal dilation with respect to itself' (Žižek 2001, 71).

The ontological completeness of reality implies the failure or impossibility of any kind of self-consciousness of the scheme or structure. There is only reality if there is a crevasse in the core of what stands for it, which allows the subject to lodge herself inside reality—that is, the mere presence of the subject does not allow reality to shutter upon itself. Here, the objective process is not immune to errors of understanding, but is its very product. Following Guardiola-Rivera, 'Reality is fundamentally open, and elements escape and withdraw from the fields and networks of relation where they become present' (Guardiola-Rivera 2009, 8). Rather than escaping potestas in a spree of Hamlet-like madness, potestas must be harnessed as the space where confrontation is possible; it must be understood as the architecture that delineates dissent and revolt.

In other words, potestas comes not before or after potentia: they are simultaneous and symbiotic. They are both placed in a conflictual yoke which cannot be set asunder by the mere strength of a weightless potentia that ignores its counterpart. Potestas builds itself in a clear contradistinction to potentia as its deterrent. Its inertia is to solidify power through the permanent hampering of potentia as it sucks the life out of its marrow. This is the locus of conflict, the extreme limit where it becomes fully visible. Hence, the point zero of power and being is not potentia on its own but, rather, the compound variations of its relation to potestas.

As we have shown, the hidden people as a permanent exercise of difference assumes potestas at its heart and thus becomes the only possibility for counteracting it. To build liberation within the fact of potestas means feeding from permanent struggle, reallocations of values, small victories and prolonged clashes over meanings which are never static and final. Language is the battle ground of meaning, superimposed in political and unstable structures and stratums that disrupt the continuity of meaning, where potentiality—far from being the negativity of potestas—is also a constitutive terrain. A beautiful exemplification of what we are trying to prove here appears in Levi Bryant's articulation of rogue objects, which

> are not chained to any given assemblage of objects, but instead wander in and out of assemblages, modifying relations within the assemblages into which they enter. Political protestors exemplify rogue objects by breaking with the norms and relations of a dominant political assemblage in order to forge new relations that challenge, change, or cast off the prior assemblage. (Bryant 2011b)

Our anchoring device is that the relation between potestas and potentia is never established in a point of equilibrium, where every fraction of reality is consumed by one or the other extreme; rather, it is a fluctuation of oppositions and (dis)encounters. What imagination meets in its hunt is not a pure object laid down with geometrical precision or a totality as a choir of angels expressing the truth of immanence. It is rather an always incomplete and shattered version of power. What imagination finds are rootless and worn-down subjectivities as well as precise methods for producing servitude and alliances of fear and consensus. It is here where politics finds its lustre, the boost to its possibility of processing the world through difference. Imagination is not a spontaneous synthesis that accesses God's substance and unifies multiplicity but is instead the pure power of dislocating and scorching reality. What imagination encounters is that it itself is a bastard offspring of potestas, and it is only after this encounter that it can become revolutionary.

FIRST DEFINITION OF THE MULTITUDE AGAINST THE PEOPLE: NEGRI'S NAÏVE ANTAGONISM

Although beautifully crafted, Negri's ethics cannot place conflict at the centre of politics. Conflict instead slides down to a sequence of a light or naïve antagonism that lacks the teeth to bite reality. It is the construction of a palace of love *for all* suspended in its own halo of ethical weightlessness. His construction of the multitude as the subject of ethics will not escape this path but will instead deepen it to a sinking point where we can show its incapacity to envisage politics through transitions and the effectiveness of power. Through the apparition of the multitude we will be able to contrast our concept of the *hidden people* as the only viable protagonist of a radical democracy and as the turning point of power as domination, that is, potestas. We will scrutinize the concept of the multitude from several directions. From its opposition to sovereignty, state, and a legal understanding of the people, we will learn that his refusal to tussle with such concepts leads to the grounding of ontology in the impossible existence of the subject of the multitude. Only when sovereignty (as state of exception) and the hidden people are fused in one can there be an ethics of the common beyond antagonism. We will also pursue another line of argumentation that sees Negri imposing on the multitude a series of necessary *prosthetics* in order to guard its full meaning that will be set asunder when we detect that the additions brought on by Negri are just that, inventive prosthetics that hold together the appearance of an articulate political subject that does not exist. This part of the book consists of four parts. First is a historical and political excavation of the multitude and its connection/opposition with sovereignty and the people. Second is the description and critique of what I call the prosthetics. In the third part, we will be *decrypting* the machine of the General

Intellect. Fourth and finally, we will return to sovereignty through the door of the state of exception.

It is useful to remember that the democracy we are seeking to unearth is democracy *not* as institutions, majorities, human rights, constitutions, and so forth, which are just secondary and aggregate properties that simulate the locus of politics. Such secondary properties can only have a resolution dependent on the first basic question of politics: *who may communicate*, taken in the strongest sense, which means that language is the axiomatic common that implies a community. As we have seen, encryption means a primal blockage and prohibition to communication as the first condition of politics. Hence, any structure that supposes a hierarchization or the imposition of conditions to the access of language is not only anti-democratic but the outright denial of politics.

Hardt and Negri tell us that the term multitude was formed in England as a technical term in the seventeenth century 'to name all those gathered together to form a political body regardless of rank and property' (Hardt and Negri 2009, 40). According to them, multitude, in its historical emergence, stands in opposition to the concept of the people. The latter means the legal organization of a body politic under the diagram of a sovereign and thus the verticality of power. The former is an open-ended multiplicity that cannot be accounted for in any system of sameness and identity, and thus is infinitely horizontal. It is the battle of titanic proportions between Hobbes and Spinoza, between majestic sovereignty and exploding multiplicity. As Paolo Virno explains:

> One must keep in mind that the choice between 'people' and 'multitude' was at the heart of the practical controversies (the establishing of centralized modern States, religious wars, etc.) and of the theoretical-philosophical controversies of the seventeenth-century. These two competing concepts, forged in the fires of intense clashes, played a primary role in the definition of the political-social categories of the modern era. It was the notion of 'people' which prevailed. (Virno 2004, 21)

Of course, these authors are narrating the birth of modern European sovereignty, a flawlessly calculated apparatus with vast extensions of parts that function in perfect synchronization. Nevertheless, there is something that obstructs sovereignty, that threatens its purity and its perfect systematization: the people, who must be then brought to a vanishing point through the imperative need to put them under the wing of a severe father. As a result of this clash, the people are not an accidental figure in modernity; they are the base that holds together the entire network of power in a solid state. Precisely because Hobbes, the architect of power and state, intends to inscribe it as the base of action and to make it coincide at all costs with sovereignty, we can denote its volatility, its capacity to destroy the state. This collectivity (people or multitude) becomes the encroachment upon power, the odd one out that does not fit but needs to fit in order for the newfound colossal apparatus of sovereignty to function. The people are the contingency at the base of the necessity of coagulated power.

Hobbes' answer, according to Hardt and Negri, is that in order for the multitude 'to become political it must become a people, which is defined by its unity of will and action' (Hardt and Negri 2009, 42). In this narration, Hobbes reduces the power of the multitude to a tamed animal in the stable of sovereignty now called the people, perfectly discernable and accounted for, inscribed in a legal text as scar tissue. As Negri explains, the concept of people 'soon falls prey to the juridical mechanism of qualification. The generic essence of the concept is reread in a constitutional key: if the "people" is the subject of constituent power, it can be so only insofar as it first undergoes an organizational process capable of expressing its essence' (Negri 1999, 97).

Henceforth, while the people stand for law and order, multitude stands for infinity against totality, potentia against potestas, and constituent power against constituted power. The multitude cannot be totalized, numerated, accounted for. It is pure intensity that cannot be divided and stratified. It opposes the people which are an unanimity formed by unitary power. Multitude does not become a totality but, rather, a set of singularities, an open multiplicity, as it lacks any pre-constituted assumptions and is the presence of a fullness of strength which signifies a truly positive concept of freedom (Negri 1999, 24). The multitude is the absolute becoming of the infinite. This is why Hardt and Negri describe the multitude in these categorical terms: 'Multitude is a form of political organization that, on the one hand, emphasizes the multiplicity of the social singularities in struggle, and on the other, seeks to coordinate their common actions and maintain their equality in horizontal organizational structures' (Hardt and Negri 2009, 110). And, furthermore, 'The multitude must always be expressed and can never be flattened into sameness, unity, identity or indifference' (Hardt and Negri 2004, 105).

On the other extreme of the spectrum, we have the people as a preordained reality that must be made into a functioning unity before it can act. This is the image of the people trapped and subdued by written constitutions and declarations of rights, always held at bay in a state of inferiority to language and precise dimensions of power. Hardt and Negri find in this dissection the fundamental subtext of modernity. The multitude has been foreclosed and buried deep inside the body of law and sovereignty and renamed the people, so a return to multitude can bring down the 'Republic of property' (Hardt and Negri 2009, 4). Through the *multitude*, Hardt and Negri aspire to comprise a subjectivity that outdoes a sclerotic notion of class struggle and at the same time is able to transcend capitalism through an intrinsic shift of the latter into *immaterial labour* which creates an *information society* that is out of the reach of control of the market and its laws. They 'conceive the multitude as all those who work under the rule of capital and thus potentially as the class of those who refuse the rule of capital' (Hardt and Negri 2004, 106).

Negri recognizes in the multitude a direct pipeline of ethical liberation in an inverse path from the traditional and hegemonic ethics that runs from Machiavelli to Spinoza to Marx (Stolze 2015). In this counter-tradition, 'the absence of pre-constituted and finalized principles is combined with the subjective strength of the multitude, thus constituting the social in the aleatory materiality of a universal relationship, in the possibility of freedom' (Negri 1999, 51). On the one side, we have the people as the final piece of the puzzle of sovereignty and as the element that regulates and brings stability to the *Republic of property*. On the other side, we have a historical abnormality, the multitude that breaks through the seams of organized power, taking advantages of its shifts into immaterial labour.

FIRST APPROXIMATION TO SOVEREIGNTY

Negri is panic-stricken by sovereignty. Sovereignty is the darkest power that absorbs all light into its own body, the touch of evil that hides the sun in a perpetual shadow and extends as a plagued wave of power, leaving no stone unturned, no crook or bend untouched by its might. The annihilation of ethics occurs when the multitude is drawn back to a point of identity with institutionalized power. Sovereignty is the emblem of power as domination, and through its sinkhole democracy and dissent disappear instantaneously.

Let us consider two depictions of sovereignty at the dawn of modernity. As Jean Bodin, Hobbes' predecessor, describes sovereignty in the sixteenth-century: 'Maiestie or Soveraigntie is the most high, absolute, and perpetuall power over the citisens and subiects in a Commonweale: which the Latins cal *Maiestatem*, the Greeks *akra exousia*, *kurion arche*, and *kurion politeuma*; the Italians *Segnoria*, and the Hebrewes *tomech shévet*, that is to say, The greatest power to command' (Bodin 1980/1596). It is Hobbes, however, who organizes sovereignty into a precise category of political and legal philosophy, boosting its overwhelming presence, not only in the apparent balance of European affairs, but as the clotting element of power. It is here where the pieces of the coming British Empire are assembled as one extraordinary machine. In *De Cive*, Hobbes delineates the blueprints of this new architecture of power:

Seeing that from the vertue of the Covenant whereby each Subject is tyed to the other to perform absolute and universall obedience to the City, that is to say, to the Soveraign power, whether that be one man or Councel, there is an obligation derived to observe each one of the civill Lawes, so that that Covenant contains in itself all the Laws at once; it is manifest that the subject who shall renounce the generall Covenant of obedience, doth at once renounce all the Lawes. (Hobbes 2000/1651, XX 73)

The magic in Hobbes' definition is that he adds a rational contract to absolute power, whereby all the members of a body politic rationally agree to be dominated by an omnipotent power. The foundation of modernity, hence, is the notarized voluntary servitude of the people . . . touché!

We will engage with sovereignty in our age and its symbiotic connection with the state of exception further down the road. Nevertheless, our exploits here will be highly enriched by establishing a thorough connection between the multitude, sovereignty, and coloniality. Negri defines the trajectory of modernity in terms of a conflict between democracy and sovereignty:

On the one hand, the idealist metaphysics that, from Hobbes to Hegel, produces a transcendental concept of sovereignty; on the other, the historical materialism that develops a radical concept of democracy from Machiavelli to Spinoza to Marx. In this framework it is evident that the opposite of democracy is not totalitarianism but the concept of sovereignty itself. (Negri 1999, 28)

This is the acutest angle in Negri's theory. Sovereignty stands in strict negation of democracy, and where one is present the other is necessarily absent. Therefore, Negri insists that 'we must specify something: here *democracy* means the omnilateral expression of the multitude, the radical immanence of strength, and the exclusion of any sign of external definition, either transcendent or transcendental and in any case external to this radical, absolute terrain of immanence' (Negri 1999, 322).

We can see how Hobbes' gambit becomes bulletproof. The degradation of the people to the presidium of law and its submission to sovereignty marks the impossibility of an immanent constituent power; autonomy is severed from the people and captured within sovereignty. Henceforth, in order to recognize any sign of democracy as the deployment of an autonomous being that weaves its own reality, it seems that we have to take democracy out of the festering claws of sovereignty.

Sovereignty is indeed a nasty business. Understood in terms of the colonial matrix, it gains a new and even more horrid dimension. Sovereignty is a multipurpose tool. First, historically, within the walls of Europe, sovereignty is the axis of a new *Nomos of the earth* which designs a legal platform that ensures that the European powers can feast on the banquet of colonization without tearing each other apart like hyenas. Second, it allows a swift transition to the secularization of power, thus challenging the axis of Spain and Portugal under the divine protection of Rome as the hegemonic colonial powers. Third, it is the ideal diagram of power to control populations within defined legal territories in Europe. Fourth, it establishes the fundamental imbalance that creates colonialism. On the one side, we have the European countries, defined through a series of characteristics that make them the beacons of humanity, reason, and civilization; on the other is the rest of the world: archaic, uncivilized, a multiplicity of lower races that destroy the syntagmatic structure of humankind. Sovereignty becomes the instrument of civilization and ethnic cleansing.

Nevertheless, the movement is incomplete until sovereignty is assigned to a very particular subject that will behold its power, and the ideal subject for such a hierarchized power is the *nation state*. In the words of Hardt and Negri, 'National sovereignty is the device that defines both transcendence and representation—two concepts that the humanist tradition had presented as contradictory—turning the contract into an intrinsic substance inseparable from an agreement of subordination' (2005, 143). Following Žižek, the nation state is the violent mutation of local communities and their traditions into the modern nation as an 'imagined community' (Žižek 2001, 183). The nation in terms of modern Europe is the repression of local and organized livelihoods that defied the new market system and their re-inscription in a new and comprehensive tradition. In terms of colonization, it is the glue of a model that defines the right race, the right life, the right speech, and therefore the condemnation of anything that is diverse from it; it is the element that converts difference into error and sin.

There is only identity in the positioning of an absolute difference that is expelled from the strict construction of the nation. Difference thus becomes negation: whoever does not conform to the precise description of the nation is expelled from its constitution. The law is the mechanism that serves the nation to contain and reduce, remove and batter any difference from the model. In colonial terms, the nation state, through sovereignty, establishes a universal model of culture and humanity that is plainly Western/European, demarcating the inside and outside of the political truth, which requires that all differences disappear and (non-)humanity passively submit to rigid meanings fabricated in the belly of European nation states. The nation becomes the essence and motor of history. The nation is built as the product of a rational spirit of history, where every history is synonymous with the history of all European nations, where all human perfection is synonymous with the ideal perfection of the nation (Hardt and Negri 2005, 146). The sovereign nation is the modern *City of God*, a perfect ideal and the funnel of production of being. Identity is conceived not as the resolution of social and historical differences, but as the product of a primary unit. The nation is the complete figure of sovereignty that is prior to its historical development, the genius who builds history as it mutilates threats of difference and multiplicity.

The solution to the crisis of modernity is the idea that nationalism is an inevitable stage of development, the final stage of history which resolves all its contradictions in one final and perfect synthesis. The nation state consolidates the particular image of a hegemonic modern society, and the victory of the bourgeoisie detaches itself from a particular narration to acquire the heroic status of the historical truth of the universe, written in the stone of the constitution. The history of the West becomes the universal history of the rest. The national becomes a powerful universal that colonizes difference and returns it to homogeneity, while economic activity is sublimated to the level of ethnic Thing (Lacan 2004), as a patriotic contribution to the greatness of the nation.

National sovereignty produces the miracle of coagulating the power of the singularities into a general will. The Roman Empire used the concentration of law as an instrument of the greater penetration and domination of its colonies. The idea of a *Ius Gentium* (a Roman universality of peoples), which purported to reflect the absolute principles that nourish the human spirit and its fate, allowed the empire to flatten any differences and establish a unique umbilical cord between the colonies and the idea of Rome. Hence, the powers of the Roman metropolis achieve the unlikely: that through *Ius Gentium*, every cultural, political, and legal difference would be reduced to the principle of the supremacy of virtue and Roman civilization. The modern international law becomes the resurrection of the Roman *humanitas* project but blown out of proportion to a global dimension. On the one hand, as we have said, it ensures the ordered and strategic occupation of territories by some European nation states, tracing precise frontiers to a law of war that allows equality and stability within the Western European geography. At the same time, it becomes the instrument to reduce the differences of a multiple colonial world to the legal unity of the nation state. This sleight of hand works beyond the legal compounds. It means that the model of humanity is enclosed within the dimensions of the nation state, and therefore the colonial world must be formed through its reflection, for therein lies the true value of humanity appraised culturally, socially, economically, and politically.

The nation establishes a particular model of human being, the European citizen, and through law it raises it to a universal value that should be copied or, failing that, violently imposed. That citizen becomes the line of demarcation of the law, the watchman who guards the border to ensure that the national group is compact and homogeneous as it prevents any leaks or alterations to the system. The construction of an absolute racial difference is essential to devise a homogeneous national identity (Mignolo 2003); this is the constitution of power in coloniality. The nation state and its two indivisible particles extend as toxic gas from the postcolonial constitutional projects. The model of nationality is transplanted to the movements of (pseudo-)independence and settles in as its axis. Thus, when decolonization struggles ripen, they tend to simply reproduce the pattern of exclusion. The new independent elites reproduce, tout court, the anatomy of colonial power; they are granted power, provided that the geopolitical clientele system of colonialism remains intact and that the internal composition of law and politics reproduce the same lines of exclusions of black, women indigenous, and the poor. The colonial model of the enlightened European man becomes transplanted to the creole elites without missing a beat.

NEGRI'S PROSTHETICS OF POWER

We will return to sovereignty and reload it with new dimensions of power that emerge out of an examination of the colonial matrix of power. Now, however, it is time to analyse the prosthetics that Negri endows the multitude with in order to protect its ontological consistency. The conundrum is manifold but intimately related to the variables of composition among the multitude, the singular, the absolute (absolute freedom, absolute government), God and eternity, and, of course, sovereignty. What the combination of these problems announces, in a manner louder than words, is the unpostponable need for action, decision, and organization as fundamental and irreplaceable concepts of politics, which the initial fabrication of potentia and potestas seemed to overthrow. In the prosthetics, we will see clearly how action, decision, and organization are not only a basic factor of any power that claims to pursue liberation but are, further, the ineradicable dimension of politics.

The first problem we will confront is the disparity between the multitude and the singularity that constitutes it. The conundrum can be posed in the following way: The multitude is a collective concept that in order to become absolute needs to reconstruct itself through the singularities that compose it, just as any mathematical infinite requires individual numbers. There is, then, a necessary degree of separation and differentiation between the multitude and the singulars. The multitude is the absolute becoming of the infinite. Nevertheless, it is inevitably also a binding together of singularities. Hence, the problem posed bluntly is if the passage from one to the other guarantees the freedom and diversity of the singular without annihilating it in a composed mass of unity. In the balance lies the question of what are the limits (ethical, practical) and extensions of the actions of the multitude. The geometrical crux of the matter is that a singularity immersed in the multitude is a subject that intersects the infinity of the multitude and the definable morphology of a singular. Hence, the underlying question is how the multitude becomes a

politically acting subject, a subject that achieves empirical and ethical transformations from a unity of action. This is the problem of the intersection of
absolute power and indiscriminate singular difference.

The second crucial problem is the imbalance brought on by two conflicting
principles installed in the heart of multitude: absolute freedom and absolute
government. Freedom must be absolute if we are to predicate any substance of
the multitude, but the only arrangement capable of ensuring freedom is absolute government, which is logically at odds with the definition of multitude.
In the TP (Tractatus Politicus) and the TTP (*Tractatus Theologico-Politicus*),
Spinoza speaks of democracy as an absolute form of state and government in
the absence of any version of the theory of contract. Given this, 'How can a
philosophy of liberty—at the margin of the contract theory—be resumed in
an absolute form of government or vice versa?' (Negri 2000, 63). Freedom
is the condition of the multitude; it is its *raison d'être*. Multitude only makes
sense as a process of liberation, and liberation is reserved as the fruit of
multitude. Nevertheless, according to the TP and the TPP, freedom can only
be guaranteed in government. So the logical impossibility lands us flat in a
planet of power beyond the perpetual becoming of the multitude. If freedom
is absolute, then nothing can contain it; but if government is absolute, it must
contain everything—including, of course, liberty, which by that same token
could not be absolute. This is the point where democracy is between the rock
of government and the hard place of freedom.

Both problems are intimately entangled as they both announce the ultimate
need of concrete action which immediately implies decision and organization. The elemental need, then, is for an acting subject which affirms itself in
reality by transforming it, thus establishing something very close to institutions, either as government or as an acting body in resistance. But with this,
the spontaneous transformation of the world stemming from the natural touch
of potentia setting in motion a domino effect seems to come to an abrupt halt.
The tension presented here seems irresolvable. In the first case, if we speak of
an infinite process, which rebuffs any kind of unity, then the freedom and difference of the singulars become indistinguishable and trampled from within.
In the second case, if we speak of absolute freedom, according to Spinoza,
such a thing is unattainable without absolute government. The result is that,
as Balibar insightfully puts it, the multitude becomes 'a contradictory power,
internally divided against itself: as such, it is unable to decide anything, an
unstable aggregate of individual passions' (Balibar 2008, 71).

Pietas, Reloading the Machine of Transcendence

How can the multitude remain perpetually open and expansive and at the same
time become an operative and concrete subject of an ethics (or of a state)

that warrants the freedom of the singularities rooted within it? Alternatively, how can the multitude assemble singularities of difference without falling to a closed totality—that is, a mere collection of parts—while at the same time being the result of unlimited singular potencies? Moreover, is it possible to avoid the multitude being deemed a mere assortment of defined elements while at the same time those elements can only be defined from within the multitude? Indeed, what constitutes the multitude? Is there a natural limit that the multitude imposes on individuality in order for the multiple to exert concrete power?

The physical relation between parts and whole is the root of the problem. It subverts the pristine relation between constituent and constituted powers. Parts would have to come before the whole as prior in time and in the order of things, as the fundamental constituent power which therefore would be the foundation. Hence, the multitude would be a clear derivative (constituted) power, a reflection of an assembly of parts. With Aristotle, we would have to ask, where is the organizing motion that bestows the form?

The problem of the absolute confronted with singular freedom and difference is at the base of the problem of infinity and totality. As we have seen, infinity is the definition of the multitude: it means the limitless and unbound expression of immanence in the becoming of being. On the other hand, totality is an accounting structure that determines a system of representation, which is in turn derivative from the act of shaping the totality. He who counts establishes the totality as a principle, with the obvious result that the totality is always secondary to he who has fashioned it, and thus a totality forms an outer limit to immanence. In short, totality is where any relation is predetermined by the normative use of a set of rules in order for language to be. Therefore, any system that predicates the need for action, decision, and organization entails the integration of a mediating point as a necessary system of accounting. The biting question is, then, whether there can be infinity under these conditions.

For Negri, the concept of the multitude is above all rooted in physical potency. He concludes: 'It is obvious that this physical horizon cannot support mediations of any kind' (Negri 2003, 74). The force of the multitude is commanded by its capacity to refine the levels of association, to develop the multiplier of the composite intersections and to accede to ever higher grades of complexity. In *The Savage Anomaly*, he adds that 'knowledge is elevated to divinity, to a superior grade of being as it traverses the imaginary and the social and is constructed by them' (Negri 2003, 208).

Given this, though, the multitude comes to a problematic crossroads: the difficulty of defining it as a political subject. As Negri concedes, the multitude, as a warped agglomeration of passions and situations, would require a 'new dislocation' and a 'corrective for its dispersion' (Negri 2000, 76). In order for it to become an ethics, a telos must be inscribed in its heart. The question becomes how to escape Rousseau's general will as a point of pet-rification and loss of immanence and at the same time determine the ethical appraisal of the multitude? How can this immanence preserve itself without any mediation? Negri's first solution is the imagination which creates from inside the potentia of the multitude. However, this solution does not suffice in grappling with the aporia of liberty and the absolute, of the infinite of the multitude and the definable singularity which partakes in this infinity. The question thundering at the core of the problem is this: how can the multitude become a machine that acts, and how can it act to preserve absolute freedom within the particular relativity of its composition?

The problem of the absolute and freedom is placed at the nucleus of singu-larities that appear as jagged fragments in a massive and unending process. But 'absolute' denotes an indivisibility of the process of becoming, where it is impossible to define the singular and her specific liberty as a body that interacts and affects other bodies in a never-stopping tombola of physical movement. The singular becomes a blur, a smudge on the canvas of mul-titude. The primordial questions are: first, how should a subject act within the open objectivity of the multitude? And second, how does the multitude remain absolute through a composition of singularities of difference? This is the unfinished part of the TP, and thus begins one of the favourite and most fruitful philosophical games: *fill in the blank*. Negri's conjecture to answer such absence must address how 'Social practice of singularities (is) laced in a process of the masses' (Negri 2000, 79).

For Negri, the key to solving this puzzle lies in the difference between totality and infinity when regarding the absolute. In the contractual system, the absolute is arithmetic; it is made to limit and hedge a totality within pre-cise bounds. In Spinoza, the only meaning of absolute is absolute potentia: 'Absolute and potentia are tautological terms' (Negri 2000, 65). Just as the absolute substance of God is not transferred but shared by men, its exercise is not exhausted by any formal and external limit; it is infinite in its becoming. Power regarded as such is not the scourge of a sovereign but the unbounded exercise of potentia within a multitude, where all causes (efficient, final) are constrained by the one and only material cause.

If the multitude, in order to become absolute, necessitates a self-recon-struction through the singularities that compose it, then there is need for a point of convergence, a point of the adherence of bodies and distribution of meanings within the multitude. But for Negri, as we have established, it must nevertheless be a point without mediation, and to reckon with this tension he turns to *pietas*, the missing link that binds and solves the aporetic condition. Pietas is defined by Negri as the 'desire to do good that is borne to life accord-ing to the guide of reason' (Negri 2000, 78). Pietas is, then, the instrument of ethical reason, which suggests that the presence of pietas as the solution to the aporia has to suppose a convergence of *cupiditates* under the guidance of reason that materially moves the individual towards the common good. Pietas is thus the synthetizing power of power, the solution of the tensions between the singular, ethics, and physics. Pietas converts the warped subjectivity of the multitude into the ontological project of collective potentia (Negri 2000, 80). It snatches the multitude from bare imagination and transforms it into political action. Negri is at pains to situate this new and uncanny element, and he ends up giving it the esoteric name of *genesis*.

Pietas, Negri maintains, is neither an aggregation nor an internal trait of the multitude; rather, it is the catalyst, the active element that dislocates the problem of the absolute and liberty by shifting its perspective. It is what makes democracy *operative*, and, hence, it is both a passion and a moral maelstrom. It is, in Negri's words, 'the soul of the multitude' (Negri 2000, 82). Talk about the recoil of metaphysics!

The circularity is obvious in this line of thought. First, the constitutive potency of the singulars constitutes the multitude. But for there to be any difference whatsoever among the singularities, and in order for the multitude to remain open as a political subject, it depends on the ethical acumen of the singularities, which must necessarily be different from that of the multitude. Now, this constitutive element called *pietas* is something that the singular does not possess ontologically: it is something added (an excess) to the equation in order for the multitude to be considered as such. If we are to preserve the integrality of the singular and the multitude, then the singular has to be *qualified as a certain something* different from being simply singular. Hence, we are not only back to square one, but something else has been added in bringing about the return: the imperative need not only for a mediator, but, more importantly, for a *constituent qualification* of the singularity. What is demanded of the singularity in order to be held as part of the multitude is a qualification of her difference beyond difference itself. This qualification stands as the zone of demarcation of the multiple, a normative hinge between the singular and the multitude. The original meaning of potentia as the melting pot of power and right becomes dissociated as another element enters to qualify it.

Only the pious subject, then, may enter the body of the multitude. At this point, not only is a mediation introduced, but there also appears a full-throttle *telos* involved in the qualification of the political. Hence, through pietas, as the buffer (mediator) between liberty and the absolute, a qualification of the ethical is introduced. Pietas becomes the holy water in the baptism of the multitude. The results openly contradict the initial construction of the multitude. To be a singular, it does not suffice to enter the multitude, and not only is the singular now qualified, but the qualification is *beyond* singularity itself. This qualification demands the representation of ethics even before ethics is ever considered or built from the base of the multitude as its precondition of existence. It is an ethos imbued in a previous ethos, ethics as the container of its production, an infinity contained by another infinity. The multitude becomes the regulative scheme of reason, and pietas turns ethics into a demand for universal morality. The irony could not be more bitter. Negri, the draftsman of the multitude, qualifies politics in the stoutest of senses in order to save the immanence of ethics. The adoration of ethics ends up destroying any possibility of democracy. The pious man replaces the civilized and the virtuous man as the new *Cerberus* of politics.

Negri is well aware of the short circuit between singularities, the multitude, and the absolute. His conjecture pretends to establish pietas as an invisible bridge, the necessary element of contrast that would render the operation complete without breaking its parts or making one of them superior to the others. Negri has to affirm that the multitude has a double function, a systole and diastole: one tends to the unity of politics while the other one spreads to the multiplicity of subjects. This raises all sorts of commotion. What happens if the singular does not meet the threshold of pietas? What happens to the scoundrel, the dissenter, and the saboteur? What if the subject immersed in the absolute potency is already tainted by potestas as forms of hegemonic selection of subjectivity? If the multitude is the high ground and the factory where words obtain meaning, how can we recognize pietas if it has not achieved the point of meaning (multitude)? In other words, if we grant that the multitude is the origin of ethics and hence of the language that defines its contours and possible combinations, how can the multitude remain absolute when its organic construction is beyond itself? When Negri introduces pietas, he introduces a previous and exterior difference to the multitude as its qualification, so singulars must first possess a property that is foreign to the compounds of the multitude.

As we have shown, granting a magical attribute to potentia where it would, of its own devices, convert potestas, is unsustainable. Now, in surveying the assortment of singular pietas and their relation to the multitude, we come to a steeper logical pitfall that takes the form of a synecdoche: the singular must already possess what is said to be the exclusive trait of the multitude! Such a trait of the multitude, admittedly, is only said to be attainable in the movement from the singular to the multiple, but this logically suggests that the multitude be understood as an aggregate of parts, a combination of fragments, which by definition makes it not a multitude but a *totality*. In order to rule out pietas as a mediator, then, it must be considered as merely an empirical subsidiary of the multitude. But if this is so, then anything whatsoever could claim the same attribute (hatred, misery, the love of domination, etc.). Why? Simply because we have no way of knowing what pietas *means* before the multitude qualifies it, and this should be impossible, as it would be presumed that the multitude would refute itself if it acts as the arbiter of difference, the gatekeeper of itself.

Negri leans on pietas, retreating from the problem without engaging its fullest intensity.[1] Pietas becomes a thin red line, an amorphous yardstick, which makes Negri finally declare: 'Evidently the relation pietas-Republica-democraticum-imperium is irresolvable' (Negri 2000, 81). Notwithstanding, he asks 'Why not consider the inconclusiveness of the relation between the social practice and the legal subject of power as a metaphysical condition of the absolute?' (Negri 2000, 84). We can do that, through an utter reconsideration of difference, transitions, subjectivity, and the dyad of potentia and potestas, under the following conditions. First, the order of production of being is always and under every condition reserved to difference and only difference. The prosthetics inverts the order of difference: difference would be a result, through the mediation of a qualification, and not the source of becoming. This means, second, that difference is not a product of qualified entanglements among singulars, but is instead the producer of every layout of being and thus of every encounter. That difference (and *only* difference) generates difference as the condition of being means that difference is not a means of contrast between identities in a secondary stage of difference which would bear the fruit of ethics; it is, instead, the primordial constitutive agent of politics. Politics in our current state of affairs of domination is only viable through transitions, which means that the subject of power is the hidden operative of difference, defined by the occultation exercised by potestas whose mere existence implies the impossibility of a structure to close upon itself. Politics cannot be the amorphous carrier of pietas, because this would insert a qualification and thus deny the principle of democracy. Power, then, shall be understood in a double and permanently opposed modality of potestas and potentia that defines each other's limits at all times and places. Hence, potentia may be fully actual, but the element of difference is not actualized in it unless it faces potestas. Hence, difference is the real infinity: as potentia, it condenses the possibility of all becoming; as actuality, it supposes the contingency of a future, which today is captured in an egg of time by hidden principles as potestas. These stipulations entail, finally, that identity (granted to the pious by Negri) cannot serve as a condition for engaging in politics. Politics is solely the product of difference. Only after its encounter—not just the encounter of individual selves but also that most dramatic and inevitably violent encounter (cataclysm) between difference (the hidden people in resistance) and power in a solid state—may we speak of potentia as a generic right to the world.

Second Prosthetic: Between Life and Death, Between Constitution and Eternity

In Spinoza's diverse treatises, 'democracy' is *said in many ways* and thus appears with a plurality of meanings. It is the common root of a great vine that climbs the walls of reality, grafting diverse nuances and tracing everything it touches. It is Proteus, shifting forms continuously. Sometimes, democracy appears as the absolute form of government; occasionally it jumps forward and turns itself into the eternal ethical flame of men assembled into a multitude; at other times, it reduces its form to a fuzzy social link; and then again, it also appears, with all its might, as the source of legitimacy of empire. There is something severely slippery in the Spinozian construction of democracy, something that refuses to be stabilized on one observable feature. It seems to be a chemical reactor that attains its particular properties depending on the specific interaction that it undergoes when combined with some other element.

The unfinished Tractatus Politicus presents a major inconsistency vis-à-vis the *Ethics*, an inconsistency which has come to be called 'the double foundation'. On one side, there is the intensive infinity of the multitude of the *Ethics*; on the other, for the TP, democracy must be understood as an absolute form of government, which lands us directly in the septic swamp of sovereignty. In the *Ethics*, democracy is the absolute becoming of the multitude which refutes on its own grounds any possibility of institutionalization, much less the absoluteness of sovereignty. It seems that from the juncture of the much slandered sovereignty and the absolute being of the multitude, there is no possible fusion or middle ground. Negri jumps from the TP to the *TTP*, weaving different textures into one fabric that can keep the consistency of democracy intact as the expression of the *Ethics* (Negri 2000, 57). Again we encounter a staunchly well-built conjecture that tries to patch the holes in Spinoza's thinking, holes that this time are due to his untimely death.

The tension that the Political Treatise and the *Theological Political Treatise* bring to the *Ethics* is not only a question of coexistence between sovereignty and multitude. It is a much more vexing question: it brings to the fore the impossibility of the multitude as an absolute process of becoming, raising the question of *legitimizing sovereignty* as the only sign of democracy.

Democracy swerves, spins, and sticks itself into different meanings in the treatises. Sometimes it is treated as the direct propulsion of the multitude as 'one mind and one soul' (Spinoza. PT. III). Yet at other times, it comes very close to Hobbes' idea of distinguishing between claimants to the 'best form of government', and at still other times it is the source of legitimacy of any government. In conclusion, democracy pulsates at the base and intersections of the state, the natural and civil right of the individual, and the right of sovereign powers. So we truly have before us three distinct and irreconcilable meanings of democracy: democracy as the generator (constituent) of government, democracy as the base of legitimacy of any form of government, and democracy as an extensive multitude that never reaches a point of friction.

Let us here illustrate the problem with a few examples. In the *TTP*, Spinoza writes, 'I prove that governments are the guardians and interpreters of religious law as well as civil law, and they alone have the right to decide what is just and unjust, what is pious and impious' (Spinoza. *TTP*. preface, 395). Later, he contends that 'if sovereignty is invested in a few men or in one alone, he should be endowed with some extraordinary quality, or must at least make every effort to convince the masses of this' (Spinoza. TP. Ch. 5, 461). And in speaking of the 'Commonwealth of the Hebrews', he adds, 'Such sovereignty Moses easily succeeded in keeping in his hands, because he surpassed all others in divine power which he convinced the people that he possessed, providing many proofs thereof. . . . He, then, by the divine power with which he was gifted, established a system of law and ordained it for the people' (Spinoza. *TTP*. Ch. 5, 439). Balibar explicates the problem for us:

> The sovereignty of the State is always absolute. If it were not absolute, it could not claim to be sovereign. Individuals, according to Spinoza, cannot withdraw their active participation from the State to which they belong without finding themselves classed as 'public enemies', with all the risks that entails. Yet at the same time, any State that wishes to guarantee its own stability must allow the individuals who live in it the greatest possible freedom of thought and of self-expression. (Balibar 2008, 25)

In the extrapolation of the imbalances between the TP and the *TTP*, we come to an intrinsic limit of the multitude. We are before two diverse movements, where one tends towards the unity and indivisibility of government and the other tends towards the absolute and infinite openness of the multitude. But the point that quakes the whole edifice is that, for Spinoza, the multitude is not only the foundation of *imperium* but its index of legitimacy and its source of law (Spinoza, PT. II, II, XVII). It is clear then that Spinoza is thinking of the multitude as an actual political subject that concentrates power—indeed, all institutionalized power—upon itself. Yet on the other side, in the *Ethics*, Spinoza insists that the movement of the multitude is plural; it tends towards infinity without any form of institutionalized capture. Again, the terrifying ghost of the sovereign and the transmission of rights and power appear as divesting features of power. In the TP and the *TPP*, the multitude is constructed as a form of legitimacy, not a form of organization of power, making it the base of the legitimacy of either aristocracy or monarchy—that is, drawn as a limit to both kinds of exercise of power (potestas).

The point is that the multitude, in this precise meaning, is neither a constituent power nor the form of the government, but instead is the *legal* base of legitimacy. Again we see the problems of identity, homology, homogeneity, and totality, as the negations of the infinite openness of the multitude, rise vertically before our eyes. In these collisions of meaning we have to ask how communication can be possible, and, furthermore, how communication can be the fundament of the political. Better yet, how can differences communicate in the absolute? The question for Negri is to figure out if there is a mode to bring together an original definition of democracy which 'is historically situated, conceptually conclusive and metaphysically structured' (Negri 2000, 59).

According to Negri, thought contributes to the cohesion of sovereignty, with the latter understood no more as the mastermind of the *scorched earth* doctrine, but now as a more benign 'continuous process of collective production'. For Negri, the multitude inherits the metaphysical power of potentia as entirely immanent, and then proceeds to invent new social relations and to create social authority through the process of constitution. Norms and rights are created from the base of society through immediate associative relations understood as a uniform base, a smooth surface that runs all through the line of immanence, a homologous power with no social distinctions. Negri fuses the Constitution-production relationship into a unitary nexus—even as he recognizes that such a thing, for example, 'does not successfully bring the antagonistic function of class struggle as foundation of reality to its full maturity' (Negri 2003, xviii).

Do Spinoza's wings span only far enough to construct the ideal empire through the legitimating basement of the multitude? This is the point where the burning question of the bridge between the TP and the *TTP* begins to swell and blister the idea of liberty. How is it possible to maintain liberty and the absolute without granting the transformation of the *corpus politicus* the need to concretize liberty as a legal standard? Or, in Negri's words, how can liberty become its own becoming without renouncing its own naturality (Negri 2000, 64)? In a world where potestas contends permanently for the status of potentia, absolute liberty is absolute nothingness, so it begs a point of capture, a mediation to render it stable and distribute its colossal weight. But—as we have already proved—legalized liberty cannot be absolute.

For Negri, the importance of democracy as the foundation of politics (Negri 2000, 42) is that it is not built on morality or religion. Hence, how the human condition begets the political constitution and the autonomy of the political can only be garnered by the autonomy of a collective subject. The absolute is 'potentia that develops as it maintains a unitary productiveness' (Negri 2003, 68). Democracy is, then, the *omnino absoluta* of government where there is no alienation of power; it is the liberation of all the social energies in a collective conatus, an organization of liberty for all.

The concept of democracy is then carved into the absolute, where the once bone-chilling concepts of *legalism* and *legality* become the natural production of democracy and where democracy is turned into an accumulative process of rules of 'consent, participation and exclusion' (Negri 2000, 57). I can't help but see in all of this a certain influence of the secular spirit of modernity that needs to divest Spinoza's politics of any religiosity, to expurgate any vestige of his Jewish tradition in order to make of his metaphysical construction a perfect fit with modern secular politics which are immune to theology. The separation of the double foundation to favour the political and the ethical can only be accomplished in a tearing apart of the theological and the isolated nurturing of the ethical. Nevertheless, this is not the main problem we have to address.

The absolute may only be conceived as the general horizon of potentia as its development and actuality. Thus, for Negri, an agreement between potentialities multiplies power. The metaphysical is a physical construct, an aggregate of singular forces, and thus the arithmetic sign of the virtual infinity. Potentia and the absolute are equivalent; they form a tautology. Metaphysics begins to be grounded and illuminated by a physical entity tending to infinity. But it is here where the aporia supposes a crack in the foundation of the supposed tautology. Negri's answer thus far does not respond to the fracture between the TP, the *TTP*, and the *Ethics* regarding the double (triple?) foundation. The said infinity would meet an internal and necessary limit if it is to remain absolute, for it must fix an allocation of power at some time or another in order to become absolute government. Hence, a precise temporal point of decision is necessitated. The tendency to the infinite is contrasted with the need for an adequate space of decision. The line that extends to every plane must be defined by one point where government would surface as an institutionalized mark of the multitude. Why, then, does Spinoza confront the multitude with the necessary stoppage point of sovereignty and state? If absolute potentia is an absolute process of openness, why must it retract to a concrete and recognizable form of power? Is this not precisely what absolute potentia shatters from the inside? Is it not the great leap of Spinozian politics to break from the alienation, representation, and mystification of power and to oust the ominous presence of the sovereign? If the potency of God is the same as the potency by which natural things act (*ipsissima deit sit potentia*) why would potency need to go beyond this perfection?

What this paradox presents us with is the necessity of drawing on a second ontology. Absolute and infinite potentia has to construct, within its own dimensions, a point of departure, a division point to proclaim its own government. To Badiou's delight, Negri's logic becomes an *axiom of choice*, a Cantor infinity defined as a totality from the axiom of government. It is the revelation of Russell's paradox: 'The set of all sets that are not members of themselves'.

Government is not simply a subsidiary expression of the multitude, a secondary manifestation of immanence which does not compromise its wholeness. Rather, as Spinoza establishes it, government is a necessary operation of the multitude within the plane of immanence. The dimensions of the contradiction are very simple: if potency is already perfect, it cannot necessitate any further arrangement, any other form of organization of space and time, because it is *itself* the organization of everything that there is. Hence, we would need to perfect what is already perfect in its own constitution from within its own constitution. Any kind of organization, as a qualification of multitude, would perfect what is already perfect. Thus, perfection as organization would be external (transcendent) to the potentia of the multitude. When we confronted the first prosthetic, pietas, we found that it brought an external qualification to the conformation of the multitude: the singular, in order to belong to the multitude, had to meet an alien qualification beyond that of plain difference. This second prosthetic, it seems, demands something even more exacting: that the qualification be internal to the construction of democracy. The mediation we are speaking of is, of course, not a mirror image of potentia as the state, or a constitutional legalized form. Rather, it is mediation not as a creation of a *tertium*, an exteriority that would come to replace the interiority, but mediation as a requisite built in from the very inside. Surely we recognize that for Spinoza the absolute is not an end in itself that would resolve, as the judge of history, all the singular contradictions in a Hegelian sense. We recognize that the absolute is the creation of power by potency in an ever-extending and intensive appropriation of truth. Nevertheless, the problem surfaces intact between liberty and absolute *within* the plane of immanence. While in Hegel the absolute is a centripetal force to ordain all singularities under the truth value of an externality, in Spinoza it is the centrifugal force that creates and ordains all measures of reality in one single and prolonged movement.

The problem in Spinoza is decisive. As recognized by Negri, in the TP the relation between potentia and the absolute is expressed in two movements. The first movement strides towards the absolute 'in a proper sense', towards the unity and indivisibility of power (Negri 2000, 69); the other is the movement of potentia within itself which is plural and unstoppable. The first scenario is the absolute detached from singular potencies, the arithmetic presupposition that a massive amount of indistinguishable parts composes the absolute with no regard to their particular differences. This answer amounts to a philosophical regression to Hobbes and Hegel, with the absolute shuttered upon itself, an accounting system of singularities indexed from within as separate natures and rights. In the second scenario, singular liberties that expand ad infinitum in their potentialities could never reach the concreteness of a political subject (multitude, people, or any other denomination) as the limit and incarnation of political reason. In the TP, Negri argues, the multitude becomes the hinge between the movements; it acts as the juridical subject of imputation and the base of legitimacy of any political construction, while at the same time it extends to infinity as the force of creation of any index of legality. But in order to achieve such dimensions, another prosthetic has to be attached to the operation: for absoluteness to be neither the absolute of the state nor the absolute sovereign nor the totality of accounting as the requisite of the political body, it must be an absoluteness demanded by reason as the logical progression of God's substance, which inevitably excludes will or idiosyncrasy.

The solution that emerges here for both Spinoza and Negri is consensus. Every aspect of Spinoza's work in the TTP poses the question of how an imperium based on consensus should be, or how it would come to be from the free exercise of potentia. In the TTP, the monarch can only rule by the consent of the multitude, and likewise for aristocracy or any other form of government. But here, with the idea of consensus, a brutal displacement of politics has befallen the idea of democracy. Through consensus, conflict is displaced irremediably to stand only as an organized byproduct of the exercise of power. In other words, conflict is thoroughly legalized and thus degraded to a role of representation of the social link. The latter means that conflict is not constitutive of the social bond but is merely represented in the law that holds it together. Hence the pact, the contract, is reintroduced through the back door of politics. If we were to stand before a monarchy or an aristocracy, this can only mean that conflict, as the constituent order of politics, has already been resolved in favour of the ruler. Hence, what follows and receives the name of *consent* is the interpretation that is demanded of a multitude in order for her to fit within the dimensions of power in a solid state. With this interpretation we are completely inside an order that comes *after* the original conflict. This order has already decided who is qualified to rule according to a pre-given set of conditions to act. 'Democracy' ceases to count as politics, serving merely as a legalizing link of legitimation for a power that already exists as the negation of democracy.

As argued earlier, there is no subject prior to politics: politics as antagonism is the place where the subject comes to full beingness. Through consensus, the multitude tumbles through the trap doors into the bottomless pit of law. Law stands as the neutralization of conflict and the cement of consensus, functioning as nothing short of a regression to the Platonic model of politics. In the Platonic tradition, politics corresponds to the allocation of power according to a natural model where democracy is anathema. According to this tradition, nature already qualifies the conditions to govern. Hence, it is natural that the wise rule over the ignorant, the rich over the poor, the mighty over the weak, all within the Platonic tradition of a natural distribution of differences established in a universal and necessary frame. Democracy is the demolition of said logic, for what is implied in democracy is the complete absence of qualifications to govern. The quintessential subject of politics is therefore the one that lacks any quality for *archein* (Ranciere 2001).

As Jacques Ranciere explains, in oligarchy, aristocracy, or absolutism, the political subject is defined by the enunciation of whoever governs. Subjectivity in democracy, however, is trapped in a multiple and complex relation where the place of enunciation is within the subject as the primal condition for the existence of politics (Ranciere 2006, 301; 2004; 2001, 14). Democracy ruptures of the logic of a top to bottom or hierarchical enunciation. In oligarchy and the rest of the legal formations, whoever governs defines the position and situation of the governed (Abensour 2007, 251), but in democracy the subject defines herself as the creation of politics. Democracy is thus the denial of the idea according to which every typology of distribution of power means a pre-existing model, an archetype; in other words, a refusal of any previous disposition or requirement to govern (Ranciere 2006, 305; 2001, 14). Democracy is the annulment of any condition to govern and is the government of those that lack any quality or disposition to govern. Only democracy can be understood as true politics, for in oligarchy or aristocracy, antagonism has been already solved through the application of natural differences and what follows is merely the legal *adaptation* of the model to reality. Democracy is the only place where antagonism has not been resolved, for it is an exceptional action that constitutes the subject.

At this point, with the idea of consent within empire, the ghost of sovereignty, instead of being dissolved, is invoked to claim power as protagonist. The virtue ascribable to the laws and conceptions of justice which emerge from the multitude are thus indentured to serve as the virtue of the imperium. The reality or power of the multitude derives from the reality or power of the imperium. Every law and each related conception is to contain the same signs of empire, for they are its replica. If consensus is taken as the locus of legitimacy, it would suppose that democracy becomes a mere pact of submission and therefore the basic renunciation of politics, with the consequence that Hobbes is revived in a bizarre invocation.

Following Baudelaire, we are in the core of a deep forest of symbols. Power is either a unique, indistinct flow that is the same as the multitude, or the multitude breaks it up and divides it into two distinctive parts. If the case is the latter, then we have one part that remains infinite, the other that incarnates the design (constitution) of the city of politics. Power is either completely indistinct from the multitude and forms with it an ontological alloy, or power is the expression of a decision and thus becomes an ontic emanation from the multitude. Negri does not read this as an anomaly, and he is instead at pains trying to fit together both the metaphysical absence of the distinction of power—as the immanent indistinction demanded by potentia—and the ethical distinction that would disappear in the political distinction. His solution is to make the contradiction run from one to the other. But, in a necessarily encrypted way, isn't Spinoza bringing out the point of transition?

The metaphysical indistinction is put at the heart of a politics, that is, built-in as potestas and thus not legitimized by potentia but opposed by it, opposed by its own ethical organization. Hence, instead of harmonizing the *Ethics* with TP and the *TTP* and bringing their apparent chiasm together, Negri opens the cracks in between them until they become fault-lines.

We are thus set against two possibilities. Democracy as *omnino absolutum imperium* (Spinoza. TP. XI) means either that the multitude is a totality that legitimizes power by consent, or the multitude must instantiate itself as a concrete form of power.

1. In the first case, we are before democracy as a *quantitative* value which levels the multitude to the *totality of citizens* as the definition of the political link (Negri 2000, 129). Quantity then means totality, the totality of the *We* of the modern constitutions or the *all* of human rights declarations. Hence, the multitude would be immediately turned to *the people* which it rejects as the original point of its conformation.
2. In the second case, we are before a *qualitative* and ontologically defined concept: democracy as the very structure of the republic, not as a frame that contains it but as the fullness that instantiates it. That the multitude is *guided as by one mind* means it is a subject of transitions, decisions, organization, and sovereignty.

Negri pursues a way out by pushing a third consideration, drafted by Spinoza as the eternity and immutability of God. Here the absolute is something which cannot be separated, that resists being made into a product or an eminent form of government. The result is that the absolute becomes eternal, and eternity guarantees the praxis of the absolute. Nevertheless, this solution supposes another prosthetic to avoid the previous displacement. Eternity would become transcendent in its own right, and God would escape the prison of immanence so carefully designed by the Spinozian architecture to claim his position as the emperor (Basileus) of truth. What Negri must uncover, to avoid transcendence, is a concept of eternity that does not place itself as a regulative idea of action before which we may only discover it epistemologically, probing its infinite and inscrutable surface. He needs an absolute praxis of a principle of action inscribed in the multitude, one that is concomitant with its own action.

Negri finds the answer to the conundrum in a very familiar space in Western philosophy, the division between *life and death*: 'When eternity opposes death freedom expresses an "eternal becoming"' (Negri 2000, 132). As we have seen, the ideal and mystical conception of the TP contravenes the materialist acumen of the second and fourth part of the *Ethics*, so they are melted into a single solution through the division of life and death. Democracy and eternity are made to cross and overlap the concepts of bodies and multitude. As the argument goes, the double foundation, as an irregularity in Spinoza's thinking, can be overcome by the fact that conatus exercises all its thrust to preserve life in a prototypical clash against death. The new ideal of the prosthetic is that freedom belongs to the man who does not think of death.

Reason is the intellectual love of God that becomes stronger as more men participate in it. The multitude is then the product of reason. If it were not for this decisive feature, the multitude could not be distinguished from an amorphous mass of contradictions. Hence reason, as the intellectual love of God, means that the multitude acts as one mind, a galvanized unity unbreakable by death.

As we have considered before, there are positive and negative affections. The interaction of singularities always brings fluctuations to power, hence conatus becomes the paradigmatic machine that augments power as it preserves life. Death is thus a bad metamorphosis, as it destroys the harmony of the parts of the body. When Spinoza asks if there are good mutations, that is, mutations as radical as death but that are capable of determining superior states of the multitude, he does not seem to arrive to an answer. The Negrian conjecture is that the answer is the positive metamorphosis of life. Life is the permanent industry of aggregating power to power, rousing cupiditas as the projection of the political body. Liberation is the condition of a body that tends to life, of the singular that tends to the multiple in one instantaneous movement. Nevertheless, such a striving for life is not solely a natural struggle to become and to preserve itself through work (Energeia), but a metamorphosis beyond life, a mystical metamorphosis of life to eternity, where cupiditas and pietas become, as it were, the 'absolute affirmative forces' (Negri 2003, 136) of such eternal becoming. All the obstacles of war and solitude, squander and resentment, will wither away under the dazzling sun of the multitude. The power of the community is thus settled in the horizon of a sole condition: the virtue of life! The intellectual love of God provides the intersection of life and death. According to Negri, 'Morality and religion are but the social nexus of a practical and rational conduct' (Negri 2000, 133).

The first glimpse of the problem with this account is that Negri has to ground the absolute of the multitude either by ascending to God or descending to the singular number, always stuffing its meaning, like implanting flesh onto the bones of a fallen angel. As he puts it, 'We can become eternal. In this mutation, the mystical (ideal) aspects of the concept of eternity are annulled by an ascetic (material) constitutive praxis' (Negri 2000, 136). The synthesis of the qualitative and quantitative principles of democracy inscribed in the metamorphosis of the individuals in the community is accomplished through the eternity of life against death. Democracy's two disparate connotations are welded together in eternity, a divine spell to dissolve the duplicity. The multitude then 'lives in eternity and is not limited by any constitution (understood as a positive political constitution) but transcends them all dynamically for it is each time more capable of perfection' (Negri 2000, 138). Terror, death, and fear are put to rest by a multitude that beyond being a form of government is the social transformation of an eternal becoming, where death is the negative and defining feature that carburizes life in common.

Negri's interpretation of the axis of life and death is utterly Christian yet at the same time uncannily nihilistic. We are in the presence of a unilateral conception of life and death, one that is to be acting as the basis of the political act and that dismisses any other conception, as it is itself enthroned as the sole metaphysical principle. The good metamorphosis is the continuation of the extravagant ideal of the West to overcome death, this time through a technology of being. But we are also deafened by the modern trumpets rattling the walls of death. The divine clash of life and death is the skin of a metaphysics of presence grafted onto ethics. Manichean death defines joy as intrinsically good and sadness as intrinsically bad. Eternity is thus defined in the oscillating cord of life and death: it is the breaking down of any barrier where virtue and potency flow as one and the same. With mercurial velocity, Negri goes back to the core of the Judeo-Christian tradition in order to defend the atheist ultra-modernity of Spinoza. It is quite curious how the modern intellectual, refusing the mysticism of modernity and trying to surpass it, ends up folding his gesture into the pure theology of nihilism, a land of zombie prophets and eerie revelations. As if the aspects of the limits of life and death, from the perspective of the negative, were less mystical than any other approximation of the idea of eternity! Negri shadows and merges the Heideggerian death as the authentic, the hidden treasure of omnipotent life that is clouded by the fear of death.

Negri substitutes the archaic and mystic concept of evil for death and replaces eternity with the actuality of work (to persevere, to create). Death is wrong! It is the absolute opposite of freedom, so we need a metamorphosis for the multitude to become eternal. The vicious fear of death as the end of the isolated individual is transfused intact into the multitude, the heroic genetic strain of life conquers death and smashes, in the same act, the fear of the living of the great unknown.

The ontological mechanics of this new prosthetic is operated by the critical experience of death and the cupiditas of life that bears eternity in its womb. It therefore becomes the spurt of the political socialization of this *lust for life*. Life is the positivity of being, death its utter negativity (Deleuze 1988b). In a sleight of hand closer to Augustine of Hippo than even to Aquinas, he elevates (or condemns) death as the negative limit of the experience of the absolute. The light of eternity, the blessed spirit of the pale ghost of the political subject, is anointed in the multitude. The sinless Adam of politics removes the thorny crown from all heads. Between the incomplete singular subject and the omnipotence of God, Negri falls head over heels towards the lethal radiation of the eternity of life. It does not get more modern or Western than this. We are before the obituary of politics.[2]

Negri thinks of the division of life and death as the primordial source of politics, and hence an origin that is itself untainted by politics. Anything that is political, then, is a derivative of the struggle between life and death. According to this line of thinking, the division between life and death is already clearly established somehow, and what is left is to persevere in life against the menace of death, which, in turn, is equated to the destruction of everything there is. Striving for life is thus the archetypal feature of politics. In accordance with this construction, life and death already have distinct definitions before they even enter the political realm. Again, Negri seems to be overseeing a frictionless world, where immanent life flows naturally and death possesses distinct features that are all too well established within the compounds of life.

There is a twofold problem with this. First, life and death in coloniality acquire a completely different relationship. Life and death overlap sometimes to indistinguishability, and as we will learn, the constitutive feature of coloniality is a stringent qualification of forms of life which brings about a rarefication of the meaning of death. In short, the qualifications of life (and death) are the key feature of power. And, second, due to the intense qualifications of life within coloniality, death becomes the site of resistance, hence death, far from being the negative closure of life, is a locus for the continuation of the political struggle.

The first problem with Negri is the symbolization of death as the descent into sheer oblivion, the absolute and eternal numbness that washes away the colour of memory into an ocean of darkness and stillness. Death, he presumes, is no more than a dim passage to the great unknown that brings about utter non-being. If we instead see the relation between life and death through the lens of coloniality, a whole different reality appears. In coloniality, the primal political decision is a division of life and death that yields a subsequent division of life into forms of dependence on universal values. It is a quite simple manoeuvre that fuses power and knowledge in one mighty agent of unification and exclusion. In order for the values of the colonizer to be deemed *universal* and *necessary*, a dividing line is established between forms of life. A division is erected between the civilized and the barbarian, the white and its negation, masculinity and its foils; the 'iconic' copies retain the fullness of the information that then builds the model of life (fullness of life), and any difference is expelled from its confines and considered as infra-life. In colonial terms, life is already qualified; indeed, the qualification of life is the essence of coloniality. Physical life is hence suspended life, docile bodies that are bled out of any substance. In that sense, the native and the black slave become the perennial symbol of coloniality. Organic life, its energy, and its capacity are incubated by power as potestas to fill in the gaps of humanity. Bodies and organs are harvested methodically as the negation of the *good* and civilized life, producing mere spectres of life in the path of devastation. Power as potestas creates a fracture in the bone that is life: it produces the good life standing on the opposite shore from those lives that are in perpetual lack of pureness and that challenge, with their very presence, the solid state's model of life. The near dead that walk among the shadows of the footpaths of civilization are, in reality, the symbols of *life* in coloniality.

In coloniality, then, the split of life and death is not an intrinsic and physiological line of division between health and illness, sensation and oblivion, positive and negative being all among equal forms of life. In coloniality, things are much more complex. Life is divided, classified, numerated, labelled and deflated until it becomes the fertilizing compost of the civilized. Life does not happen among equals; it is, rather, the yardstick of differentiation, functioning primordially through race. It is the construction of race which determines a position towards life and death, a biopolitical arrangement which is at the heart of the colonizing enterprise.

Santiago Castro-Gómez recuperates the following divisions made in the thick of Spanish colonization of Nueva España (Mexico), corresponding to a usual pictorial practice that established a taxonomy of race that defines the function of life in a descending pyramid of social immobility (Castro-Gómez 2005, 75). In the first scale, we find purity in the Spanish unmixed blood and then a precipitous slope descends us into mixtures that mean impurity, and impurity establishes the position of body in a social scale. Here the ability to use language and to perform a function within the social edifice is determined fully, and with it comes a particular legal position towards life and death. As we descend in this ghastly scale, every level is more paralytic and less prepared for autonomy, until the final scale defines the antithesis of the apex of the pyramid: sheer immobility and pure negation of being.

Above all the others stand the Spanish begotten by Spanish (as you can see, they are not even included in the numeration). Following them are those:

1. Born from a Spaniard and an indigenous woman, *mestizo*
2. Born from mestizo and a Spaniard woman, *castizo*
3. Born from castizo and a Spaniard woman, *español (Spanish)*
4. Born from a Spaniard and a black woman, *mulato*
5. Born from a Mulato and a Spaniard woman, *morisco*
6. Born from a morisco and a Spaniard woman, *chino*
7. Born from a chino and an indigenous woman, *salta atrás (jump-back)*
8. Born from a salta atrás and a mulata, *lobo (Wolf)*

9. Born from a lobo and a china, *jíbaro*
10. Born from a jíbaro and a mulata, *albarazado*
11. Born from an albarazado and a black woman, *cambujo*
12. Born from a cambujo and an indigenous woman, *zambaigo*
13. Born from a zambaigo and a loba, *calpamulato*
14. Born from a calpamulato and a cambuja, *tente en el aire (floater)*
15. Born from a tente en el aire and a mulata, *no te entiendo (Literally translated, 'I don't understand you')*
16. Born from a no te entiendo and an indigenous, *torna atrás (go back)*

As can be seen, each genetic division begets a racial abomination that degrades the purity of the white and must then be allocated a proper place within the map of functionality. Before anyone can invoke life and death as an unequivocal organization of meaning, a previous and more profound split has taken place, one that defines the threshold not only of life and death but of the sundry qualifications of life.

The catalogue dictates a few instructions of colonization: suspend life and turn it into a universal donor of identity, labour, and science; suspend difference and construct it under precise codes of racial origin; suspend the model of humanity in one particular meaning and then define any difference as its negation. The concentration camp is not a phenomenon born from the loins of the twentieth-century but is an architectural construct of the very dawn of modernity; the 'politicization' of bare life (Agamben 1998, 10) is the womb of modernity.

Negri seems only capable of observing the split between individual life and death *as if* life was always the expression of a *proper life* equal for all. Life is understood as if it were already organized and qualified through a certain meaning and structured through certain ethos that are nurtured from inside the beliefs and values of an already existing community moving in a straight-line march of history. For Negri, life and death as the symbiotic link of ethics occurs in a *communion* and not in a community, in life marked as a *certain something* that is valuable (bios) and not on intense divisions and qualifications through a constant political decision over the meaning of life. More importantly, Negri neglects the power of potestas to establish the legal catalogue of who deserves to live and who does not. Our point is very simple: the divisions between life and death and between diverse and qualified forms of life are the origin of coloniality; it is power as potestas that defines the anatomy of this power.

In coloniality, life is splintered into many planes of race, gender, age, and nationality that determine the functionality of biological life for the production of identities and commodities. Thus, the lines of inclusion and exclusion are the paradox of biological life, since life is always an appendix of a political fabrication extended as a function within the social body. Life is always in a deep connection with race and race with function. The *good life* is reserved to a discrete minority that possesses it naturally as the gift of purity of race. In contrast, organic life is not dumped into a wasteland but kept alive artificially to feed the greedy paunches of the *good life*. We are not referring to bygone times, as these same presuppositions inject themselves fully into coloniality in the processes of independence. Here we can see Agamben's *homo sacer*, but above all we see Fanon's *damné*. The damné is placed in a permanent state of exception as it stands for the negative of the norm, the very place from where the norm is created. It is a relation that cannot be sundered; it is symbiotic, permanent, and decisive. The blood of the bare life, of the damné, is the ink from which the scriptures of modernity are written, and from the methodical extraction of her skin the geography of modern science is spliced; the law and the state as well as the sublime and the eternal are all built on the carcass of this living-dead creature.

The first conclusion is that power in the solid state of coloniality is built from the division of life and death in a complex and constituent manner. First the division of bios and zoē, the good and the bare life, then further divisions between bare life according to a function within the production of power (identity, personality, constitution, etc.). The divine curtain between life and death is already defined by a constitutive political creation within potestas which blends one into the other permanently through the manipulation of aesthetics, law, and the production of wealth.

The living dead is the symbol of civilization. It brings together life and death in a single body. It is where death is already present as a long shadow of destruction and where life necessitates that even the simple expression of a breath, a sigh, or a lament shall be captured, controlled, and utterly immobilized. The living dead, the hidden people, are the exception of humanity: on the one side stands humanity defined as the *good life* that is civilized and racially pure, on the other stands the exception that confirms the rule and which must be kept outside the gates of civilization as bare life.

The political split within colonization is the rift of civilization and barbarism, of tradition and the archaic, of race and gender. Death can only be thought from the *good life*, from a qualification that inserts life in a direct correspondence with death. In this sequence, death becomes an individualizing feature of life. Nonetheless, for the outcast, the marginalized, for the displaced, in short, for the being of coloniality, the experience of death is not an individualizing factor, but the constitution of reality itself (Maldonado Torres 2007, 254). For the hidden people, death is always crouching in every turn of the body; there are no casual encounters. Death is a constant companion; it is stuck to the bone and haunts the core of being.

The splitting and qualification of life and its continuity in death is the form of coloniality. Life is always in direct submission to extreme apparatuses of classification and degradation until it becomes unrecognizable. It is here, however, that death becomes the place of resistance. With the *bestialization of life,* as Foucault calls it, politics becomes a technology of the body and the tissues of bodies fashion aberrant sets of pluralities. The collective being does not emerge from an individual encounter with her personal mortality; rather, her existence is signed by the *bios mori.* Being is built not only with desire (Douzinas 2008, 284) but with the need to evade the qualifications of life as well as death, which is always in reference to the absolute other. In coloniality, subjectivity is designed as dependence to an absolute other: being is being *for* the absolute other, within the reality and the rules created by the absolute other, in full submission to the absolute other. Life is reduced to a form of physicality, to bulges of flesh and blood that are instrumental in carving out the creature of power.

Precisely because coloniality means a permanent disposition of the body to death, the encounter with death is not only constant but is also shared with others who are placed in a position of exclusion as inclusion, shared with other and multiple beings displaced from reality as the very constitution of reality. Here we see the face and feel the heart of the true other, and what joins this multiple other is a link of solidarity that offers a sense of amalgamation of the precariousness of life and the ever presence of death. For the outcast and displaced, death is a strategy of resistance.

The quintessential question of coloniality is *why not embrace nothingness?* As Lewis Gordon emphatically puts it, rather than the angelic question of philosophy—*why is there something rather than nothing?*—the question for the colonized is *why go on* (Gordon 2005)? Short of a complete capture of all vital spaces, not even death guarantees liberation.

One of the most spectacular and beautiful wonders of resistance in America has been syncretism, which amounts to the undoing of coloniality from its very seams. For the Catholic dominators, death is the redemption of life and the promise of eternity in a pure form of afterlife, attainable only through conversion through an ethnic cleansing of the skin, the soul, and language. Syncretism defuses eternity and turns death into a celebration of life, not its prolongation and redemption but as the point of resistance. For example, in Brazilian Umbanda or Candomblé; or in Santeria all across the Caribbean, the balance of life and death is supported by the dead not the living. Death does not mean to enjoy the paradise of the afterlife or to transcend to a land of plenty and thus to gain access to eternity; rather, the mission of the dead is to help the living through the tribulations that are proper to life. The finality of life is not immortality or eternity but death as a passage where the spirit becomes first and foremost an aide of the living. Death composes an intensive community of dead and living, a unique force that slides in and out of death to underscore the possibilities to resist. Umbanda is erected to contradict the vision of death as the promised land of eternity, physical death and spiritual oblivion; it is meant to anchor a symbiosis and not a separation of the community. Suffering and compassion are deferred to the dead whose only vessel of communication to life is to embrace the fight of the living, to guide it, to protect the poor and discouraged lives, not with the promise of redemption but through the buffering of the energies of the body.

In Mexico, anyone who has attended the celebration of the 'Day of the Dead' in San Andrés de Mixquic understands that the umbilical cord of life and death is the electric rod of resistance. The feast takes the place of the liturgy, and death as the Western end of life is mocked, challenged not as metaphysical presence but as well-known friend who is worthy of a dance, a joke, a spin. Life and death share the common land of the feast, not to appease the formidable and negative power of death but to celebrate a community that does not distinguish one from the other. Life is in a deep symbiosis with death; they come together in the feast which means the lack of language. In the feast, to shout, to scream is to celebrate the meaninglessness of language and its hierarchies, to possess the moment when words mean nothing; it is not only the advent of the unusual but the celebration of nothingness as the only residue of the lack of language. It is underlining the basic fact that life, and not death, is orphanhood.

THE SOCIAL BRAIN: DECRYPTING MARX'S IDEAL MACHINE

The bolts and knobs of capitalism, the industrial chimney, the draconian foreman, and the line of production seem to pale and wither away as they become secondary to a massive change in the logics of capital. Big Data emerges, with information circulating and endlessly connected at every point of seemingly infinite lines of extension, creating multiple and overlapping social and economic relations faster than the speed of light. This seems to be the new order of production in post-Fordism. We are all irremediably connected. A million tongues and ideas speaking at unison in a boiling, Babel-like hive, discerned and decoded infinitesimally, mustering totally new forms of communication and modes of cultural interaction that seem to expand endlessly. Information seems to escape the prison of hierarchies and becomes accessible to a multitude aggregated as a social entirety. A click in 'the City' executed by a vegan hipster and thousands of acres disappear in the Amazon rainforest. A click in Silicon Valley executed in a 'game lounge' and half the planet enters into its fifteen minutes of popular ecstasy. A click at a pharmaceutical and half the population of a country becomes vulnerable to one specific disease. A click in a military bunker and a drone destroys a hospital in Afghanistan, though for the operator this is just like playing Xbox. But there is another side: a *social brain* is connected, creating art and new forms of communication in horizontal lines of interaction, and discrete realities that were ostracized jump to the fore with all the intensity of a new life. There are no apparent high grounds from which to control the ever-extending flow of life, no tribunals to decree the right order of combinations and no locution to stop the extension of knowledge. The *arcana imperia* become fragile to new availabilities of connections and social interactions. There is something amazingly new, terrifyingly exciting, pulsating at the heart of this new life.

The blueprints of a new cardinality of emancipation were drawn by several authors[3] around a special journal of *Futur Antérieur* (2006/1994) devoted to studying the shift of power within the frame of the *General Intellect* established by Marx in the 'Fragment on Machines' in his *Grundrisse*. The core argument is that the relations of power in post-Fordism develop a new logic based on immaterial labour. The rise of the machine implies the reduction of labour within the field of production; it demands a permanent subordination of the worker regarding the mighty machine. Nevertheless, a contradiction brews in this relation: in order to keep the automaton of capitalism riding at cruise control, a whole new field of cooperation and massive creativity must arise within the workforce which displaces knowledge and its organization from the capitalist to the worker, allowing what these authors call '*mass intellectuality*'.

The intimate link of politics and Entelecheia becomes ever more evident in our post-Fordist times, where the core of work and the production of surplus hinges on *immaterial labour* and dense webs of communicative strata yoked in indivisible forms of the production of signs and images. Labour is best defined by the performative ability of communicators and not by the image of workers tied down to an archaic assembly line. In post-Fordism, labour produces immaterial goods through cognitive and intellectual labour which supposes that the meaning of productivity shifts drastically to become the unharnessed spark of art and intellect. Post-Fordism depends on the technical production of immense packages of information, where all the energy of the *social brain* must be drained to produce lifestyles, 'victimless' wars (from the vantage of the assailant), social aesthetic models, and fifteen-minute icons through the simulacra of affects. For the likes of Paul Mason, Hardt and Negri, and the Accelerationist movement, this new rule of labour implies an incalculable expansion of cooperative communication, of spontaneous and un-regularized processes of creativity that cannot be guided or controlled by a niche of power. The key for them is that a magnificent modification has occurred from industrial capitalism to post-Fordism: labour power has become separated from the control of capital, and, hence, capitalism, in order to succeed, must let immaterial production become autonomous; 'Production becomes hegemonic over all other valorization processes' (Hardt and Negri

2009, 25). Specifically, for Hardt and Negri, the result is that the shift allows the multitude, as the bearer of the general intellect, to transcend the contradictions of capital without engaging with any institution and thus to create a post-capitalist Arcadia. What connects all these theses is the belief that the expansion in the need for communication and its free flow harvests a deep contradiction within capital that will ultimately make it blow sky-high without the need of direct confrontation.

The fundamental question is this. Capitalism in order to sustain itself needs private property as one of its bastions. Nevertheless, immaterial labour ferociously changes the scope of private property, because if the true production process is based on the creation and free stream of information, then this kind of property must be by definition common. Information by definition soars freely at high speeds and nobody has the capacity to pack it up and preserve it in stable points of capture. As Paul Mason lucidly explains, intellectual property escapes any possibility of being calculated as prize value: 'Something is broken in the logic we use to value the most important thing in the modern world' (Mason 2015, 4). 'Cognitive' capitalism is a completely new form of capitalism where the content is more valuable than any composite of the material used to create it. It dwarfs the merchant, the industrial as well as the slave capitalism that precedes it. According to Mason, the incapacity to produce a precise balance book for this strain of capitalism lies in the fact that its logic is 'anti-capitalist'. In order for capitalism to function as an information society, it must emancipate the nodes of information and the lattices from where it is programmed. There is an intrinsic impossibility of power as capital to control all of these diffuse processes: in order for immaterial labour to succeed it must be free, it must circulate in a frictionless manner. Therefore, ironically enough, the success of capitalism seems to hinge on an impossible combination; it must free information and the forces that drive them while at the same time it must control its outcome. Consequently, as Mason acknowledges, free information as the backbone of capitalism is at odds with the need of capital to hierarchize and vault the information. According to Mason,

> [One] defense mechanism is to form monopolies—the giant tech companies—on a scale not seen in the past 200 years, yet they cannot last. By building business models and share valuations based on the capture and privatization of all socially produced information, such firms are constructing a fragile corporate edifice at odds with the most basic need of humanity, which is to use ideas freely. (Mason 2015, 4)

Capitalism must freeze and underutilize information, it must sweep the surplus of information under the carpet; but if it does so, it is negating the free market in the very same act. As Mason states, 'The business models of all our modern digital giants are designed to prevent the abundance of information' (Mason 2015, 4). Hence, according to Mason, an economy based on the full utilization of information cannot tolerate a free market based on absolute intellectual property rights. In conclusion, immaterial labour holds the key to the destruction of capital; it is a force that capitalism necessitates but cannot control if it is to deploy all of its potential.

At this point, Paolo Virno poses the right question: 'Is it possible to move from the 'ancient alliance' of Intellect/Labour to a 'new alliance' of Intellect/political action?' (Virno 2004, 68).

A new and vigorous movement seems to offer an answer: the *Accelerationist* (Williams and Srnicek 2013). The basic thesis is that capitalism itself is the great hindrance for the dream of the Enlightenment, and that any blockage to creativity and technological innovation lies in the heart of capital. Thus, pushing capital to its own limits will liberate reason and science as the bastions of a new dawn of humanity. For the Accelerationist, the purpose of any movement of transformation and resistance to capitalisms is not an attempt to return to a 'Golden era' of post-war Fordism or to advance to a techno-utopianism; rather, the ultimate goal of this project is '*a new post-capitalism technosocial platform*'. This process entails four specific traits: (1) accelerate the process of technological evolution—that is to say, to harness every technical advance that allows a reconfiguration of the material platform of today's society; (2) take sociopolitical action to open the pathway to a real self-mastery of the society; (3) develop an '*ecology of organisations*' that combines '*legitimate vertical authority*' and distributed horizontal forms of sociality (in this sense, the key lies in avoiding becoming '*slaves of either a tyrannical totalitarian centralism or a capricious emergent order beyond our control*'); and (4) in general, work towards the objective of creating the conditions for a real democracy (self-mastery of the people) and a material platform that enable a new hegemony that overcomes the value system of capitalism. According to their manifesto, 'The left must take advantage of every technological and scientific advance made possible by capitalism society' (Williams and Srnicek 2013).

In order to evaluate all of these proposals, we must turn to their prophetic origin, Marx's description of the *general intellect* and of *objectified labour*. The key to understand the crossroads of post-Fordism lies in the combinations of living labour and fixed capital as well as their profound transformation in the appearance of the machine as the new sign of capitalism.

As reiterated by Virno, Marx describes labour as an abstract element of purposeful activity aimed at the production of use-values; it is, then, the organic renewal between man and nature (Virno 2002, 66). Levinas gives us a wonderful opening for this discussion: 'The way of access to the fathomless obscurity of matter is not an idea of infinity, but of labor' (Levinas 1979, 159).

Within the grasp of labour, matter remains absolutely indeterminate, and the finality of matter to be a form of commoditization is eschewed, for commodity imposes a finality while labour only returns to the relation as the source of movement; the finality and the source become one, the common. Labour defines matter in the continuum of doing and being. The ruse of capitalism is to turn labour itself into a thing to be devoured, a thing to be possessed. As an extension of the relation, the relation of labour to a thing is not transformative, it is creative, and its aim is not to grab a definite possession over the thing but to liberate its access without destruction and alienation. The potentiality of a thing is not its primordial matter but rather the open access to it through labour, its coming forth as exteriority through its enjoyment as a being in common. Labour has always been the immeasurable menace of the transformation of movement, that which dislocates the idea from its abstract pureness. Labour is the axe of the venerable substance, what transverses it and unveils the movement from thing to being. Capitalism is its inversion, for the relation always has to be mediated by whatever stands in the place of substance, a pre-given that determines the outcome of the relation, a *qualification* as we have proved extensively. Labour turned into property is the final eradication of living labour's potentia. Potentia is not in the matter but in labour. Its aim beyond itself is not to be useful—for this would reintroduce a finality of the thing—but to be shared, which already expresses need: the need of life and the life that needs.

The conclusion flashes with simplicity: living labour is tantamount to being singular plural. As pictured by Levinas, 'Labor does not consist in being first in a continuous chain of causes' (Levinas 1979, 166). Living labour consists in the actuality of the immanence of the encounter. It binds potentiality and actuality in an equilibrium of forces and brings things to intellection. Living labour is the possibility of beginning of a world that commences to condense itself as political. Not the *where* of politics but the *how* of the world. In the sense of final causes, labour is its own cause; in terms of efficient cause, the relation is the cause of labour, which makes every relation a relation of labour and through labour. Labour sets the *what for* of the thing as an umbilical cord to the encounter. The quiddity of things is expounded in work, and the finality of labour is to lose itself in the sharing of labour as the quiddity of things. Negri sees this clearly:

> This necessity resides at the core of Marx's theory of capital, where living labor appears as the foundation and the motor of all production, development, and innovation. This essential source also animates the center of our investigation. Living labor against dead labor, constituent power against constituted power: this single polarity runs through the whole schema of Marxist analysis and resolves it in an entirely original theoretical-practical totality. (Negri 1999, 32)

According to the prevailing interpretations, Marx's construction of the general intellect provides the implicit and direct conditions for superseding capitalism within capitalism. Accordingly, the apparition of the machine as a form to uniform knowledge opens capitalism wide open to the intervention of a general intellect that will liberate labour from the tenets of capital and regenerate the capacity to immanently become autonomous. The *general intellect* is, then, a communicative principle, a connection beyond its parts that shares information at high speed; it is the self-reflection of the human activity in concert. As Mason recounts, 'Marx imagined information coming to be stored and shared in something called a "general intellect"—which was the mind of everybody on Earth connected by social knowledge, in which every upgrade benefits everybody. . . . And, he wrote, its existence would "blow capitalism sky high"' (Mason 2015, 6).

Let us try to summarize Marx's prophetic answer to the mechanization of capital as a brand new shift in the relations of power. Our aim is to establish if Marx did indeed propose a kind of an immanent tear of the capitalist order from within. Our thesis, in line with the other arguments advanced in this book, is that something else is required to achieve this, something beyond the simple inner contradiction in capitalism through its own mechanization. Our thesis is that a political shift is necessitated at the root of the mechanization. The general intellect cannot free itself unless the origin of the liberation lies in the hidden people. Our understanding is that Marx is already signalling towards such path and that his idea of the *machine* is basically an expression of encryption, perhaps the most basic and fundamental encryption of power.

Marx begins to build his ideal machine in his traditional description of capital:

> Originally, when we examined the development of value into capital, the labour process was simply included within capital, and, as regards its physical conditions, its material presence, capital appeared as the totality of the conditions of this process, and correspondingly sorted itself out into certain qualitatively different parts, *material of labour* (this, not raw material, is the correct expression of the concept), *means of labour* and *living labour*. On one side, capital was divided into these three elements in accordance with its material composition; on the other, the *labour process* . . . was their moving unity, the product their static unity. (Marx 2015/1857, 691)

Nevertheless, for Marx, something amazing occurs within the logic of capital that transforms the whole picture, introducing a novelty so strong that a new definition is required. The key to it all is the definition of *fixed capital* (means of labour). As we know, fixed capital is regarded as the part of capital which is locked into the production process (machines, buildings, warehouses, land, equipment, etc.). While floating capital is consumed, fixed capital is merely used in the extended process of production. Here is Marx's astonishing conclusion:

> [O]nce adopted into the production process of capital, the means of labour passes through different metamorphoses, whose culmination is the *machine,* or rather, an *automatic system of machinery* (system of machinery: the *automatic* one is merely its most complete, most adequate form and alone transforms machinery into a system), set in motion by an automaton, a moving power that moves itself; this automaton consisting of numerous mechanical and intellectual organs, so that the workers themselves are cast merely as its conscious linkage. (Marx 2015/1857, 694)

According to Marx's amazingly sharp insight, means of labour are transformed from use value to fixed capital. This is the crucial transition in capitalism that turns the machine into the ideal form of the concentration of power. If the means of labour remain as such, that is, as a simple part of the realization process of capital, then labour merely suffers a formal modification within the process. Nevertheless, when it enters into the process of production it is elevated by capital to stand as the vortex of all the system and all of the processes. The machine accomplishes a crucial feat for capitalism: it snatches the use value away from the means of labour and turns them to represent the entirety of the capitalist process as fixed capital. Hence, when the means of labour stood on their own they were necessarily connected to labour as living labour, but now as fixed capital, living labour is absorbed, granting capital ideal conditions for appropriation. Hence, in Marx's words, 'In no way does the machine appear as the individual worker's means of labour' (Marx 2015/1857, 693).

The fundamental twist accomplished by the machine is to mutilate as it inverts the relation of labour to means of labour. Hence, if the labourer passed onto the means of labour his own virtuosity and sealed its own finality through his own creativity, now the relation is the opposite: it is the machine that transfers to the worker its own virtuosity. Virtuosity is passed from the machine onto labour. 'Rather, it is the machine which possesses skill and strength in place of the worker, is itself the virtuoso, with a soul of its own in the mechanical laws acting through it' (Marx 2015/1857, 694).

The transformation is political at its roots and economic in its consequences. When the machine was seen from the optics of means of labour, it was utterly available to labour; labour commanded it and created reality from its use, so the means of labour simply expressed living labour. But when the machine is transformed to fixed capital, the labourer is separated from it and becomes its appendix. Thus what is fundamental to understand in Marx's diagnosis is that the machine organizes, directs, and makes labour dependent. The machine subordinates and 'objectifies' labour. In other words, through the machine the productive relation is encrypted and solidified in a political decision that is previous to the relation itself. When the relation sprouts out in materiality, any outcome is already ingrained in the machine. The point of rupture of living labour is that the machine concentrates a planned and centralized outcome of labour as capital. The machine is what ultimately guarantees the conversion of living labour to dead labour and hence to capital. We are before a new category of labour that is decided by the intervention of the machine: objectified labour. In Marx's words, 'a power which, as the appropriation of living labour, is the form of capital' (Marx 2015/1857, 694). What becomes clear is that there is a previous and defining political decision that establishes the relation of fixed capital and labour. And although Marx sees in this new composition the possibility of an internal shock of capitalism, he is also signalling that the production of such a reality is rooted in a political decision.

The transition accomplished by capital is fundamental if we are to understand the capacity to break free from capital, because it ultimately entails the most pervasive way to solidify power and make potestas immune. As Marx states, 'In machinery, objectified labour confronts living labour within the labour process itself as the power which rules it' (Marx 2015/1857, 693). The fundamental aspect is that objectified labour confronts and subordinates living labour not only by appropriating it, but also by becoming the sole producer of any social process itself.

The ideal machine subsumes all of the factors of production and it automatizes them under one rule. The fundamental shift is this: Fixed capital escapes its relation with capital as a mere product or as the means of labour and literally becomes the machine of the concentration of all aspects of capital. This conclusion is formulated by Marx as follows:

> The *production process has ceased to be a labour process* in the sense of a process dominated by labour as its governing *unity*. Labour appears, rather, merely as a conscious organ, scattered among the individual living workers at numerous points of the mechanical system; subsumed under the total process of the machinery itself, as itself only *a link of the system, whose unity exists not in the living workers, but rather in the living (active) machinery*, which confronts his individual, insignificant doings as a mighty organism. (Marx 2015/1857, 697)

Human labour becomes a robotics of power under strict rules of operation. We are before Isaac Asimov's three rules applied backwards: the machine determines what labour can do under the legal constitution of the invariants of capital. We are before the perfect description of encryption. Marx is not thinking of a material machine locked down in some bunker connecting all the data systems draining them in one shaft of information. Nor is he thinking of an autonomous cybernetic brain that determines the livelihood of all others. What Marx is describing is a dispositif that rules social production through the reduction of labour to obedience. This is also the reduction of labour to a state of incapacity, because there is a machine that withholds all the codes, signs, signifiers, graphs, and ciphers of communication. We are before a new lexicon of power, a new constitution of language through a strictly scrutinized determination of its meanings where signification is bottled up in an apex that is utterly controlled.

Before everything else, the machine stands for a method of absorption of knowledge. The general intellect connected to the machine hierarchizes knowledge as it hides differing kinds of *knowledges*. In plain sight, it erects a pyramid of the uses of knowledge, the keys and codes to encrypt it, and it determines the few that are authorized to use it. It is, to my knowledge, the only time that Marx uses the term *social brain*:

> The capital accumulation of knowledge and of skill, of the general productive forces of *the social brain*, is thus absorbed into capital, as opposed to labour, *and hence appears as an attribute of capital*, and more specifically of *fixed capital, in so far as it enters into the production process as a means of production proper. Machinery appears, then, as the most adequate form of fixed capital, and fixed capital, in so far as capital's relations with itself are concerned, appears as the most adequate form of capital as such.* (Marx 2015/1857, 694)

We have, then, the complete landscape of the operation. While the first part of the operation was to turn means of labour to fixed capital, the second one accomplishes something even more powerful. All the knowledge in the world is absorbed by the machine and thus knowledge (creativity, cooperativity, memory, action) is absorbed into capital and begins to appear simply as a discrete part of the production process.

To be sure, it is impossible to absorb *all* of knowledge: it is a physical impossibility to count something immaterial as material—but this is precisely the point! This is the unprecedented sleight of hand of capitalism, its *magnum opus*. We are before the exact definition of power in a solid state. The great power of the machine is to determine that there is something monolithic and stable called knowledge, and thereunto to define the possible combinations that would render it the *only* knowledge. And to be sure, for a certain form of knowledge to be deemed the only knowledge, it must be valued as expedient to capitalism.

It is here that the recent work of Colombian philosopher Gabriel Mendez-Hincapie is more than illuminating. According to Mendez, the stage of modern politics is set for the struggle between the social brain (*Das gesell-schaftliche Hirn*), which embodies the utter self-determination of the general productive forces, against the potestas of the individual intellect incarnated in what Hardt and Negri would call the *republic of property*. Accordingly, the machine stands for the *actuality* of power as potestas since it bottles up all knowledge and turns labour to conditioned labour while it converts the means of labour into fixed capital. According to Mendez, potentia must be conceived as equivalent with the social brain, while potestas is equated with the individual intellect that encrypts all knowledge and conceals it. Consequently, actuality is marked by the fact that all knowledge is 'locked up' in the machines, and thus it constitutes an alien power utterly opposed to the people and to democracy. Mendez invites us to think what would happen if the *damné* would seize the control of cyberspace. According to Mendez, 'at this moment an Event of incalculable proportions would take place, all the knowledge accumulated by humanity from its diverse origins would be actualized continuously in the brains of the excluded creating an authentic social brain' (Mendez-Hincapie 2015a). I believe Mendez-Hincapie delivers one of the most overwhelming and precise interpretation of Marx's manoeuver. The social brain supposes that living labour is the undying open point of creativity and of sharing. Capitalism, in order to be what it is, must appropriate the social brain and turn it to a particular form of controlled knowledge. The way to suffocate it is to encrypt every action and creation of living labour into a machine that absorbs and conceals knowledge, that is, to turn the commonality of potentia to a particularity of potestas. If the concealment of power was achieved politically by deciding who is included in knowledge and who is not, the appropriation of power must also be a political act that decides the demolition of the act of exclusion. The point being that the simple continuation of the flow of information under the same conditions established by the ideal machine of capital only serves to ensure its posterity.

Of course, to gain way into the ideal machine, we must confront and decrypt singular machines and their operation. Machines, as information technologies, remain as a strong variant of physics in the solid state. Along with the insights provided by the Accelerationist, we must begin to master these technologies through their sophisticated artificial languages that are encapsulated as brain functions and laced in networks. The culture of the machines should not remain hidden from the hidden people. As maintained by Méndez Hincapie (2015a), radical democracy needs to connect to the masterminds of the general intellect. We need to connect with these layers of the middle class that are experts in programming and thus encrypting the language of machines. Only with their help can the hidden people take control of the solid state.

Encryption signals to the way a faction of the middle class became expert in sophisticated languages, which, as one definition of encryption reads, 'retain the possibility of enunciation of truth and define the scope of the problems and their solution' (Méndez Hincapie and Sanín-Restrepo 2012). For this reason, machines have a major role to play in the emancipation. Just imagine the prodigious force of all that knowledge that is bottled up in a summit being released through the commons. While such a thing happens, machines are still being programmed by expert elites trained in sophisticated languages that define their areas of possibility, while the purpose of the machines serves only the power of capital; the machine remains utterly encrypted and is still a weapon in the hands of capital.

This is Marx's point of the encryption of labour in fixed capital through the machine. Insofar as machinery develops with the accumulation of society's science, of productive force generally, general social labour presents itself not in labour but in capital, and science does not present as open to society but shuttered inside a solid power. As Marx concludes, as long as the productive force of society will continue to be measured as fixed capital, 'Capital appropriates knowledge free of charge' (Marx 2015/1857, 696). Ultimately, then, the machine is the organization of power, and this is the point, it is the means of encryption of all the social energies (Energia) and all social productions.

When Virno is thinking of the machine, he imagines the possibility of a contraption that absorbs all knowledge like a super turbo funnel: 'Even if social knowledge was really ever fully absorbed in the technical machines in the era of industrialization, this would be completely unthinkable in the post-fordist context' (Virno 2004). But I believe that Marx's point is not the idea of an actually existing machine which you could sabotage with hammers, clubs, and pikes, but rather a system of encryption that acts like a code that decides what knowledge is and feeds production from the top. Marx's point is that, if the general intellect is kept as fixed value, then the core of capitalism is retained by capitalist rule. Again, the point is not that all knowledge can be concentrated in one specific materiality, the point is that the simulacrum of the ideal machine creates the fantasy of such possibility and with it erects a wall of prohibition to the access and use of language as its first and utmost political deed. We can even extend this insight to its full-blown possibility: the fact that there is a decision through which knowledge composes capital means that the social fabric is simply its composite and thus secondary production, and hence communication, is severed from the beginning.

According to the likes of Virno and Negri, living labour incarnates the general intellect (the 'social brain'), which Marx called the 'pillar of production and wealth'. But according to them, the general intellect is no longer absorbed in fixed capital: it no longer represents only the knowledge contained in the system of the machines, but rather it is fashioned in a horizontal and smooth surface of integration. The incapacity of structures of power to capture this living intellect is due to its intense mobility, to the capacity of verbal cooperation of a multitude of living subjects to create new sets of meanings, as an abstract apparatus of consciousness reflected in a web of endless communication that cannot be stopped or enumerated by capital. In Virno's words,

> It seems legitimate to maintain that, according to the very logic of economic development, it is necessary that a part of the general intellect not congeal as fixed capital but unfold in communicative interaction, under the guise of epistemic paradigms, dialogical performances, linguistic games. In other words, public intellect is one and the same as cooperation, the acting in concert of human labor, the communicative competence of individuals. (Virno 2004, 65)

I think, then, that they are missing the crucial point that Marx is trying to put across. Marx's point is that the general intellect as a structure of power is encrypted, which rests on the capacity of capital to outrageously claim to have accumulated the whole of human knowledge. What truly has been accumulated is the political power and legal capacity to denote such power, to inscribe it within stringent zones of control of its enunciation. Take, for example, another key claim made by Virno: 'In Post-Fordism, the general intellect does not coincide with fixed capital, but manifests itself principally as a linguistic reiteration of living labor' (Virno 2004, 106). Definitely, the information society unleashes an unparalleled quantity of information that serves as the concretion of materiality and that depends on ever-rising creativity and means of circulation. Nevertheless, what Marx is signalling is something deeper: knowledge and the access to it are already organized as an epistemological paradigm. And though it is true that this change in the nature of 'real abstractions' entails that social relations are ordered by abstract knowledge rather than the exchange of equivalents, it is also true that such an abstraction is not garnered from within the communication itself. Rather, the possibilities of communication are established beforehand in a political decision that determines who has access and to what. It is thus not true that communication, as the immanent and constitutive zone of knowledge, erects a materiality named from within communication; rather, communication is a derivative of the power to define communication within the machine. The machine is the ideal contraption, the figure of the organization of energies that transforms Energeia into Entelecheia before communication has even begun. In this sense, the machine is a kit of instructions, a law vested with the power to organize matter into a certain form, into a certain substance. The ideal machine is, in Gramscian terms, the inner code that organizes hegemony. It is ultimately the constitution of the rules of language. The machine not only turns fixed capital into the preeminent form of capital, even more so, it organizes capital as a certain organization of knowledge that cannot escape the rules of its own organization. The machine draws the perfect circle of power: it determines not only the meaning of language but also the zones that are legitimate to activate it or silence it. It determines in one swift and self-contained gesture the limits of knowledge—and, thus, the limits of power.

In brief, we can describe the main features of Marx's ideal machine of power as follows. The machine, rather than being a material apparatus, is the organizational technology of the system, and through it the mystification of the social relations is complete. If social relations are mystified, that immediately means that any production through communication is also mystified. As long as communication depends on an elitist programming that determines its possible combinations and outcomes, communication remains the optimal servile weapon in the hands of capital. The ideal machine is not a totality of *knowing all* but a system of discernibility of language that controls and guides its own application. It cannot capture all the information but it can direct all partial intelligence towards particular aims and has the capacity not only to store huge amounts of data but also to select the relevance of such data and its pragmatic use. In the same sense, it possesses a centripetal movement of absorption of information and a centrifugal movement in which all its parts communicate with singular instances of power. The principal trait of the machine, according to Marx, is to direct the force of production while it directs the processes of social life. The ideal machine acts as the scheme of production in a descending scale, so the importance of the machine is not so much about *what* it knows but *how* it knows it. Knowing is always social, always in an open-ended and uncontrollable swarm. Hence, what the ideal machine controls are the access points of knowledge and the catalogued order of its relevance. Put simply, the ideal machine is the *simulacrum of the social brain*. Therefore, the machine is before all the point of absorption of knowledge into one solid form, one particular design of power as the utter mechanization of power. Ultimately, the ideal machine solves the primordial conundrum of conflict within capitalism. The machine guarantees that any contradiction between economic and political powers, as the essence of capitalism, will always be solved in anti-democracy.

Marx knew all too well that the machine is above all the operation that encloses the knowledge and skill of workers and scholars as objectified knowledge and skill, opposing the scattered workers as a dominant power. Hence, the intellect is absorbed and encrypted in potestas as a mere particularity, an extension that captures the channels of communication and binds them together, directing them to the core of the system. However, the self-active machine is more than a technical mechanism. The machine does not appear here limited to its technical aspects, but rather as a mechanical-intellectual-social assemblage; it is the face of power, the mechanism of potestas—in brief, the concentration of power in a solid state. The machine as the simulacrum of the social brain becomes the perfect system of appropriation of all the living energies in a concatenation of power as knowledge and knowledge as technology of being. The machines mediate every and any aspect of social production

Following Deleuze and Guattari, the machine is a topological knot where everything is connected without confusion, where everything flows together and is distributed (Deleuze and Guattari 1983, 242). It is thus the crown and throne of the encryptor. The machine concentrates the technical, the mechanical, and the social as one and the same thing. As recognized by Marx, the ideal machine would cost nothing; it adds no value to the production process and thus reduces the cost of labour to virtually zero and would reverse the logics of surplus and exploitation one after the other like falling domino pieces.

As a machine of knowledge, its programming is fairly simple. A very elemental set of rules embodies the science inscribed in it. It reduces the complexity of laws, while life is reduced to infinite combinations of binary numbers and very finite results. It is ultimately a processing machine that selects the information relevant to commoditization. If the machine is something, it is first a filter and then a centripetal motion, but, more importantly, it defines the usefulness of other machines. Under these terms, the ideal machine is literally a *deus ex machina* that resolves the thread of life. As Aristotle announces in his poetics, it is something that breaks the casual stream of events; it brings the unwarranted result to the fore, a final conclusion that orders the particles of time (Aristotle. Poet. 1454a33).

Continuing Marx's elaboration, we find that, if anything, what capitalism has accomplished through this mechanization is the encryption of living labour. In Marx's words, 'The quantitative extent and the effectiveness (intensity) to which capital is developed as fixed capital indicate the general degree to which capital is developed as capital, as power over living labour' (Marx 2015/1857, 699). This is the X that marks the spot of a major shift of power. Accordingly, capital can only become omnipotent when fixed capital determines the power over living labour. The fundamental transformation of power is that machinery escapes its mechanical nature to become the ultimate determinant of social relations through the absorption and control of knowledge.

What is crucial to Marx's analysis is that the ideal machine creates a social subjectivity that is central to its own conformation. The machine is the simulation of the capacity to create those subjectivities. In other words, as soon as knowledge is built in the machine as a certain distribution of codes and interactions, it is also ingrained in the subjectivities that participate in it at the same speed and intensity. Henceforth, the development of the social individual which appears as the great foundation stone of production and of wealth is simulated inside the machine, and its power to distribute identities is tied to particular forms of knowledge. The machine thus creates its own point of vulnerability: it has to be fuelled by intellects that are constantly displacing information. Yet the point Marx is making is that what has to be decrypted is the particular organization, the modes in which singularities are plugged into the great machine of production. As he explains,

> On the one side, then, it calls to life all the powers of science and of nature, as of social combination and of social intercourse, in order to make the creation of wealth independent (relatively) of the labour time employed on it. On the other side, it wants to use labour time as the measuring rod for the giant social forces thereby created, and to confine them within the limits required to maintain the already created value as value. (Marx 2015/1857, 706)

The key concept we have to clutch onto is that the machine stands for the accumulated knowledge of society; it is the physiological accumulation of the social brain. Nonetheless, it is above all the ideal scheme for exclusion of diverse knowledges and the ultimate hierarchization of the valid knowledge of social production. Hence, the first thing we must acknowledge is that the place for production of the political moment is actuality as Energeia that opposes and undermines the ideal machine, which amounts to politics as Entelecheia. Better yet, the key point to grasp is that the machine is itself the process for the transformation of Energeia to Entelecheia.

Would it not be true, then, that where Hardt and Negri see the blossoming of a multitude connected by this new principle of cooperation and zigzagging of know-hows as the principle of deterioration of Empire (and thus the opportunity of overcoming capitalism), we are forced instead to see an even more stringent form of conducting politics as Entelecheia? Where they see a smooth navigation of the multitude to the shores of democracy, we identify a brutish hand kneading a mass to a blob. The kernel of immaterial and intellectual work is that it is directed to very specific *telos* that the work itself is not capable of determining, so the political landscape not only remains empty but is simulated by forms of creativity that already have precise slots to fill within capital.

As Nick Dyer-Witheford reminds us, regarding the criticisms directed at the authors of *Futur Antérieur*,

> Perhaps the most serious of these objections is that, in its capitalist form, 'general intellect' is not 'general' at all, but rather structured by an intensely hierarchical division of labour. This restricts crucial knowledges to a narrow stratum of privileged, and hence loyal, employers, leaving the rest to suffer the effects of technological deskilling. (Dyer-Witheford 1999, 503)

We have already made clear that this 'biopolitical' transition of power, as Hardt and Negri call it, is insufficient to give a complete picture on its own of the complexities of power in our times of 'porous sovereignties'. Hence, immaterial production cannot become an over determining factor of power; it cannot sway away from servitude, classic forms of slavery, biopower, and stringent forms of sovereignty (borders, irregular wars, prisons, armies). These all act as a compound of power and its privation, where, as we have shown, the true overdetermining concept is the separation of the people and the hidden people. But even granting the biopolitical thesis a proficiency certificate to explain power, it would do so in the adverse way in which Hardt and Negri intend it to be. As a mere descriptive device, it fails to capture that the producer, no matter how advanced and detached from control she is, is still dependent on a major split within politics which they seem to pass over.

The social brain considered from Energeia (living labour) is already a disposition of organized parts as an actuality that is not qualified, while the outcome of what it can do is not decided beforehand but will only come about as what the mutual affections of an infinity connected freely to language might determine. The latter means that there is no previous condition or principle that orchestrates its composition from outside of it or its finality. Common life is its beingness, but, nevertheless, the defining instant of capitalism is that it must pervade Energeia in order to transform it into an Entelecheia, and to garner said transformation it must encrypt the common language and the open sources of communication into a controlled and hierarchized knowledge and know-how. The 'virtuosity without a script' that Virno assigns to *dunamis* as the production of a common language with no further qualifications would render itself helpless before the might that potestas has of severing and disconnecting its parts in order to direct labour into a finality. The only remaining possibility, then, is to politize the situation. Only when a clash occurs between politics considered as Energeia and politics considered as Entelecheia can we behold the true meaning of politics. In other words, the potential of a common can only be exercised once politics is considered to be the actuality of Energeia.

This suggests that letting the genie of potentia out of the bottle requires a previous act of politicization—not so much through an organization of particulars in a predefined disposition, but rather by the opening of such a possibility. The *social brain* as potentia is subdued by the organization of capital, and thus plugged into the machinery of surplus value through a systematic practice of organizing labour. Nevertheless, the social brain is also kept as a mere potentia through the atomization of subjects by the rule of law, and the patching of interests and appetites through the piecemeal of public administration and public policies. At the same time, it is thrusted onto the spectacle of political simulacrum through a toxic assortment of false decisions: to elect, to choose liberty, to uphold the principles of liberal democracy.

The coercive presence of encryption is achieved through a hierarchized society acting as a funnel of information to implant its own version of knowledge at the top of the pyramid. Through the privatization of the common of language, the free use of ideas is still commoditized and *price* is still the prohibitive barrier. The privatization of language is done through the neoliberal privatization of education and telecommunications of all sorts. As long as a minority controls the mobility and legal determination of language and holds the panhandle of the flux of money, the general intellect is simply an echo of power in a solid state, a mimicry of communication. Following Paul Mason, 'Neoliberalism, then, has morphed into a system programmed to inflict recurrent catastrophic failures' (Mason 2015, 3). For that reason, the machine keeps on crushing the working class in Flint, Michigan, Dubai, or anywhere it pleases, as the industrial reserve army grows exponentially and technology becomes more chic and available to all. Hence, as long as it remains encrypted, the liberalization of knowledge has an infinitesimal capacity to avoid the precarization of life. We are all connected to a network, but it is a two-way street. We are built into the machine through bits of data, and the most minute information about ourselves, our tastes, and our debilities are used to reboot the network and feed back into it a detailed profile of docile costumers—no longer the docility of the body on its own, but the docility of our thirsts, tastes, and inclinations. Such information is used as a tool to capture the future by big companies that share the profile with retailers as well as with the NSA or the CIA. What an Edward Snowden or Julian Assange has accomplished is fundamental for emancipation, but not because their acts feed a horizontal general intellect: rather, because those acts decrypt the true order of the enclosed and hierarchized general intellect. The order of the ideal machine is to monopolize data and to absorb the information into commerce. We are still in a world of abundant information and political and material scarcity. This is the reason why 3D printers are not used to combat hunger but to create more commodities. That is why a person at the top of the hierarchy can literally buy ten or fifteen years of life from an illness that kills millions, without the access to medical technology, within weeks. Each time we are astonished by the new tech trend, then, the first question we must ask is, *is it decrypted, and does it really belong to all of us?*

Automated machines produce gigantic amounts of information that the machine itself can dissect, separate, classify, and turn into feedback to strengthen the rule of capital. Hence, decryption of information from such machines cannot simply be done by relying on the capacity of information to separate itself from the source that commands it; rather, it must be a political act that recognizes such order of things as anti-democratic, and as anti-political.

It has become clear in this book that the *acceleration* of modernity is just the acceleration of coloniality if what is at its base is not the destruction of the division of the hidden people and the people as a totality. If this is not the root of change, acceleration will remain but a sexy and misleading sound bite. Certainly, movements like *#Accelerate* offer a fertile ground for new forms of resistance. For example, the accelerationists highlight the importance of becoming literate in technical fields like mathematical modelling in economics, and decryption will make it possible to understand the political and social grounds of this kind of model and thus determine the direction needed to obtain true fields of emancipation. We need movements and counter powers, organizations and alliances, hactivists and cyber-poets, all connected through one common truth: that the only viable action of politics arises when we move from within the actuality as Energeia of the hidden people. And, furthermore, when we comprehend that politics is anchored in the principle that the hidden people must become 'the people'.

NEW SOVEREIGNTY, OLD TRICKS

The difficulty—and, indeed, impossibility—of identity in relation to totality, is, as we have shown, that totality is a Moebius strip: it is totality to the extent that interiority and exteriority are mutually suspended and imply each other at the same moment. Not only does this appear as an aberration vis-à-vis the principle of non-contradiction, but it is a contraption for making impossible the fullness of individuality. The finality of such a construction is that any individual is forced both to belong and to be excluded from the totality, to yield individuality as soon as it comes in contact with the totality.

What we are aiming at is subjectivity not as an idea which has to be haunted because it is always on the move, nor individuality as a lavish automaton moved by the lever of moral judgement, and we are certainly not advancing individuality as the mirror of death. What we are aiming at is individuality as the foundation of the idea of infinity: individuality as the magnetic field of the production of being. Production is the factory of being, and only in the encounter can there be a production of life, a setting in motion of affections and its modes as the creation of meaning through the other. Truth produced in totality is an evidence of simulacra. When the truth of totality is imposed upon the encounter, subjects become players adjudicating meaning as a procedure to accomplish the totality which evades them, thus playing the game of lack that can never be fulfilled and that, furthermore, exists precisely on condition that it never be fulfilled.

'Infinity does not first exist, and then reveal itself. Its infinition is produced as revelation, as a positing of its idea in me' (Levinas 1979, 26). The self contains a surplus that does not dwell in his solitary pre-identity. Infinity is what cannot be ascribed to an individual or to a sum of individuals; it is, rather, the product of indefinite encounters, not as a mystical echo but as mathematical exponential. Or, as Levinas put it, '(subjectivity) accomplishes the impossible feat of containing more than it is possible to contain' (Levinas 1979, 26).

Infinity is not a programme installed in individuals as a repetition of the totality which is activated by contact. Infinity, rather, is the name of that contact that shatters totality and its duplicity of inside/outside. Production or labour functions as the spark plug between potentia and actuality that creates infinity. Infinity of being is not, as Heidegger would have it, a containment of fullness of self within itself, an inward sinkhole of being, thought for the sake of filling up the self, but is instead a facing towards the other that means nothing less that the bypassing of any totality meant to inscribe the relation within itself.

To cross the barriers of immanence, Levinas' idea of infinity is a potential that is actualized in the encounter and only in the encounter, where labour and production break through as the backbone of reality. Infinity is only realizable through this contact, through labour. What is substantial—and is more than a mere attitude—is the *letting be* of the other as the only condition of the community. That means not shrouding otherness in a model or totality which will speak for him as representation. The other, recognized through the standard of the law of totality, is what turns the community to a ceremony, the gratification of a protocol which is exactly what the totality aims for, all that totality wants to say is that *all is said*.

Finally, we come across the unavoidable of power: sovereignty. As I believe I have proved, there is no going around it and no leaping over it; any movement within power will have to lock horns with it. Nevertheless, the problem is not only the perseverance of the definition of power that sovereignty ensues, but its capacity to mutate into different forms and qualities that make it so evasive. Certainly, when we stand today before an opaque manifestation of power we cannot recognize in it the same traits that defined it in the times of Bodin or Hobbes or even Schmitt; its focus and standard have shifted into something new. Notwithstanding, I will set out to prove that even the most profound variations still hold a nucleus, an atomic composition that cannot simply be removed from the charts of power and that continue to define power as domination. We will prove as well that there is something particular, definitive, and constitutive in every coinage of power as domination that carries the seal of sovereignty with it. Even if we speak of its transmutations into biopower, biopolitics, disciplinary societies, or post-Fordism, the essential component of traditional sovereignty is still its beating heart. But we are committed to demonstrate something even deeper than its perseverance. We are set to demonstrate that *only* when we attain a fusion of sovereignty and the hidden people can democracy be obtained.

Earlier we gave the orthodox definition of sovereignty, which we will now take onto new domains. The hard rock definition of sovereignty that became a spoke in the wheel of modern politics is given by Carl Schmitt, as Giorgio Agamben describes:

> Carl Schmitt's definition of sovereignty ('Sovereign is he who decides on the state of exception') became a commonplace even before there was any under-standing that what was at issue in it was nothing less than the limit concept of the doctrine of law and the State, in which sovereignty borders (since every limit concept is always the limit between two concepts) on the sphere of life and becomes indistinguishable from it. As long as the form of the State constituted the fundamental horizon of all communal life and the political, religious, juridi-cal, and economic doctrines that sustained this form were still strong, this 'most extreme sphere' could not truly come to light. The problem of sovereignty was reduced to the question of who within the political order was invested with cer-tain powers, and the very threshold of the political order itself was never called into question. (Agamben 1998, 13–14)

As we have proven in chapter 2, the power of the state has receded from its eminent place of power but only to combine and reinforce other types of power as domination. What became clear in that definition is that, even with the apparent absence of the state in the violence bestowed upon the hidden people, the fundamental and corrosive traits of sovereignty do not wither away but, rather, are included even more doggedly and in increasingly com-plex formats of power.

Consider the following examples. Complex mathematical models that pre-dict the failure of a harvest in China will make a handful of new billionaires, who in turn spike the prices of housing in London, expelling entire popula-tions from the city and generating squander and violence. Colombian farmers are sent to jail because they kept some rice seeds from the previous harvest in order to plant the new one; in doing that, they broke the law that forced them to plant only the genetically modified seeds sold by Monsanto who in turns owns the intellectual property over them.[4] Think of people shouting their lungs out at a girl in a call centre who barely makes ends meet. Think of the mortal crossing of the Mediterranean, of the dispossession of farmers in Africa in order to plant soybeans, of the taking over of Greece by a '*troika*'. Think of how in the richest country in the world 'one in three black males born today can expect to spend time in prison during his lifetime',[5] and how those prisons function as a pseudo-slave appendix of the big corporations, as new industrial concentration camps.[6] Can you consider these realities and still attempt, in seriousness, to tell me that sovereignty is not the juice that commu-nicates all of the pipelines of power as domination in these human disasters? A stern decision of who is included in the law and who is not is the mainstay of all these operations. Sovereignty is what makes all of these expressions of domination come full circle; it maintains them and directs them in line with the legitimacy of capital. All the victims described above are victims of the same garden variety of virus, sovereignty. Not only is the presence of sovereignty felt in the very air we breathe, but all of its components are still present even if dislocated from the state as its primary protagonist.

In all of the facts depicted above, violence is still made possible thanks to the act of a sovereign who decides the law and its limits, its point of reverberation and of banishment. Sovereignty still defines an act of a sovereign—a diffuse sovereign, but a sovereign nonetheless, as he who decides on the state of exception, as a suspension of the validity of the law, garnering an inside and outside of the legal order at the same time. The state as the sole incarnation of the sovereign may have shifted and trickled into different and prolix nodules of activation, but sovereignty, as *he who decides over the exception*, is still at the core of operability for the machine of power as domination.

One of the most lucid insights into the paradox of sovereignty is provided by William Rasch:

> The sovereign, whether individual and collective, does not stand like some lonely deity at the pinnacle of an earthly triangle, surveying its domain, but rather stands both inside and outside the law, both inside and outside the systems of norms that it both follows and fashions. In fact, precisely where and how distinctions are drawn remains oddly hidden by sovereignty. It remains undecidable from which side of a differentiation the line is drawn. (Rasch 2008a, 2)

The trademark of the sovereign is to create order and with it its externality. The sovereign, as the origin of language, declares both what is inside and outside of it. He determines normality and abnormality in the same drive. The decision on the differences (between the political and the legal, for example) is not inside or outside the difference, *it is* the difference itself; it is the constitutive gap of such inside and outside; in other words, it is the state of exception (Rasch 2008b, 43). Only from this paradoxical place can the sovereign decide on the undecidable. The key to grasp here is that *only* from the state of exception can the difference between inside and outside be accomplished. The barbarian to be civilized, or the underdeveloped to be developed, justifies at once the system that excludes her. In addition, only in the state of exception can the sovereign subordinate the bare life (that problem called *the people*), which is the adulterated but true origin of the legitimacy of sovereignty which needs to be constantly neutralized. Only in the state of exception can law suspend its validity, and therefore normality, to act on the dispossessed and marginalized outside the norms of law but with all the violence of the legitimacy of the law. Hence, when the system comes into contact with bare life, it suspends its validity as a direct formula both of integration and exclusion. One may retort that law within normality is enough to deprive the marginalized, to keep them at bay from the ambrosias of law. This would be partially right; it is the normal horizon of inequality through the thick and thin of law. But precisely in order for the law to act as *norm* it depends on creating a constitutive exception where the law itself is enabled to act as the floodgate of subjectivity. The point we are making is that such division signals a major short circuit in sovereignty which represents the nucleus of the fundamental split between power and democracy in the modern world.

As Agamben neatly proclaims, the paradox of the law is that it is placed by sovereignty *outside itself*: 'I the sovereign standing outside the law declare that there is no outside the law' (Agamben 1998, 17). Exception becomes the form of exclusion as both concepts become indiscernible. The excluded, the hidden people, are kept in a relation to the norm in the form of a suspension. The norm withdraws from the exception as soon as it creates it, thus, they are both in an intimate relation, and only the sovereign can decide the outcome. The original structure of the law is preserved in its suspension as it irradiates to what it excludes. What law generates in this queer actuality is the power to create the exteriority in a complete dependence to the interiority as the *band*, as the quintessential cusp of *abandonment* (Agamben 1998, 23). But the fundamental issue is as follows. Sovereignty, if it is to retain any classical feature (Bodin), has to remain the highest, most absolute, and perpetual value of power—which includes excluding. The sovereign is thus he who decides on the regulation of the rules of inclusion/exclusion through a law that suspends itself to claim the utter exteriority from the exception. The rule, the norm, can only be proved in its exception, and so, Benjamin declares, 'the state of exception in which we live is the norm' (Benjamin 2010).

Hardt and Negri demonstrate that the traditional Westphalian sovereignty has suffered a deep transformation where it has dissociated itself from the national state as its natural home. In the same analysis, it is also true that law is no longer the single propeller of power. Nevertheless, and against Hardt and Negri, the same cannot be said for sovereignty as power of domination which continues to define the contours of the world. As Costas Douzinas holds, sovereignty perseveres as a quotidian power (Douzinas 2013, 102). Sovereignty is present whenever the sea is declared '*nostrum*' and thousands of immigrants drown in its coastline, whenever a sanitary wall is built to keep out the poor and needy and wherever women are confined to a nurturing activity. All of these acts of power, even if they interact as formally independent of the state and the law, are supported by the metaphysical manifestation of sovereignty. The very qualification of migrant, poor, and feminine suppose a previous legal act of subjectification that maintains the perfect resonance of the harmony between inside and outside and between exception and norm.

The totality of the people can only act as a consistent simulacrum when there is something outside of it that acts as its fundament of legitimacy and validity.

Agamben asks what the relationship between politics and life is, if the latter is presented as something that should be included through an exclusion. The focal point of Agamben's thesis is that the *homo sacer*—who, before modernity, law pushed outside where anyone could dispose and bestow death upon him—is included by modern biopolitics to the point that law coincides exactly with him, *but it does not include him in the norm, but in the exception* (Agamben 1998, 14). The stronghold of Agamben's thesis, which we share to a great extent, is that the sovereign of modernity, no matter with what name he is baptized and what forms he may incarnate, is whoever decides on the exception. Deciding on the exception means an integration of the *homines sacri* or bare life not completely within the order (norm), or completely outside of it (chaos), but on the fringes, on the threshold between one and the other (state of exception).

The critique stemming from Hardt and Negri is that to focus excessively on sovereignty produces what they call an *Apocalypticism*, and places power as a frame of knowledge very close to *new fascisms* (Hardt and Negri 2009, 3). The problem with this picture, according to them, is that it focuses on transcendent authority and violence instead of immanence and the multitude, thus mystifying the daily functioning of constitutional processes. Excessive focus on sovereignty becomes a sort of theological adoration of power, not in the sense of divine authority but in the sense that sovereign power begins to occupy with it a transcendental position above society and outside its structures (Hardt and Negri 2009, 4)

It is obvious that sovereignty has fluctuated and accommodated to ever-changing conditions at a ravaging speed, but this is not the point. Our point is that no matter how intense the changes are, power in coloniality depends on one thing, and one thing only, the creation of a hidden people, and such a feat can only be accomplished through the exercise of sovereignty. Furthermore, the magma that moulds power relations in coloniality is only possible through sovereignty as a coagulation of power and an extreme and violent decision on who and what is inside the norm and who and what in the state of exception. Sovereignty is not the tenuous glimmer of a bygone time but the very site of decision that defines the world. Sovereignty welds neatly together power as domination and legitimacy, and, more importantly, it maintains any kind of violence and the dissolution of the social tissue as a legalized consequence of capitalism.

Take, for example, biopower as a mutation of sovereignty into a new dimension of power. According to Foucault, the synthesis between new social sciences and the need to control emerging populations produced an upsurge in the technologies of power that do not fit with a classical definition of sovereignty. Through statistics, census, medicine, prisons, and schools, the *docile* body is controlled through structures of discipline which are a swarm of institutions that extend beyond the state and its law. What is controlled? The body, the manners, the interactions, desire, and knowledge. This kind of power is symbolized by the *panoptic,* an eye that sees everything without being seen, and 'Its first axiom is that bodies are the constitutive components of the bio-political fabric of being' (Hardt and Negri 2009, 31).

The accommodation of power does not stop there, as Dreyfus and Rabinow explain:

> The other pole of bio-power centered on the body not so much as the means for human reproduction, but as an object to be manipulated. A new science, or more accurately a technology of the body as an object of power, gradually formed in disparate, peripheral localizations. Foucault labels this 'disciplinary power' and he analyzes it at detail in Discipline and Punish. (Dreyfus and Rabinow 1983, 134)

Yet another phase of the transmutations of power is the societies of control. These intensify the rule over the docile body. Every aspect of human activity is controlled, not only by the state, but by every organization that stratifies singularities homogenizing them. Nevertheless, the fundamental feature is that every individual becomes a source of control of itself. The enemy is not only exterior (the terrorist, the fundamentalist), but also interior. The body becomes a site of terror; the enemies are the carbs and gluten, the heart and the belly in its most organic sense. Models of beauty and good sense are erected to be carbon copied. Deleuze speaks of a network of dispositifs where the model is defined by the confession within a *pastoral* diagram of power.

Another phase of the shift of power comes along in post-Fordism. And even though we analysed extensively in the previous section, let us simply signal some of its basic traits in line with our argument. Besides neoliberalism and its machine of privatizations and off-shores and a global interconnected economy through *big data*, the frontiers of power become fuzzy and mobile. For example, national borders as an archetype of national sovereignty become rigid for some people (Mexicans, Syrians) but are always open for money (fiscal paradises). It is the epoch of financialization, which means the great control of money soothsaying the future, the time of 'shadow' banking systems and free trade agreements. It is a time signalled by transformation of property rights into intellectual rights. War on terrorism becomes the privatization of war in a crucial transformation of what Schmitt termed the 'nomos of the earth' as traditionally modern (Schmitt 2006). Nevertheless, for Hardt and Negri, the key to it all is *cognitive capitalism* and *immaterial labour.*

Massive amounts of information are produced, so communication becomes the sign of a power that cannot be controlled by typical standards of power, much less sovereignty.

Yes, all this is true, and it is very powerful stuff, and without the monumental work of the likes of Foucault we would still be trying to measure power through general theories of the state, trying to weigh it by tons. Power as domination is protean, opaque, dispositional; it curves, swirls, and twitches. But in what we have defined coloniality, its defining feature is sovereignty. Our point is very simple. When we talk about the liege of science and power, the panoptic as the ideal architecture of power, or the outsourcing of war and labour, the common bonding force is sovereignty as an act of exclusion and inclusion. The proposition is thus not that power from the sixteenth-century has suffered many dislocations where one of its poles was (national) sovereignty. The correct proposition is that there is a common denominator for power in the last five hundred and so years, and it is called coloniality, and coloniality is a form of power that depends fully on sovereignty as the division of a people as a totality and its hidden counterpart. Hence, even if it is true that forms of power have come and gone, coloniality is still the matrix that defines the configurations of all those variables, which are ultimately the result of keeping the people as both the exception and the false totality of their own makeshift composition. In short, sovereignty is the substance of coloniality, it is the active *machine* of power in coloniality.

TO ESCAPE SOVEREIGNTY IS TO SEIZE IT: THE FUSION OF THE HIDDEN PEOPLE AND SOVEREIGNTY

There is a second dimension in the relation of the people to sovereignty that binds all our pursuits: constituent power. Here the paradox of power becomes the tectonic plate that divides oceans and continents of meanings. Let me formulate the necessary gambit in coloniality that brings everything together in a preposterous foundational paradox: the people must be both the exception and the (simulated) sovereign!

Our wager is that escaping sovereignty is escaping the very possibility of politics. And this is so not because we profess an adoration of sovereignty as eminent, but because it is the very site where the constituent power of the people is abducted. Far from maintaining that politics should always refer to sovereignty, we are making a practical historical claim: coloniality as the factory of potestas depends on proclaiming the sovereignty of the people only to shutter the people inside the prison of sovereignty, deflecting the power to decide to other sites of power. As we have seen, the defining signature of the liberal simulacrum is to allocate sovereignty to the people as the foundation of modernity and coloniality. Without a simulated totality of the people as sovereign, the whole extension of the apparatus of liberalism would be but a stump. It is within the simulacrum where the conversion of the people to sovereignty happens as the elemental particle of power as domination. Modernity has to marshal a contradiction lodged in its core. The people must be kept in the division as hidden or in totality, and the hidden can only be considered as such in the exception, but, at the same time, the liberal simulacrum must elevate the totality to the place of the sovereign. Hence, '*We the sovereign people*' is the crowning masterpiece of the simulacrum. Nevertheless, the simulacrum/exclusion is drawn in a way in which it becomes its own contradiction. How must the liberal apparatus of power respond to this? Drown the constituent power (people as sovereign) in the constituted power (state, the spectacle of the market, people as totality, etc.). We are standing before the collapse of the constituent power to a constituted power, a collapse that defines a paradox that we must unravel in order to pull democracy from its entrails.

The paradox produced between constituent power and constituted power illuminates while it overshadows the entire landscape of political philosophy; this is the enigma of sovereignty and hence of democracy. If it is true that the sovereign is he who decides on the exception and within the exception, then the empire of law, deemed from constituent power, depends, in the last instance, on an abysmal act of violence founded solely on itself. The original act which founds the symbolic, originating the word of the law, is an act that resists validity, for *it is* validity as such. Any positive statute to which this act refers to legitimize itself is imposed as a self-referential act (Žižek 2001). There is no ahistorical point of origin that could contain it within another act, and any effort to find it within what is already constituted will then be futile.

Constituent power escapes any possibility of being understood within the normal forms of the legal system; its shape is incongruent with the order, and to the extent that it establishes the order, it cannot be comprehended in the order itself. When the constitutional tradition of liberalism encounters this monumental hurdle, it overlaps constituent and constituted power and collapses the political within the legal and multiplicity within unity. This misplacement allows liberalism to maintain the very fragile facade of relation and consistency within the terms of the established legal order—a facade that is made solid through the ideological strata of the totality of the people. Nevertheless, it remains a complex shuttered within its own logic because constituent power frontally challenges the very foundations of order.

As Antonio Negri perfectly rounds out the idea of the short circuit between constituent power and sovereignty,

The foundation is inverted, and sovereignty as *suprema potestas* is reconstructed as the foundation itself. But it is a foundation contrary to constituent power; it is a summit, whereas constituent power is a basis. It is an accomplished finality, whereas constituent power is unfinalized; it implies a limited time and space, whereas constituent power implies a multidirectional plurality of times and spaces; it is a rigidified formal constitution, whereas constituent power is absolute process. (Negri 1999, 12)

While constituent power in its nude presence is incomprehensible and escapes the channels of normality, constituted power fits perfectly within the internal logic of the order, because it becomes its mirror. It is thus so much easier to dissolve or convert the constituent within the representational space of the constituted (Badiou 2003). As we have shown, Negri categorically affirms that any actualization of potentia is necessarily its denial (Negri 1999, 21). His argument is that to the extent that the power of the constituent is an absolute, unlimited, and expansive process, its actualization as sovereign power means the destruction of its constituent features, for the only absolute that pervades sovereignty is domination (Negri 1999, 12). The problem of sovereignty announced by Negri is as follows: every actualization of the potentia of constituent power implies necessarily that potentia transforms itself as power as domination. To our amazement, Negri is describing the cellular compound of the problem, but he refuses to take it to its conclusion and transform it into something else. Precisely what we are pointing at is that in order for the architecture of potestas in modernity to remain unfettered, it must accomplish the rarest of feats: it must first organize people as sovereign and then snatch sovereignty as constituent power from her hands. Consequently, it must paradoxically fuse the hidden people as sovereign and exception through the collapse of constituent power to constituted power and thus to sovereignty.

Constituent power determines that the event of creation of the juridical is not juridical in itself. It is in the event of the very creation of the legal where the complete absence of law is captured. The paradox is entrenched in the very origin of the institution, but the institution cannot account for it. Of course, modern horror over lack of precise origins, as well as the need for masters that lead us to stupefaction and command our thoughts and deeds, ignites the legal apparatus to move the centre of imputation of the decision to transcendent and hypothetical models. However, the constituent power of democracy as the index of legitimacy of the system is also its major abnormality, an irreparable contradiction which determines the whole of the system.

A constituent power meets no other limit but itself. It fractures order and pierces the appearance of consistency and stability of the legal system. The internal problem for the system then becomes how to tame its unlimited origins that stubbornly refuse to agree with the system itself. Hence, the key to order, of every regime of liberal power, lies in transmitting the belief in a rationality that sutures each of its productions and that the belief in such a gambit is provable when the effects of the law are rolled back to an original cause (a supreme law, *à la* Kelsen's Grundnorm) that cleanses its torrid past and declares it ahistorical.

'All violence as a means is either lawmaking or law-preserving. If it lays claim to neither of these predicates, it forfeits all validity. It follows, however, that all violence as a means, even in the most favorable case, is implicated in the problematic nature of law itself' (Benjamin 2010, 287). In these terms, Benjamin differentiates constituent power as violence that founds law and constituted power as violence that preserves law. The sovereign is the point of indifference between violence and law, the verge at which violence becomes law and law becomes violence (Agamben 1998, 68). It is not possible to cross directly from the pure normative order to the real social life. Therefore, an act of will, a decision based entirely on itself, is utterly necessary to inaugurate the order and to define its precise hermeneutics. Any legal order, taken in itself, is stuck in an abstract formalism; it cannot bridge the gulf that separates it from real life. 'However (and this is the core of the argument of Schmitt) the decision that crosses the gap does not impose a *concrete order*, but primarily the *formal principle of order* as such' (Žižek 2001, 153). There is no positive content that can be assumed as a universally proven framework to define the principle of order. It is precisely the decision of the sovereign that creates such a framework—that which we call *the principle of order*.

Hobbes was the first to explicitly describe the distinction between the *principle of order* and *any specific order*. The violence that establishes law is the principle of order, an unfounded and extreme decision, decentred and absolute. On the other hand, law as a specific order can only aspire to the violence that preserves law as a *concrete order*. Regarding this relation, Benjamin emphatically states, 'One might perhaps consider the surprising possibility that the law's interest in a monopoly of violence vis-a-vis individuals is not explained by the intention of preserving legal ends but, rather, by that of preserving the law itself' (Benjamin 1986, 281).

According to its canonical meaning, the sovereign is he who decides the exceptional, and in order to do so he needs to be within the exceptional. We have then three compartments: (1) order, (2) exception, and (3) absolute exteriority (chaos). To define what order is and who belongs to the order is therefore to declare who and what is outside of the order. The key in understanding Benjamin's division is that the decision may not come from the order itself, but from the exception, because if it comes from the order we would be before a power that was established by the sovereign and obviously lacks its power. The following passage from Hobbes' *De Cive* illustrates the point we are getting to:

> Moreover, because our Saviour hath not shewed Subjects any other Lawes for the government of a City beside those of nature, that is to say, beside the Command of obedience, no Subject can privately determine who is a publique friend, who an enemy, when Warre, when Peace, when Truce is to be made; nor yet what Subjects, what authority, and of what men, are commodious, or prejudiciall to the safety of the Common–weale. These, and all like matters therefore are to be learned, if need be, from the City, that is to say, from the Soveraign powers. (Hobbes 2000/1651, XI, 97)

What we are detecting progressively is that the violence that preserves the law is not only limited to preserve the particular order as a derivation of the violence that founded the law. Hence, it's not limited to exercise the violence *of the law* and *for the law*, but it stretches much further, and this is the step that Benjamin provokes us to take. When the law exercises violence to preserve the law, in the same act it gives a qualitative leap and seizes formally the gap between constituent and constituted power. Law thus colonizes the violence that founded the law, which is an aberration for it is the violence that identifies the constituent power. It is the violence that is the sole property of constituent and not constituted power. However, the juridical, stemming from the exception, stands as a kind of interface that yields the place of the constituent, achieving the fusion between both brands of violence. This is proven simply by the state of suspension that the hidden people are put to as a result. This is the place for a chain of disastrous confusions: the principle of order is confused with the particular order, constituent power with the law, and democracy with its nothingness.

Hence, the first step taken by liberalism to cauterize the bleeding of constituent power as its matrix of power was to collapse constituent power in the constituted and defer all violence to the state. The constituent power of the people as the first rule of operability of liberalism meets it choking point when sovereignty is anointed in a totality that represents the people in the form of the state. Traditional theories of the state, starting with the contract theory in Hobbes and perfected in Locke, are directed mainly to reduce democracy to impotence at the same time that they place all the power of the sovereign in the state (commonwealth). According to all mainstream theories of the social contract, when the colossal monument of the state is erected, it means that democracy, as a will, has been exhausted in its exercise of granting to the sovereign all rights. The theory of the transfer of rights means that constituent power itself as the initial mark of the sovereign is incorporated into a civil state that surpasses and inhibits the emergence of violence that has no purpose other than the protection of the state. In other words, the place of the people is shuttered and its constituent power is extinct.

We have proven that the fantasy of the totality of the people is structured from exclusion; this is the constituting basis of the simulacrum. Hence, when people are included within the social contract as equals, the inaugural law makes no distinction between excluded and included, for they are all included as free wills that contract with the same qualities and interests. In this order of things, any possibility of rebellion against the sovereign state, then, is inhibited, because, not being considered as *abandoned* or bare life but rather as part of the state, such a possibility is forbidden. This allows Agamben to affirm that 'The understanding of the Hobbesian mythologeme in terms of *contract* instead of *ban* condemned democracy to impotence every time it had to confront the problem of sovereign power and has also rendered modern democracy constitutionally incapable of truly thinking a politics freed from the form of the State' (Agamben 1998, 66).

The hidden people are in a position of absolute dependence to the law as a passive subject of obedience, but beyond even this—still outside the law so it may dispose of life and death—is the place of the colonial subject. Only here is the complete substitution of the sovereignty of the people for the sovereignty of the state. We come thus to an unnerving but fundamental conclusion, the state of exception is the inferno of modernity, reserved only for two inhabitants: the sovereign (who decides normatively who lives and who dies) and the hidden people (absolute disposition to death). Only in this descent to hell is the abduction of sovereignty and its complete reversal in perfect symmetry. This state of affairs may become reversible from what Walter Benjamin called divine violence (Benjamin 2010, 32), but this in another topic.

As a first conclusion we find that in modernity, the space of the sovereign has been conquered by an element that is inside the order, whose distinctive feature is that it ontologically belongs to the constituted power—that is, it is an ontic reflection of the sovereign. First the state and later other forms of institutionalized power have arrogated for themselves sovereign power, so thereafter power can only be dealt with as domination. What we find in all tracks of modernity is that sovereignty is folded into particular subjects as the measure of power as domination.

Hence, we meet yet another point where Negri's theory abandons democracy to its own devices. To ignore sovereignty as the place of coagulation of power is to ignore the machine that creates power as a *certain something*. That is, sovereignty creates potentia already suspended and derivative of potestas. What we have held time and time again—that potentia on its own cannot bring down the walls of potestas—makes all the more sense here. Only when the hidden people as an *actuality of being at work of difference* confront the hideous separation between sovereignty and constituent power as the very matrix of the simulacrum of politics may we think of democracy.

Thinking outside of the box of sovereignty allows Hardt and Negri to propose the multitude as the prototypical subject of politics. Notwithstanding, any energy that the multitude produces is produced outside of the true extension of power of sovereignty; thus, it is energy in a vacuum and becomes an act as fruitless as pedalling a bicycle without the chain attached to the crankset. The multitude washes away coloniality, for it presupposes a direct passage from potentia to power without any mediation of potestas. As we have just proven, potestas in its highest form of sovereignty marks and composes a gapless reality. Henceforth, we cannot deem potentia as a physical law of dynamics that is transferred in a *pure state* from the world of singularity to the world of the multitude without potestas defining its affect. The multitude, as it skips the fundament of power, is turned into a rule of life as domination as a mere ahistorical counterpart meant to never *interact* with its negation, allowing the negation to colonize power in a frictionless and *irresistible* manner.

Hardt and Negri see constituent power through multitude as something that western civilization lost and must recover, something which would reload civilization from the inside (Hardt and Negri 2004, 352). But given that we are not thrown onto a fresh and unconstructed natural world but a secondary and artificial nature, potentia on its own is incapable of restoring the natural order. The multitude is everything the hidden people are not. It is not the excluded middle of anything; it is not the remnant which is at the same time the fundamental but false base of the system. Ultimately, it is not the exception that creates the norm as an act of power. Multitude is therefore odourless, invisible, and harmless. The multitude lacks the dialectical component; it opposes no negativity whatsoever; it is itself the ontological completeness of life in another planet of power. In Spinozian terms, as an anticipation of modernity, the infinite being has been reduced to particular powers and the determinism of nature has been made contingent. There is already a full set of norms that pre-form a definite space of recognition, of command, of division, and of exclusion that the multitude cannot override as it is not even present in them; it is insubstantial to potestas. On the other side of the spectrum, the hidden people incarnate the fight for the right to become a commonality when potestas has been confronted in its own burrow of darkness.

The hidden people stemming out of the organization of power of liberalism and coloniality is the empirical fact of difference, its bone-crushing truth, so difference is the ontological necessity of democracy. In the same order of things, the multitude, and also dictatorship, would be a legitimate claimant of constituent power if sovereignty is not taken to be the core of its definition. Obliterating the exception would not be the necessary exercise of constituent power as potentia and openness. Potentia can only remain potentia when it closes the tremendous gap: the bleeding machine of sovereignty that will simply not go away by ignoring it.

The primordial effort of political philosophy must then be directed to synthesize sovereignty and people as true democracy, which modernity severed with its division in the state of exception. This is the only way to make the pest of sovereignty go away. Only when the one that is inert and helpless before death occupies the position of deciding her own life will there be democracy, and only in such a synthesis will the requirement of a total exteriority that is always vulnerable to death disappear. With it, the authentic conditions for politics and law will be replenished.

The only history that should matter to a real political philosophy in the twenty-first century has to be precisely those legal and political schemes from where the absolute and irreconcilable detachment between the people and democracy was planned and executed. Political philosophy must encounter head on the way the people have been replaced—first by a dense image of a people as an impossible totality that depends on a fundamental exclusion, and then by the production of institutions deriving their hidden legitimacy from this image. Ultimately the first question has to concern how a democracy can function without a people or a substitute that is only nominal and empty. To continue to omit sovereignty is to help the executioner blindfold his victims.

In conclusion, we will remain looking down the barrel of sovereignty as long as we keep ignoring it. The banishing point of sovereignty only comes about when it is seized by those who are placed in the exception. Only when the exceptional (the hidden people) seizes the exception may sovereignty disappear. Sovereignty repeats itself in a vicious cycle as long as the exception is not seized by the exceptional.

NOTES

1. Hence Negri wagers on the non-solution of the aporia, bringing to the fore another basic Spinozian concept: tolerance as the basic republican virtue that solves the aporia by leaving it intact. Tolerance means the respect of consciousness, and the liberty to philosophize freedom constitutes the multitude through reason as tolerance. Tolerance is the spur of freedom and the absolute; 'it allows every singularity to "transfer" to society her own initiatives and values' (Negri 2000, 77). Balibar argues that tolerance emerges 'because men's opinions are, for the most part, a product of the imagination, and the imagination of each individual (the stories he puts together, the images he projects onto the world) depends irreducibly on his own "complexion"— what Spinoza calls, using a term that has no direct equivalent in English, his ingenium (which we might translate as "nature" or "temperament")' (Balibar 2008, 29). Again, tolerance falls into the same deadlock since it is not a primal expression of the mind but one mediated by intense forms of imposition through potestas as the furnisher of

language. Tolerance could not, then, avoid being tainted by prejudices and a specific use of language imposed by structures of power where its introduction as the link within the smooth space of immanence reproduces its fundamental progeny. In short, without undoing potestas, tolerance becomes an instrument of obedience.

2. We will not even pursue an attack on Negri through his composition of time. It will suffice to say that this version of eternity paralyses time and thus becoming, and it freezes the power of time to create and destroy. In eternity, the succession of time cannot be spatialized, interpreted, or recreated. Subjectivity and any type of autonomy that can be a predicate of it become inert. Negri is talking about divine intervention, time as an unmovable structure that is naturally immune to change. It is an onto-theology that makes death and time the product of transcendence.

3. Among them Antonio Negri, Paulo Virno, Michael Hardt, Jean-Marie Vincent, and Maurizio Lazzarato.

4. https://www.youtube.com/watch?v=kZWAqS-El (retrieved 12 of April 2015).

5. http://www.naacp.org/pages/criminal-justice-fact-sheet (retrieved 21 of November 2015).

6. http://www.globalresearch.ca/the-prison-industry-in-the-united-states-big-busi-ness-or-a-new-form-of-slavery/8289 (retrieved 10 of November 2015).

Bibliography

Abensour, Miguel. 2007. *Para una filosofía política crítica*. Barcelona: Anthropos Editorial – UAM.

Adorno, Theodor W. 2004. *Negative Dialectics*. London: Routledge.

Agamben, Giorgio. 1998. *Homo Sacer: Sovereign Power and Bare Life*. Stanford: Stanford University Press.

Agamben, Giorgio. 2011. 'Bartelby o de la Contingencia'. In *Preferiría no hacerlo, Bartelby el escribriente*. Valencia: Pre-textos.

Agamben, Giorgio. 2015. *A Potência do pensamento (ensaios e conferencias)*. Belo Horizonte: Autêntica Editora.

Alexander of Aphrodisias. 2013. *On Arsitotle Metaphysics 5*. Translated by William E. Dooley. London: Bloomsbury.

Aristotle. *Categories*. 2015. Perseus Digital Library. http://www.perseus.tufts.edu/hopper/.

Aristotle. *Metaphysics*. 2015. Perseus Digital Library. http://www.perseus.tufts.edu/hopper/.

Aristotle. *Nicomachean Ethics*. 2015. Perseus Digital Library. http://www.perseus.tufts.edu/hopper/.

Aristotle. *Poetics*. 2015. Perseus Digital Library. http://www.perseus.tufts.edu/hopper/.

Badiou, Alain. 2003. *Infinite Thought: Truth and the return to Philosophy*. London: Continuum.

Balibar, Etienne, and Wallerstein, Immanuel. 1991. *Race, Nation, Class: Ambiguous Identities*. Translated by Chris Turner. London and New York: Verso.

Balibar, Etienne. 2008. *Spinoza and Politics*. Translated by Peter Snowdon. London: Verso.

Balibar, Etienne. 2014. *Equaliberty: Political Essays*. Durham: Duke University Press.

Beere, Jonathan. 2006. 'Potentiality and the Matter of Composite Substance'. *Phronesis LI/4*. Leiden: Koninklijke Brill NV.

Benjamin, Walter. 1986. *Reflections: Essays, Aphorisms, Autobiographical Writing.* Translated by Edmund Jephcott and edited and with an introduction by Peter Demetz. New York: New York Schocken Books.

Benjamin, Walter. 2010. *Para una crítica de la violencia.* Madrid: Biblioteca Nueva.

Bodin, Jean. 1980. *Selected Writings on Philosophy, Religion and Politics.* Edited with an introduction by Paul Lawrence Rose. Genève; Townsville, Qld: Librairie Droz in association with James Cook University of North Queensland.

Bryant, Levi. 2011a. 'The Ontic Principle: Outline of an Object-Oriented Ontology'. In *The Speculative Turn: Continental Materialism and Realism.* Melbourne: Re.press.

Bryant, Levi. 2011b. 'Rogue Objects'. https://larvalsubjects.wordpress.com/2011/05/25/rogue-objects/.

Bryant, Levi, Nick Srnieck, and Graham Harman, eds. 2011. *The Speculative Turn: Continental Materialism and Realism.* Melbourne: Re.press.

Buber, Martin. 1996. *I and Thou.* New York: Simon & Schuster.

Castro-Gómez, Santiago. 2005. *La hybris del punto cero.* Bogotá: Editorial Universidad Javeriana.

Césaire, Aimé. 2000. *Discourse on colonialism.* New York: Monthly Review Press.

Cohen, S. Marc. 2009. *A Companion to Aristotle.* Edited by Georgios Anagnostopoulos. New Jersey: Blackwell-Wiley.

Connelly, Stephen. 2015. *Spinoza, Right and Absolute Freedom.* London: Birkbeck Law Press.

Debord, Guy. 1977. *The Society of Spectacle.* Kalamazoo, MI: Black & Red.

Deleuze, Gilles, and Felix Guatarri. 1983. *Anti-edipus Capitalism and Schizophrenia.* Minneapolis: University of Minnesota.

Deleuze, Gilles, and Felix Guattari. 1987. *A Thousand Plateaus: Capitalism and Schizophrenia.* Minneapolis: University of Minnesota Press.

Deleuze, Gilles. 1988a. *Spinoza: Practical Philosophy.* Translated by Robert Hurley. San Francisco: City Lights Books.

Deleuze, Gilles. 1988b 'Deleuze: Abecedare. Episode 3: Power (Potentia) vs. Power (Potestas): The Story a Joyful Typhoon'. http://thefunambulist.net/2013/03/26/spinoza-episode-3-power-potentia-vs-power-potestas/.

Deleuze, Gilles. 1990. 'Control and Becoming: Gilles Deleuze in Conversation with Antonio Negri'. *Journal Futur Anterieur* 1.

Deleuze, Gilles. 1992. *Expressionism in Philosophy: Spinoza.* New York: Zone Books.

Deleuze, Gilles. 2001. *Pure Immanence: Essays on a Life.* New York: Zone books.

Deleuze, Gilles. 2004. *Difference and Repetition.* London: Bloomsbury.

Deleuze, Gilles. 2014. *Michel Foucault y el poder. Viajes iniciciáticos.* Madrid: Errata Naturae.

Derrida, Jacques. 1968. 'Ousia and Gramme: Note on a Note from Being and Time'. In *Margins of Philosophy.* Translated by Alan Bass. Chicago: University of Chicago Press.

Derrida, Jacques. 1973. '*Speech and Phenomena' and Other Essays on Husserl's Theory of Signs.* Translated by David B. Allison. Evanston: Northwestern University Press.

Derrida, Jacques. 1986. Foreword to *The Wolf Man's Magic Word: A Cryptonymy*, by Nicolas Abraham and Maria Torok. Minneapolis: University of Minnesota Press.

Derrida, Jacques. 1993. *Aporias*. Stanford: Stanford University Press.

Derrida, Jacques. 1997. *Of Grammatology*. Translated by Gayatri Chakravorty Spivak. Baltimore: John Hopkins University Press.

Derrida, Jacques. 2001. *Writing and Difference*. London: Routledge.

Derrida, Jacques. 2004. *Dissemination*. London: Continuum.

Derrida, Jacques. 2005. *Two Essays on Reason*. Stanford: Stanford University Press.

Douzinas, Costas. 2008. *El fin de los derechos humanos*. Bogotá: LEGIS.

Douzinas, Costas. 2013. *Philosophy and Resistance in the Crisis*. Cambridge: Polity.

Dreyfus, Hubert L., and Paul Rabinow. 1983. *Michel Foucault: Beyond Structuralism and Hermeneutics*. Second Edition. Chicago: The University of Chicago Press.

Dussel, Enrique. 1995. *The Invention of the Americas, Eclipse of 'the other' and the Myth of Modernity*. New York: Continuum Intl Pub Group.

Dyer-Witheford, Nick. 1999. *Cyber-Marx: Cycles and Circuits of Struggle in High Technology Capitalism*. Urbana-Champaign, Chicago, and Springfield: University of Illinois Press.

Foucault, Michel. 1977. 'Nietzsche, Genealogy, History'. In *Language, Counter-Memory Practice: Selected Essays and Interviews*, edited by D. F. Bouchard. Ithaca: Cornell University Press.

Foucault, Michel. 1978. *The History of Sexuality Volume I: An Introduction*. New York: Pantheon Books.

Foucault, Michel. 1980. 'The Confession of the Flesh'. In *Power/Knowledge: Selected Interviews and Other Writings*, edited by Colin Gordon. New York: Pantheon Books.

Foucault, Michel. 1995. *Discipline and Punish: The Birth of the Prison*. Translated by Alan Sheridan. New York: Vintage Books.

Goetschel, Willi. 2004. *Spinoza's Modernity: Mendelssohn, Lessing, and Heine*. Studies in German Jewish Cultural History and Literature Series. Madison: University of Wisconsin Press.

Gordon, Lewis Ricardo. 2005. 'Problematic People and Epistemic Decolonization: Toward the Postcolonial in Africana Political Thought'. In *Not only the Master's tools*, edited by Lewis R. Gordon and Jane Anna Gordon. Philadelphia: Temple University Press.

Gordon, Lewis Ricardo. 2006. *Disciplinary Decadence, Living Thought in Trying Times*. London: Paradigm Publishers.

Gousis, Konstantinos. 2011. 'Critical Perspectives on Slavoj Žižek's Perception of Commons'. Paper prepared for CUA (Commission on Urban Anthropology) Annual Conference, 'Market vs Society? Human Principles and Economic Rationale in Changing Times'. Corinth, May 27–29.

Grosfoguel, Ramón. 2011. 'Decolonizing Post-Colonial Studies and Paradigms of Political-Economy: Transmodernity, Decolonial Thinking, and Global Coloniality'. *Transmodernity: Journal of Peripheral Cultural Production of the Luso-Hispanic World* 1(1). http://escholarship.org/uc/item/21k6t3fq. Retrieved May 2014.

Guardiola-Rivera, Oscar. 2009. *Being Against the World. Rebellion and Constitution.* London: Birkbeck Law Press.

Guha, Ranahit. 2000. 'On some aspects of the Historiography of Colonial India'. In *Mapping the Subaltern Studies and the Postcolonial*, edited by Vinayak Chaturvedi. London: Verso.

Hardt, Michael, and Antonio Negri. 2004. *Multitude: War and Democracy in the Age of Empire*. New York: Penguin Books.

Hardt, Michael, and Antonio Negri. 2005. *Imperio*. Buenos Aires: Editorial Paidós.

Hardt, Michael, and Antonio Negri. 2009. *Commonwealth*. Cambridge: Harvard Press.

Hardt, Michel and Paolo Virno, eds. 2006. *Radical Thought in Italy. A Potential Politics*. Minneapolis: The University of Minnesota Press.

Harvey, David. 2011. *The Enigma of Capital and the Crisis of Capitalism.* London: Profile Books.

Hegel, G. W. F. 1991. *Elements of the Philosophy of Right*. Translated by H. B. Nisbet. Cambridge: Cambridge University Press.

Heidegger, Martin. 1996. *Being and Time*. Albany: State University of New York Press.

Heisenberg, W. 1958. *Physics and Philosophy*. London: Penguin Books.

Hobbes, Thomas. 2000/1651. *De Cive*. London: Blackmask.

Lacan, Jacques. 1994. *The Ethics of Psychoanalysis*. London: Routledge.

Lacan, Jacques. 2004. *El seminario: los escritos técnicos de freud*. Buenos Aires: Paidós.

Lambert, Gregg. 2002. *The Non-Philosophy of Gilles Deleuze*. New York and London: Continuum.

Legendre, Paul. 1979. *El amor del censor*. Barcelona: Anagrama

Levinas, Emmanuel. 1979. *Totality and Infinity: An Essay on Exteriority*. The Hague: Martinus Nijhoff publishers and Duquesne University Press.

McDonald Angus. 2014. 'Pots, Tents, Temples'. *No Foundations* 11.

Macherey, Pierre. 1997. 'The Problem of the Attributes'. Translated by Ted Stolze. In *The New Spinoza*, edited by Warren Montag and Ted Stolze. Minneapolis: The University of Minnesota Press.

Maldonado-Torres, Nelson. 2007. 'On the Coloniality of Being'. *Cultural Studies* 21: 240–70.

Marx, Karl. 2015/1857. *Grundrisse. Foundations of the Critique of Political Economy.* http://www.marxists.org/archive/marx/works/1857/grundrisse/index.html. Converted to eBook by Andrew Lannan.

Mason, Paul. 2015. 'The end of Capitalism has begun'. Upcoming in *Postcapitalism a Guide to our Future*. London: Penguin Books.

Massumi, Brian. 1987. 'Realer than Real. The Simulacrum According to Deleuze and Guatarri'. *Copyright* 1: 90–97.

Meiksins-Wood, Ellen. 2002. *The Origin of Capitalism. A Longer View*. London and New York: Verso.

Meiksins-Wood, Ellen. 2004. *El imperio del capital*. Barcelona: Ed. El Viejo Topo.

Meillassoux, Quentin. 2008. *After Finitude. An Essay on the Necessity of Contingency*. Translated by Ray Brassier. London: Bloomsbury Academic.

Mendez-Hincapie, Gabriel, and Ricardo Sanín-Restrepo. 2012. 'La Constitución Encriptada. Nuevas formas de emancipación del poder global'. *Redhes, Revista de Derechos Humanos y Estudios Sociales*, Número 8. Universidad Autónoma de San Luis de Potosí.

Mendez-Hincapie, Gabriel. 2015a. Sobre 'El Fragmento de las máquinas' de Karl Marx y el enigma del Poder -como 'Desencriptación' del Big Data- (Manuscript with the author).

Mendez-Hincapie, Gabriel. 2015b. *El tercer principio de la justicia. La encriptacion del poder y la desestabilización de la Justicia como Equidad*. Universidad Complutense de Madrid. Disertación Doctoral. Suma Cum Laude.

Merton, Robert K. 1948. 'The Self-Fulfilling Prophecy'. *The Antioch Review* 8(2): 193–210.

Mignolo, Walter. 2001. *Cosmopolis: el trasfondo de la Modernidad*. Barcelona: Península.

Mignolo, Walter. 2003. *The Darker Side of the Renaissance: Literacy, Territoriality, and Colonization*. Ann Arbor: The University of Michigan Press.

Morris, Martin. 2004. 'The Critique of Transcendence: Poststructuralism and the Political' *Political Theory* 32(1): 121–32.

Mouffe, Chantal. 2013. *Agonistics, Thinking the World Politically*. London: Verso.

Nancy, Jean-Luc. 2000. *Being Singular Plural*. Stanford: Stanford University Press.

Negri, Antonio. 1999. *Insurgencies*. Minneapolis: University of Minnesota Press.

Negri, Antonio. 2000. *Spinoza Subversivo*. Madrid: Ediciones Akal.

Negri, Antonio. 2003. *The Savage Anomaly: The Power of Spinoza's Metaphysics and Politics*. Translated by Michel Hardt. Minneapolis: University of Minnesota.

Nietzsche, Friedrich. 1996. *Human, All too Human*. Cambridge: Cambridge Texts in The History of Philosophy.

Power, Nina. 2010. 'Potentiality or Capacity?—Agamben's Missing Subjects'. *Theory & Event* 13(1): 121–29. Baltimore: The Johns Hopkins University Press.

Priest, G., and T. Smiley. 1993. 'Can Contradictions be True?' *Proceedings of the Aristotelian Society* 68(Supplement): 17–54.

Proudhon, Pierre-Joseph. 1846. *The Philosophy of Misery*. https://www.marxists.org/reference/subject/economics/proudhon/philosophy/.

Quijano, Anibal. 2001. *Colonialidad del Poder, Globalización y Democracia*. Caracas: Instituto de Estudios Internacionales Pedro Gual.

Ranciere, Jacques. 2001. *Ten Theses on Politics*. Baltimore: John Hopkins University Press.

Ranciere, Jacques. 2004. 'Who is the Subject of the Rights of Man?'. *South Atlantic Quarterly* 103(2–3): 297–310.

Rancière, Jacques. 2006. 'Democracy, Republic, Representation'. *Constellations* 13(3): 297–307.

Rasch, William. 2008a. *The People: Before, Within, and Beside the Constitution* (Manuscript with the author).

Rasch, William. 2008b. *Sovereignty and Its Discontents*. London: Birkbeck Law Press.

Ricoeur, Paul. 1981. *Hermeneutics and the Human Sciences. Essays on Language, Action and Interpretation*. Edited and translated by J. B. Thompson. Cambridge and New York: Cambridge University Press.

Sachs, Joe. 1995. *Aristotle's Physics: A Guided Study*. New Brunswick: Rutgers University Press.

Sachs, Joe. 2005. 'Aristotle: Motion and Its Place in Nature'. *Internet Encyclopedia of Philosophy*. http://www.iep.utm.edu/aris-mot/#H2.

Santos de Souza, Boaventura. 2010. *Para descolonizar occidente: más allá del pensamiento abismal*. Buenos Aires: Consejo Latinoamericano de Ciencias Sociales - CLACSO; Prometeo Libros.

Schmitt, Carl. 2006. *The Nomos of the Earth in the International Law of the Jus Publicum Europaeum*. Translated and annotated by G. L. Ulmen. New York: Telos Press Publishing.

Smith, Daniel W. 2012. *Essays on Deleuze*. Edimburgh: Edinburgh University Press.

Spinoza, Baruch. 2002. *Complete Works*. Translations by Samuel Shirley. Indianapolis/Cambridge: Hackett Publishing Company, Inc.

Stolze, Ted. 2015. 'Revisiting a Marxist Encounter with Spinoza: Alexandre Matheron on Militant Reason and Intellectual Love of God'. *Crisis and Critique* 2(1): 153–67.

Studtmann, Paul. 2014. 'Aristotle's Categories'. *The Stanford Encyclopedia of Philosophy* (Summer 2014 Edition). http://plato.stanford.edu/archives/sum2014/entries/aristotle-categories/.

Tlostanova, Madina, and Walter Mignolo. 2009. *Global Coloniality and the Decolonial Option*. Kult 6 special edition. Roskilde: Roskilde University Press.

Virno, Paolo. 2002. 'Entry'. In *Lessico postfordista. Dizionario di idee della mutazione*, edited by Adelino Zanini and Ubaldo Fadini. Milano: Feltrinelli.

Virno, Paolo. 2004. *A Grammar of the Multitude: For an Analysis of Contemporary Forms of Life*. LA: Semiotext.

Wall, Illan. 2012. *Human Rights and Constituent Power, Without Model or Warranty*. London: Routledge.

Wedin, Michael V. 2000. *Aristotle's Theory of Substance: The Categories and Metaphysics Zeta*. Oxford: Oxford University Press.

Williams, Alex, and Nick Srnicek. 2013. #Accelerate Manifesto for an Accelerationist Politics. Critical Legal Thinking. http://criticallegalthinking.com/2013/05/14/accelerate-manifesto-for-an-accelerationist-politics/.

Žižek, Slavoj. 2001. *El sujeto espinoso*. Buenos Aires: Editorial Paidós.

Žižek, Slavoj. 2011. *Visión de Paralaje*. Buenos Aires: Fondo de Cultura Económica.

Žižek, Slavoj. 2012. *The Year of Dreaming Dangerously*. London: Verso.

Index

#accelerate, 177;
    ecology of organizations, 179;
    resistance, 193;
    social brain the, 185;
    techno-utopianism, 179

Abensour, Miguel, 167
aberrant communities. *See* community
absolute freedom. *See* freedom, absolute
absolute government. *See* government,
    absolute
absolute other. *See* coloniality, absolute
    other
accelerationists. *See* #accelerate
action. *See* power, as action
actuality:
    definition, 76, 84–87, 96, 98–99;
    difference and, 49, 64, 71, 105, 133,
        191, 193–94;
    Energeia and Entelecheia, difference
        between. *See* Energeia;
        Entelecheia;
    finality, as. *See* Energeia;
        Entelecheia;
    existence, 87, 100 (*see also*
        coexistence);
    impotence, 95, 104, 107 (*see also*
        Agamben, Giorgio, impotence;
        potentia, privation);

necessary, 91, 96, 194;
and potentia, 68, 82, 85, 194;
definition of relation with, 87, 96,
    191 (*see also* potentia);
of power, 71, 85, 106, 111, 91;
as potestas, 69, 106, 185;
previous in logos, 96, 104; previous
    in time, 95; primacy of, 50, 69,
    89, 91, 92, 95; primacy of the
    present, 96–97
as property of the self, 105 (*see also*
    Energeia);
qualification of, 99, 100, 105;
of time, 86.
    See also Aristotle; Energeia;
    Entelecheia
actualization of difference, 44, 49–51, 64;
    definitions, 68–69, 105–9, 160;
    as Energeia, 72, 103, 105, 107–9,
        191, 193–94, 205;
    necessity of, 65–70, 71–72, 105, 108,
        111, 205;
    as potentia, 123, 160, 191, 193, 205;
    power and, 69, 105, 107, 129,
        133, 160;
    qualitative leap, 67, 70, 105,
        193, 205;
    source of truth, 66;
    subject of, 67, 106

About the Author

Ricardo Sanín-Restrepo is a member of the Caribbean Philosophical Association and a professor of legal and political theory at several institutions across Latin America, including Universidad Autónoma de Mexico (UNAM), Universidad Central de Quito, Universidad San Luis de Potosí (Mexico), PUC Rio de Janeiro, and Universidad Javeriana in Colombia, among others.